Regional and
Urban Location

Regional and
Urban Location

Colin Clark

St. Martin's Press
New York

© University of Queensland Press, St Lucia, Queensland 1982

All rights reserved. For information, write:
St. Martin's Press, Inc., 175 Fifth Avenue, New York, NY 10010
Printed in Australia
First published in the United States of America in 1982

ISBN 0 312 66903 8

Library of Congress Cataloging in Publication Data

Clark, Colin 1905-.
    Regional and urban location.

    Includes bibliographical references and index.
    1. Regional planning. 2. City Planning. 3. In-
dustries, location of. 4. Transportation planning.
5. Land use. I. Title.
HT 391.C49 1982   338.6'042   81-21510
ISBN 0 312 66903 8

Contents

Tables

Preface

There has been far too much theorising on the subjects of regional and urban location, and too little factual study. This book is not intended as a comprehensive reference book, which would have to be very long and quite unreadable, but is designed to give a general view of the subject on an international scale, to geographers, planners, and economists other than specialists. Specialists too may find that it opens up some new lines of research.

The modern practice, in learned books and journals, of collecting all the references at the end of the chapter, is based on the assumption that the reader is possessed of three thumbs, and does not mind repeatedly having to turn over pages: while the practice of spelling out the initials of authors, the full titles of articles referred to and their paging, is clearly designed to make work for printers and professors' research assistants. This book adheres to the old custom of giving references in footnotes to each page, on the assumption that the reader wants to be able, as he reads, to know immediately whether it is a source with which he is already familiar, and also to make some judgement on its reliability. Title of book or periodical, name of author, and date of periodical gives all the information required by anyone seeking to follow up the reference.

1

Transport Costs in Simple Economies

Our studies of the location of population, agriculture, and industry usually take for granted the existence of a system of transport and communications similar to that which we now enjoy. We would do better however to begin by considering communities whose transport systems are, by our standards, totally inadequate. These still represent, after all, the manner of life of a large part of the world's population and one which, until comparatively recently, was universal. We would also do well to study what information is available about the transport and economics of the ancient and mediaeval worlds. Many of the problems which they faced bear a striking resemblance to those of present-day Asia and Africa.

The phrase "subsistence agriculture" unfortunately has confused meanings. Literally the word "subsistence" means the physiologically necessary minimum of food supply, though its meaning is often extended to include also estimated minimum requirements of clothing, fuel, housing, etc. But the phrase "subsistence agriculture" has come to mean not necessarily living at subsistence level, as above defined, but the production of crops primarily for consumption by the farm families and villagers themselves, rather than for sale in distant markets. It must be noted that even the most primitive communities have need for some commodities to be obtained by trading outside their borders, though the crops traded in exchange may represent only a small fraction of their total output.

A method of measuring the agricultural productivity of Asian peasant economies was developed by DeVries, a Dutch economist who had spent most of his life in Indonesia. Dealing with economies whose staple crop was rice, he expressed the output of all other agricultural and livestock products in terms of their economic equivalents in kilograms of milled rice. This was not a calorie equivalent (which would have led to the complete exclusion of such crops as cotton) but an economic equivalent, based on the comparative prices of agricultural products in the local markets (which may have differed widely from the prices in outside world markets).

A similar method was used by J. L. Buck[1] except that rice is a staple crop in certain regions of China only, and in other regions Buck took as a standard the staple grain of the particular neighbourhood.

DeVries found that agricultural output, expressed in kilograms of milled rice equivalent, per head of population, gave a good measure of the degree of agricultural advance of different communities. A figure of 250 kilograms/person/year represents the minimum, or chronic (rather than occasional) hunger line. It is not that this figure represents the physiological minimum requirement of cereal consumption; but allowing for the need of some diversification of the diet, of some small quantity of textile fibres for clothing, and a few other inescapable requirements, for storage losses, and for the need to keep some reserve against emergencies, the figure of 250 kilograms has been taken as the minimum. Between 250–300 kilograms per head we must expect to find nothing more than the simplest type of agriculture or grazing, with use only of hand tools. Between 300–500 kilograms per head agriculture is still practised with hand tools — there is no margin of fodder to feed draft animals — but a certain amount of the product will be traded away from the village to purchase other urgent needs. At about 500 kilograms (rather lower in the special case of India, where the monsoon season is unusually short) agriculturalists can afford to support draft animals, and raise herds to provide draft power, meat, and milk. It is only about 750 kilograms that what we might call our "eggs and bacon" type of diet becomes possible, with a large part of the cereal output being fed to livestock in order to produce indirectly more expensive products.

A study has been made of the proportion of agricultural output traded, as opposed to consumption within the village, in peasant agriculture at these various levels.[2] Making some further estimates of the varying proportions of the population engaged in non-agricultural activities, these results, based on the assumption that at the productivity level of 250 kilograms per head almost the whole output will be consumed, show the proportion consumed falling to eighty-three per cent at three hundred kilograms per head output, sixty-four per cent at four hundred kilograms, fifty-two per cent at five hundred kilograms, and forty-one per cent at seven hundred and fifty kilograms. The differences represent the amount expected to be traded outside the village.

It is only with sales outside the village that there is any demand

1. J. L. Buck, *Land Utilization in China* (Nanking: University of Nanking, 1937).
2. C. Clark and Jones, Oxford Agrarian Studies (1977).

at all for transport. These figures give us some idea of the factors determining the growth of such demand.

To us, both output and transport costs are measurable in money. But this is not a suitable measure for peasant economies, whether in the present or in the past. Quite apart from the difficulties of comparing the value of currencies in widely different times and places, we must remember that money transactions only play a limited, and often unrepresentative part in peasant economies, whose main concern is the production of basic foodstuffs.

The costs of transport, which can be physically quantified in tonne-kilometres, are therefore also expressed in terms of the quantity of grain (choosing whichever grain is most used in the neighbourhood) exchangeable for one ton kilometre of transport.

This, of course, would be a most unsuitable method for measuring either output or transport costs in advanced economies, where prices of grains may vary widely, often because of political decisions; and in any case represent only a small fraction of the whole output of the economy. But it is a suitable method in economies where grain represents a large proportion of the entire output.

We now come to a proposition so obvious that it is usually overlooked. Consider a peasant family who have produced a tonne of grain. If, as in some extreme cases, transport costs, expressed by the above measure, amount to 30 kilograms of grain equivalent per tonne-kilometre of transport, then transporting grain to the market for sale, over a distance even as short as 20 kilometres, is economically out of the question — more than half the value of the grain would have been used up in transport costs.

Thus we have the basic proposition that high transport costs compel peasant economies to remain at subsistence level, whether or not they would have preferred to have produced a larger output for sale.

The converse also holds. The first need for the economic advancement of a subsistence agricultural society is the provision of transport.

"The material development of Africa may be summed up in one word — transport". So wrote Lord Lugard,[3] the outstanding administrator, who, at the end of the nineteenth century, virtually created what is now Nigeria out of a chaos of warring tribes and slave traders.

We have some actual examples. Japanese farmers encouraged to settle in Ecuador in the Upper Amazon valley to grow rice for sale had to abandon their farms because of transport costs.[4] In vacant land

3. Lord Lugard, *The Dual Mandate in British Tropical Africa* (Edinburgh: Blackwood, 1922), p. 5.
4. Professor Sasaki, Eichi University, private communication.

now being settled in Mindanao in the southern Philippines, where adequate roads are lacking, some farmers are finding that the transport agent charges as much as one kilogram of rice for every two kilograms transported (presumably by porterage).[5]

The administrators of the Australian Northern Territory in the 1920s hoped that the Territory could be developed for agriculture, not solely for cattle grazing. Though modern means of transport were available, the distances to the markets were so great and transport costs so high, that the projects soon had to be abandoned.

A number of costs expressed in terms of kilograms of grain per tonne-kilometre of transport of the different forms of transport available to less-developed communities, both present-day and historical have been tabulated,[6] and the following is a general summary of these and further data

Transport by porterage, usually head loading, is a necessity where only rough tracks are available, or where the villagers cannot use animal transport because of their poverty, or (as in Africa) because animals die from tse-tse fly infestation.

Where transport is by porterage, costs range from a lower quartile of 7.8 kilograms grain/tonne-kilometre to an upper quartile of 19.6 — quite high enough to discourage production for marketing. These costs represent solely payment for labour. It is to be expected therefore that they would be low in the lowest wage countries (China and Bangladesh). They are seen to be high in some African countries. When countries have reached the level of economic development of say Malawi or Ghana, wages rise, and in regions without adequate roads transport becomes very costly. We thus have the unfortunate paradox that development of some regions in an African country, by raising wages, actually increases the degree of isolation of some remoter regions and drives them further back towards subsistence agriculture — until roads and motor vehicles eventually become available.

There is wide diversity of evidence,[7] regarding the loads and daily distances which can be accomplished by head loading. This method of transport, which seems so strange to us, nevertheless gives "complete control and a stable centre of gravity".[8] Dr Phillips considers loads of thirty to thirty-five kilograms for twenty kilometres/

5. Philippines Central Experimental Station, Bulletin No. 1, 1957.
6. M. R. Haswell and C. Clark, *Economics of Subsistence Agriculture,* 4th ed. (London: Macmillan, 1970), pp. 196—201.
7. *Ibid.,* pp. 202—30.
8. P. G. Phillips, "The Metabolic Cost of Common West African Agricultural Activities", *Journal of Tropical Medicine and Hygiene* 57, no. 12 (1954).

Table 1. Transport Costs Expressed as Kilogram Grain Equivalent/Tonne-Kilometre.

	Lower quartile	Median	Upper quartile	Minimum costs	Maximum costs
Porterage	7.8	11.4	19.6	China, Bangladesh	Ghana, Malawi
Bicycle		20.0			
Pack animals	3.1	5.0	6.1	Middle East 19th century Nigeria 1926, Sudan	East Africa
Carts & wagons	2.3	3.6	5.2	19th century France 11th century China	Malawi, Nigeria, Vietnam 13th century long journeys
Boats	0.4	0.8	2.1	Ancient Egypt & China	West Africa
Steamboats		0.4			
Early railways	0.3	0.4	1.0	Saudi Arabia, Pakistan	Australia 1850s, England 1830s
Motor vehicles	0.5	1.0	1.7	Metalled roads	Rough tracks
Sea transport	.07	.16	.8		

day not excessive, if the carrier is able to rest on the return journey. Considerably higher figures, up to fifty-nine kilograms and fifty kilometres have been estimated for China, however even the strongest man can only do such work for twelve days a month, and receives two or three times the wages of an ordinary agricultural worker.

The wheelbarrow is said to have been a Chinese invention, and greatly reduces transport costs where animals are not available. (That Chinese porters used to fit sails to their wheelbarrows to catch favourable winds may be no more than an entertaining legend.) Its use however requires, not necessarily roads, but at any rate well-paved footpaths, which were probably available in China long before they were available elsewhere. Russia in the 1930s, as Sidney Webb pointed out with wry amusement, still had not discovered the wheelbarrow — nor, he added, the mop, as was shown by the state of public conveniences.

One or two examples of bicycle transport, from Africa, Malaysia, and Vietnam, have been costed. It proves to be a very high-cost form of transport; but it has been analyzed separately, because an erroneous idea is now in circulation to the effect that bicycles will solve the transport problem of developing countries. Riding a bicycle is very laborious when carrying any weight. It should also be observed that in a country which can afford bicycles, wages are likely to have risen to a level which will make this form of transport inordinately costly.

However bicycle transporters in Malawi, when faced with competition from other vehicles, were able to reduce their charge by forty per cent.

Where the economy and climate permit the breeding of livestock, but where there are still no adequate roads, transport will be by pack animal. Pack animals have to be accompanied by drivers and the cost of such transport therefore also contains a considerable wage element. Once again we find very high costs in East Africa, where wages are comparatively high. The camel carries a heavy load and can be operated at a comparatively low cost. In general, pack animal transport effects a big saving on porterage.

There are however circumstances under which pack animal transport is more costly. This appears to be the situation in China[9] where a detailed analysis has been made of the comparative costs, with China's wages and conditions, of the two forms of transport. Pack horses have very short working lives, can only carry ninety

9. Hsiao Ting Fei and Chih-i Chang, *Earthbound China: a Study of Rural Economy in Yunnan* (London: Longmans, 1966).

kilograms, only move 1.5 times as rapidly as porters, and also require one day's rest in five. In mediaeval Europe[10] wagons were used for local and medium distance transport but "continental commerce was carried on pack animals, or where the roads were steep, as on the Alpine passes, on the backs of porters". In other words, men are more efficient than animals on very steep slopes. Even in modern Hong Kong, a relatively high-wage economy, supplies to some Army outposts on very steep slopes are carried by porters.

As the roads improved pack animal transport gradually gave place to wagon transport, but only, as is seen, with a comparatively limited reduction in costs. Even in eighteenth century England much transport was still by pack animals, and oxen were only gradually being replaced by horses, which constituted a higher capital investment, both for breeding and feeding. On a very bad road, with the possibility of getting stuck in wet weather, a wagon shows no great advantage. It is interesting to see that wagon transport could attain low costs on the reasonably good roads of nineteenth century France, or of eleventh century China. De Foville's figures for France show that improvements in wagon design played an important part in reducing costs: but these in their turn were only made possible by improvements in the roads. After 1780 the metalling ("macadamizing") of roads led to large reductions in transport costs in England; and further large reductions of wagon charges were made as soon as the railways began to compete.

Costs are again found to be high in partially developed countries. Some interesting records are available from thirteenth century England of payments under army transport contracts. While the costs of short-distance transport were about what was to be expected, costs were more than three times as high for long-distance transport, where the driver was away from his familiar surroundings, and indeed could not be sure of getting home again. But even in more peaceful circumstances charges have been much higher for longer journeys.

In the Australian gold rush of the 1850s transport to the Victorian goldfields was by ox-wagon. Compared with previous times, money costs of transport more than doubled, real costs rose by one-third. This however was only in the summer, when the tracks were dry. In the winter, when the tracks were muddy and the farmers needed their oxen for ploughing, charges might rise five-fold. After the gold rush real costs stabilized at a much higher level, due to the rise in real wages.

The really striking reduction in transport costs appears when it is possible to use boats. We find low costs in records from Egypt in

10. D. Hay, *Europe in the Fourteenth and Fifteenth Centuries* (London: Routledge and Kegan Paul, 1948).

the third century A.D., with easy transport on the Nile using boats of over five tons capacity, and also from ancient China, which pioneered the construction of canals. African costs are high, mainly because of the turbulent and shoaly nature of the rivers. Costs have to be expressed per kilometre of direct distance, not of the much longer distance which the waterway sometimes takes; and it is also necessary to distinguish charges for river journeys downstream from the higher upstream costs.

The introduction of steamboats further reduced costs, about to the level of those of early railway systems.

Australia in the 1850s showed exceptionally high railway costs, principally explained by the sparsity of traffic.

Motor vehicles, when first introduced, were substantially more costly than railways, even under the rare circumstances when they could be provided with metalled roads. Where tracks are exceptionally steep and rough (New Guinea provides an example, also the mountainous African country of Lesotho) transport by air may prove more economical – even small aircraft can work at a cost of about 6 kilograms grain-equivalent/tonne kilometre. Conversely, the surfacing of only eight kilometres of road to a Syrian village reduced its transport costs to seaport from 2 to 1.35 kilograms/tonne kilometre.

But by far the cheapest form of transport was by sea.

Nearly all of such international commerce as developed in the pre-railway age was carried by sea. Real costs in the Roman world were estimated by Jasny to be no more than three times present day sea transport costs.[11] Wheat could be shipped from Asia Minor to Western Spain in the fourth century A.D. at a charge equal to only twenty-six per cent of its price.[12] Mediaeval costs were higher, and cargoes of grain could not stand long voyages, though there was some traffic from the Baltic to western Europe. For instance, transport of grain from Danzig (Gdansk) to Bruges added forty-eight per cent to its cost, and salt from Portugal to Bruges added eighty-five per cent.[13] For products of higher value per unit of weight the burden was less – the transport of wine from Gascony to England or Ireland only added ten per cent to its price.[14] Cloth could travel

11. N. Jasny, *Wheat Studies* (Stanford: Stanford University, 1944).
12. F. W. Walbank, *The Awful Revolution: The Decline of the Roman Empire in the West* (Toronto: Toronto University Press, 1969), p. 85.
13. D. Hay, *Europe in the Fourteenth and Fifteenth Centuries* (London: Routledge and Kegan Paul, 1948), 360–363.
14. F. Braudel, *Capitalism and Material Life, 1400–1800,* trans. by M. Kochan (London: Weidenfeld and Nicholson, 1973), p. 320.

across Europe for a sixteen per cent addition to its price, and raw wool for a twenty-seven per cent addition.[15]

However, it is only where there is a properly organized shipping service that these low charges prevail, and sometimes shipping is much more costly. Thus the eighteenth century service conveying wool from Bilbao to Nantes cost as much as three units (kilogram equivalent/tonne-kilometre); and it was stated that sea transport in the Mediterranean was even more costly, because of the danger of piracy at that time.

Shipping always has been, as it is now, a business of highly imperfect competition in which shipowners, by agreement among themselves, are able to charge according to the nature of the goods, and not simply on tonnage. Thus in the early nineteenth century a tonne of wheat could be transported across the Atlantic for an expense equal to 135 kilograms, that is about .04 kilogram/tonne kilometre; whereas charges on cotton were ten times as high, though rapidly falling.

Table 2 covers only historical data, before 1920 (including those already published in *Economics of Subsistence Agriculture*) which are of course much scarcer than current data, and deemed to be of greater interest (refer to footnote 16).

15. G. Luzzatto, *Storia Economica dell Italia nel medio evo,* Annali di economia II (Padova: Traduzione di G. Luzzatto, 1936), pp. 307–311.
16. A complete set of the original data, with their source references, is too voluminous to print here; copies may be obtained on application to the author at the Department of Economics, University of Queensland, St Lucia, Australia 4067.

Table 2. Historic Transport Costs.

Mode of Transport	Country or region	Date	Length of journey km.	Transport costs (original measure)	Grain equivalent used (if not wheat)	kg grain equivalent/ tonne km.	Reference
Porterage	France	1880		3.33 francs/tonne km.		12.0	A
	Tanganyika	19th c.			Maize	30	B
Wheelbarrow	Japan	1884			Milled Rice	31	C
	China	11th c.		30 cash/tonne km.	Milled Rice	2.7	G
Pack Animals:							
Camel	Middle East	1880		0.87 francs/tonne km.		1.7	A
Horse	England	1655	190	8 pence/tonne mile		4.1	D
Horse	England	1754		12 pence/tonne mile		6.2	D
Mule	France	1880				3.1	A
Horse	U.S.A.	1790		5½ shillings/tonne mile		7.5	V
Wagon	Australia	1795		20 pence/tonne mile		2.8	E
	"	1839	58	8 pence/tonne mile		1.4	E
	"	1839	225	24 pence/tonne mile		3.4	E
	"	1854		42-66 pence/tonne mile		3.6-5.6	E
	"	1860		24 pence/tonne mile		5.6	F
	China	11th c.		.022 cash/lb mile	Milled Rice	1.2	G
	England	13th c.	Long distance	3½ pence/tonne mile		8.0	H
	"	13th c.	Short distance	1 penny/tonne mile		2.3	H
	"	14th c.	80			3.0	I
	"	Early 19th c.		13 pence/tonne mile		5.7	J
	Flanders—Italy	1864	30	6 pence/gallon milk		16.4	K
	France	14th c.	750	20 lire/wool bale (149 kg)		3.7	L
	"	17th c.				5.4	A
	"	1750				3.0	M
	"	1775				1.5	M
	"	1810-50	30	15 sous/quintal (coal)		1.0	M
	"	1815-24		35 centimes/tonne km		1.2	M
	"	1825-34		25 centimes/tonne km		1.0	N
	"	1912		60 centimes/tonne km		2.2	O
	Germany	1815	short	(firewood)	Rye	3.1	P
	"	1815	37	(rye)	Rye	2.7	P
	"	1815	166	(butter)	Rye	7.5	P
	India	1848	800	17.5£/tonne		2.4	Q
	Roman Empire	3rd c. A.D.		37 denarii/tonne mile		3.2	R

Category	Region / Place	Date	Size/No.	Rate	Commodity	Value	Key
(heading cut off) Provinces		3rd c. A.D.		20 denarii/1200 lb/mile		4.4	S
	Russia	19th c.	1600	1.15 roubles/pood	Rye	5.0	T
	Spain	18th c.	short	10 maravedis/fanega/league		1.9	U
	"	18th c.	250	18 do		4.0	U
	U.S.A.	1790–1818	Over 300	21 cents/tonne km.		3.5	V
	"	1790–1818	Under 300	13 cents/tonne km.		2.2	V
	"	1800		15 cents/tonne mile		1.6	W
	"	1820				4.5	X
	"	1887		20 cents/tonne mile		4.9	Y
	"	1896		25 cents/tonne mile		7.4	Z
	"	1918		33 cents/tonne mile		3.8	Z
Boats (Inland)	China	11th c.		5 cash/tonne km.		0.5	G
	Egypt: Canal	3rd c. A.D.		1 drachma/tonne mile		1.1	AA
	Egypt: River / Nile	3rd c. A.D.				0.3	AA
	England	14th–19th c.				0.8	D, I, BB
	France	Early 19th c.				0.2	N
	Germany	14th c.		5.8 centimes/tonne km.	Maize	0.3	CC
	Ghana	1900	1700			5.8	DD
	Poland	1830	43			0.3	M
	Russia	11th c.	270	12 shillings/quarter		1.0	T
	U.S.A. Canal	1810	650		Barley & Rye	2.2	EE
	do.	1810	450			0.4	V
	Mississippi Upstream	1810	30			4.8	V
	Mississippi Downstream	1820				0.9	V
						0.5	X
Early Railways	Australia	1850s		6 pence/tonne mile		1.4	F
	"	1870s		Wheat 2 pence/tonne mile		1.2	F
	"	1870s		Machinery 7 pence/tonne mile		4.1	F
	England	1830s		3.1 pence/tonne mile		1.0	D
	France	1841		25 centimes/tonne km.		1.1	A
	"	1870		12 centimes/tonne km.		.5	M
	"			6.1 centimes/tonne km.		.2	M
	Sudan	1910	1700	Wheat 1.8£/tonne		.17	FF
	"	1910	1700	Cotton 3.8£/tonne		.34	FF
Motor Vehicles	U.S.A.	1918		15 cents/tonne mile		1.7	Z

Table 2. (cont.)

Mode of Transport	Country or region	Date	Length of journey km.	Transport costs (original measure)	Grain equivalent used (if not wheat)	kg grain equivalent/ tonne km.	Reference
Sea Freights	Danzig-Bruges	15th c.	2000	480 kg wheat/tonne		0.5	CC
	Hull-London	15th c.	410	6 shillings/tonne		0.5	BB
	London-Calais	15th c.	180	2% on price of wool		1.3	I
	Newcastle-London	15th c.	560	11 shillings/tonne		0.8	I
	Danzig-London	1839	2000	60 shillings/tonne		0.16	M
	Bilbao-Nantes	18th c.	500	220 francs/tonne		3.0	M
	Hobart-Sydney	1839	1300	1.5£/tonne		0.23	GG
	Sydney-London	1839	18000	7£/tonne		0.08	GG
	Antwerp-New York	1822	3500	78 francs/tonne		0.09	M
	Antwerp-Hamburg	1822	650	18.8 francs/tonne		0.12	M
	UK from Baltic	1820-29	1900	9% of C.I.F. wheat import price		0.06	HH
	UK from US	1820-29	3200	12% do.		0.04	HH
	UK from Black Sea	1820-29	6700	20% do.		0.04	HH

A   De Foville, La Transformation des Moyens de Transport.

B   International Economic Association, Economic Development of Africa South of the Sahara (London: Macmillan, 1964), p. 97.

G   S. Kuznets, W.E. Moore, and J.J. Spengler, Economic Growth – Brazil, India, Japan (Durham, N.C.: Duke University Press, 1955).

D   W.T. Jackman, The Development of Transport in Modern England (Cambridge: Cambridge University Press, 1916). Canal and river charges are expressed per kilometre of road distance.

E   E. Dunsdorfs, The Australian Wheat Growing Industry (Melbourne: Melbourne University Press).

F   E. and G. Shann (eds), Economic History of Australia (Cambridge: Cambridge University Press, 1948).

G   R. Hartwell, Journal of Economic History (March 1966), pp. 35, 37.

H   M.M. Postan, Economic History of Western Europe (London: Methuen, 1967).

I   M.M. Postan, ed., Cambridge Economic History of Europe (Cambridge: Cambridge University Press, 1952), Volume II, p. 152.

J   Baxter, Journal of the Royal Statistical Society, 1866.

K   K.R. Gasson, Geography (1966).

L   G. Luzatto, Storia Economica dell Italia nel medio evo, Annali di economia II (Padova: Traduzione di G. Luzatto, 1936), pp. 307-311.

M   P. Bairoch, Revelution Industrielle et Sous-Developpement, pp. 78, 329.

N   Toutain, Les Transports en France de 1830 a 1965 (published by ISEA).

O   Bernard, Le Progres Agricole.

P   J.H. Von Thunen, The Isolated State, trans. P. Hall (Oxford: Pergamon Press, 1966).

Q   Bourne, Railways in India.

R   F.W. Walbank in the Cambridge Economic History of Europe (Cambridge: Cambridge University Press, 1952), Volume II.

S   N. Jasny, Wheat Studies (Stanford: Stanford University, 1944).

T   J. Blum, Lord and Peasant in Russia from the Ninth to Nineteenth Century (Princeton: Princeton University Press, 1961).

U   D.R. Ringrose, "Transportation and Economic Stagnation in Eighteenth Century Castille", Journal of Economic History 28, no. 1 (March 1968).

V   Carnegie Institute, History of Transport in the United States before 1860 (1917).

W   Cochran and Miller, The Age of Enterprise.

X   E.F. Renshaw, Journal of Political Economy (June 1963), p. 289.

Y   A.D. Welk, Recent Economic Changes (1889).

Z   L. Moses and H.F. Williamson, American Economic Review (May 1967), p. 214, quoting the United States Department of Agriculture; and private communication.

AA Johnson, Economic Survey of Ancient Rome (Baltimore: John Hopkins Press, 1933-40.)

BB P.J. Bowden, Agrarian History of England and Wales, Volume iv, p. 62.

CC D. Hay, Europe in the Fourteenth and Fifteenth Centuries (London: Routledge and Keegan Paul, 1948).

DD Anyane, Ghana Agriculture.

EE E.F. Renshaw, Journal of Business (Chicago) (Oct. 1960).

FF D.J. Shaw, private communication.

GG A.G.L. Shaw, The Economic Development of Australia (Camberwell, Victoria: Longmans, 1973).

HH D.L. North, Journal of Economic History (Dec. 1958).

2

The Effects of High Transport Costs

Communities facing such high transport costs, whether in the past or the present, have to live within an economy of small regions, each with only a few transactions with other regions. In the 18th century Cantillon[1] took it for granted that food would not normally be transported more than fifteen kilometres from its place of origin. The maximum distance over which vegetables could be transported in nineteenth century Japan was estimated at twelve kilometres.[2] Under these circumstances, to provide for the region's comparatively few needs of commercially supplied non-agricultural goods and services, a closely-spaced pattern of villages and small towns will grow up (which patterns in older-settled countries are still with us). A city of any size, by its nature, requires substantial inward transport, not only of food and raw materials, but also of large quantities of fuel and building materials; with a lesser weight of outward transport of manufactured goods. For obvious reasons therefore, until the coming of the railway age, all large cities had to be built where they could use sea or good river transport. The Aztecs, an inland civilization without draft animals and dependent upon porterage, built their capital city on the shores of a large lake. The Maya civilization in Central America, also dependent on porterage, collapsed, Gourou suggests,[3] through inability to meet rising transport costs to their capital city when the gradual exhaustion of soils in the neighbourhood of the city, brought about by their primitive agricultural methods, necessitated transporting food supplies over much greater distances. The Inca civilization in Peru, also dependent on porterage, could exploit more fertile soils (irrigation of arid lands); but even so the Incas faced

1. Quoted in J. J. Spengler, "Richard Cantillon, First of the Moderns", *Journal of Political Economy* 62, no. 4 (1954), pp. 281–295 and 62, no. 5 (1954), pp. 406–424.
2. Lockwood in Economic Growth – Brazil, India, Japan, S. Kuznets, W. E. Moore, and J. J. Spengler (Durham, N.C.: Duke University Press, 1955).
3. Gourou, *Le Monde Tropical.*

an acute transport problem and every able-bodied man was conscripted for a large part of the year for transport duties.

There is one outstanding exception which "tests" (not, as the proverb is sometimes misquoted "proves") the rule, namely Madrid.[4] Unlike other capital cities, Madrid, far from any sea or navigable river, was "planned" in the sixteenth century by King Philip II, concerned by the separatist tendencies of the Spanish provinces, and desiring to centralize his administration. But he was unaware, apparently, that the high land around Madrid was unsuitable for wheat growing, and that very high transport costs, about doubling the price, would be incurred by transport from the wheat-growing districts, over high mountain ranges, in the roughly-built wagons of the period. With these high transport costs, the lower-paid labourers in Madrid were living at near-starvation level.

High transport costs also cause "transport bias" — that is, unusually low prices in regions remote from the main markets. These are accentuated if substantial export taxes are imposed (as in Thailand, and in some other countries). In Thailand[5] in the central and southern provinces the price of rice was 82 per cent of that in Bangkok, but in some of the remoter regions less than half the Bangkok level. This difference, of course, does not represent transport costs alone, but also merchanting charges. Silcock believes that in the remoter provinces the farmer is faced with a considerable measure of oligopsony (inadequate competition between buyers) on the part of Chinese merchants.

For Vietnam we have historical records going back to 1898[6] comparing rice prices in Saigon and in a rice-growing district approximately one hundred kilometres distant. Here the price difference per tonne per kilometre (obviously including substantial merchanting charges and profits), rose from five kilograms of rough rice/tonne kilometre to seven in the 1920s and still higher in the 1930s. But for 1941 and 1958 the figure had been reduced to two, owing to improved road transport and increased competition between merchants.

In mid-nineteenth century Ghana[7] the only currency was in cowries

4. D. R. Ringrose, "Transportation and Economic Stagnation in Eighteenth Century Castille", *Journal of Economic History*, 28, no. 1 (March 1968), pp. 51–79.
5. C. C. Zimmerman, "Siam Rural Economic Survey 1930–31" in T. H. Silcock, *Economic Development of Thai Agriculture* (Canberra: Australian National University Press, 1970).
6. J. Symonds, private communication.
7. Reindorf, "History of the Gold Coast and Asante" (Basel: 1895), quoted in Anyane, *Ghana Agriculture*.

(a rare kind of sea-shell), four or five of which could be exchanged for a penny. The price at which maize could be purchased in this currency was as low as one-fifteenth of its current world price (about £7/ton).

A little less extreme was the situation in the northernmost part of Malaya,[8] which had no road communications until 1920. About 1880, when the only communications were by small boats, and probably subject to piracy, the local price of rough rice was about £1.7 ton, when its world price was over £7. By 1890 however, with improved communications, the price had risen about seventy per cent. By 1940 rice prices had risen to £8/ton rough rice, approaching world level. The terms of trade between fish (comparatively unchanged costs, with no transport), and rice, had changed nearly three-fold between 1880 and 1940.

Sweet potatoes are admittedly a cheap form of food. But in rural Indonesia in the 1920s[9] they were selling at 4 Dutch guilders (1.6 dollars)/ton. The internal price of maize in East Africa in the 1930s[10] was only £3.3/ton, a little over half the world price.

A very clear example of transport bias is provided by the history of rice prices in India,[11] which were very low in relation to European prices in the eighteenth and early nineteenth centuries, and were raised by the gradual increase in commerce, the coming of steamships, and the Suez Canal (opened 1869) (Table 3).

Table 3. Price Indexes 1899-1901 Base.

	1861-9	1841-53	1760-85	1704-49
Wheat (U.K.)	176	192	176	112
Rice (India)	66	25	38	19

Likewise regarding eighteenth century China, Adam Smith wrote[12] "Rice in China is cheaper than wheat is anywhere in Europe".

8. R. W. Firth, *Malay Fishermen: Their Present Economy* (London: Routledge and Kegan Paul, 1946).
9. J. H. Boeke, *Economics and Economic Policy in Dual Societies, as Exemplified by Indonesia* (Harlem: H. D. Tjeenk Willink and Zoon, 1953), p. 191. p. 191.
10. F. Couchman, *East African Journal of Agriculture* (March 1939).
11. Data back to 1841 from Dharma Kumar, *Land and Caste in South India*, Cambridge Studies in Economic History (Cambridge: Cambridge University Press). Earlier from Brij Narain, *Indian Economic Life* (Lahore: 1929).
12. Adam Smith, *Wealth of Nations*, Everyman Library No. 412 (London: Dent, 1910), Book I, Chap. 9 in a digression concerning variations in the value of silver.

Chisholm[13] quotes an interesting example from the Kasai region of Zaire in 1951, where manioc (cassava), which is transported for sale in the mining towns, sold at 1.5 Bfr/kg (30 $/tonne) within 15 kilometres from the railway, and at prices progressively descending to 1 Bfr at 150 kilometres distance. This implies 3.3 kilograms manioc or only 0.8 kilograms wheat equivalent/tonne kilometre of transport — presumably on fairly good roads.

But we get also examples of the opposite phenomenon from some low-income agricultural areas which import staple cereals, or at any rate produce only just enough for their own requirements, depending mainly on cotton, cocoa, or other export crops. Thus, at the time when Fuggles Couchman found maize prices so low in East Africa, Beckett[14] found the internal price of maize in a cocoa-growing district in Ghana over £9/ton. Internal prices of sorghum and millet in Cameroun, Senegal, and Uganda have been found much above world price.

Both phenomena were apparent to Lesotho in 1839[15] where sorghum sold at only £2/ton, but at six or seven times that price in Carlsberg, 320 kilometres distant.

We may expect high transport costs also to be reflected in prices paid for land. In some newly-settled areas in Mindanao[16] where good roads are lacking, near to markets a hectare of land sells for the equivalent of 3 tonnes of rough rice (750 pesos), whereas at 3–4 kilometres distance the price falls to 2 tons equivalent, and at 4–6 kilometres to 1.75 tonnes. If we assume that these differences in land prices represent a capitalization of transport costs at a rate of ten per cent per year, and an average yield of 1.2 tonnes/hectare rough rice, transport costs work out at 20–25 kilograms rough rice/ tonne kilometre transport. The report stated that in newly-settled areas in Mindanao, transport (by agents) might cost 500 kilograms for one ton delivered to market — this is possible if the new settlement is 20–25 kilometres distance from the market.

These deduced transport cost figures are however somewhat exaggerated. The farmer will also take into account transport costs for farm inputs, household needs, and personal travel, and perhaps also take into account the lessening of security as distance from the town increases.

Farmers wishing to sell crops for cash but faced with high

13. M. Chisholm, *Rural Settlement and Land Use: An Essay in Location* (London: Hutchinson University Library, 1962).
14. Beckett, *London School of Economics Monograph in Social Anthropology*, No. 10.
15. Blackhouse, *Basutoland.*
16. Philippines Central Experiment Station, Bulletin No. 1, 1957.

transport costs, whether due to high costs per tonne-kilometre or to distance from markets, may be expected to look to products with a high value per unit of weight. An outstanding case is that of Tanzania,[17] where nineteenth century transport was mainly dependent upon head porterage (there were some ox-wagons but the cattle were liable to tse-tse fly infestation). Transport costs were estimated at as high as six shillings/tonne mile, under which circumstances the only product worth bringing from the interior was ivory — up to the mid-nineteenth century also slaves, who could be made to walk to market. Conversely, in 1857, the explorers Burton and Speke found — "In the bazaar [at Kazeh, some 700 kilometres from the coast]

> most articles essential to East African trade were on sale, though at prices about five times higher than in Zanzibar".[18]

Preferred crops include tobacoo (value per unit of weight 8 times grain) or coffee (5.6 times) — provided that the farmers' own skill, the productive possibilities of the soil and climate, and the availability of markets permit such trade, which is by no means always the case. In one extreme case in Malagasay[19] a village whose only means of transport is by foot track open in the short dry season of two months a year, can only sell coffee, which has to be transported by head loading for fifty-six kilometres, at a cost which absorbs twenty-five per cent of its selling value — that is, twenty-five kilograms grain equivalent/tonne kilometre. Other high-value crops suited to this climate are pyrethrum and vanilla. Costly and uncertain means of transport compel traders to carry exceptionally large stocks and also lead to sudden changes in prices, greatly harmful to poor farmers, who may be driven into debt on very disadvantageous terms.

In Thailand, where transport is inadequate, Zimmerman[20] found that the fertile delta region of the Menam Plain suffered violent fluctuations in the local price of rice, which threatened to disrupt the whole social economy, arising from the fact that certain areas almost entirely lacked normal marketing and transport facilities. There appeared to be many regions in Thailand, at that time almost uninhabited, which could be made very productive; others,

17. International Economic Association, *Economic Development of Africa South of the Sahara* (London: Macmillan, 1964), p. 97.
18. Alan Moorhead, *The White Nile* (London: Hamilton, 1960), p. 47.
19. *Analyse de la Structure des Prix et des Circuits Commerciaux Internes* (Malagasay: Ministery of National Economy).
20. C. C. Zimmerman, "Siam Rural Economic Survey, 1930–31", in T. H. Silcock *Economic Development of Thai Agriculture* (Canberra: Australian National University Press, 1970).

such as the fertile alluvial soil region in central Thailand, are apparently already very densely populated. A transfer of labour from one region to the other would benefit everybody, but this could not be considered till transport had been improved.

Within a single village in West Bengal[21] there was evidence that, as access to markets improved, a larger proportion of the crop was offered for sale, even by the poor cultivators.

The comparatively low income elasticity of demand of Japanese cultivators for the food which they had produced themselves, and the correspondingly high income elasticity of demand for other goods, could not have been possible except in a country with good transport and communications.

Some isolated mountainous regions in Macedonia specialize in tobacco production for the same reason; but here they have a long tradition of skill, and access to European markets once the crop has been transported to the railway. The inhabitants of some isolated mountain regions in Kentucky have as their principal saleable product "moonshine" (illicitly distilled whisky). Geographers who have examined, with all the apparatus of dot maps, the distribution of such stills point out that farmers in these remote districts could not stand the transport costs of the more bulky raw maize.

Some of the most isolated farming communities in Asia cannot even face the transport costs and production and marketing difficulties of tobacco. So they earn cash by selling opium, which has a very high value per unit of weight. In spite of international agreements on the suppression of the drug traffic, the political authorities in control of these regions are reluctant to deprive these tribesmen of their means of livelihood. It has been seriously suggested[22] that arrangements should be made to enable such tribesmen to follow the example of another community still more isolated by high transport costs, namely the Swiss in the early nineteenth century, who turned to a manufactured product with an exceptionally high value per unit of weight, namely watches. A valuable load of this product could be carried on one man's back (and is carried to this day by smugglers across the Swiss frontier). Transistor radios were another suggestion. But the Swiss watch trade was not established in a day, and a long period of preliminary subsidization would be necessary.

21. Mandal, "The Marketable Surplus of Aman Paddy in East Indian Villages", *Indian Journal of Agricultural Economics* (Jan–March 1961), p. 51.
22. W. Klatt "Problems of Food and Farming in Asia" *Asian Affairs* 57, no. 1 (Feb 1970), p. 4–18.

Dr Klatt goes on to add that Asia urgently needs more watches —
without them people will never get down to the routine of modern
working life.

By the early years of the nineteenth century, with improvements
in roads and in wagon design, transport costs had reached a lower
level than previously. At this point there appeared a highly scientific
analysis of the effect of transport costs on the differentiation of
agricultural production (and also, by implication, upon the rents
and prices of land). This was Von Thünen's *The Isolated State.*[23]
It is probably the case that Von Thünen's work, which applies only
in a horse-transport economy, has received too much attention from
geographers; but it has certainly received too little from economists
and economic historians.

Von Thünen, a German estate manager in Mecklenburg, was
preparing his studies during the early years of the nineteenth century
(apparently undisturbed by the Napoleonic Wars), but did not publish
his book until 1827. This was to be regretted; because by this time the
unduly   simplified   Ricardian   theorem   of   rent   had
taken a firm hold in the intellectual world (Ricardo made his
analysis in the terms of only one agricultural product, whereas
Von Thünen, a practical man, differentiated them). His work was
remarkable for the thoroughness and precision with which he kept
records of transport and other costs; and also for the skill with
which he generalized the experience of his own and neighbouring
estates, and submitted the results to economic analysis.

The region in which he worked was entirely dependent on land
transport (by horse wagon); Von Thünen pointed out that the results
would have been different in a region where transport costs were
reduced by the existence of a navigable river.

We have to make a considerable effort of the imagination before
we can visualize agricultural life in those days. One unfamiliar feature
is the production of vast quantitites of horse and cow manure, all of
which was diligently ploughed back into the land, in the absence of
chemical fertilisers. (It is true that "natural" manure helps to preserve
the physical structure of the soil, but in the chemical ions needed for
plant growth, which are the same from animal manure and from
artificial fertilisers, the supply was gravely deficient.) The towns
were dependent on horse transport, and also had a large amount of
manure to be carried away, including substantial quantities of cow

23. P. Hall, trans. *The Isolated State* (London: Pergamon Press, 1966). A fuller
    commentary is given in Chapter 2 of C. Clark, *The Value of Agricultural
    Land* (London: Pergamon Press, 1973), reprinted from *Oxford Economic
    Papers* (Nov. 1967).

manure. The high transport cost and perishability of milk, as compared with the lesser transport cost and perishability of feeding stuffs, led to the establishment of many dairies within the town (it was a cow kicking over her lamp in a town dairy which started the great fire of Chicago in 1871). Of all products, manure was the most costly to transport in relation to its value. In consequence, it was all ploughed into the soil in a small zone in the immediate neighbourhood of the town, whose land thus became exceptionally fertile (and highly priced), and was used for the production of fresh vegetables and milk, commodites which in any case could not stand transport costs over any greater distance.

The next circumstance to which we must advert is the absence of coal. The only possible fuel was wood, to which we must add substantial requirements for building and other purposes. Forests in close proximity to the city, carefully managed with cycles of replanting, were thus an economic necessity. In Von Thünen's region, at any rate, these forests were apparently established by private land-owners. In later years they were generally taken over by the local authorities. The abundant forests which add so much beauty to the German landscape, not to mention their value for recreation and sporting purposes, began as an economic necessity. However, Von Thünen points out that the land owners must have been running them, in effect, as a public service; he calculated they could not have made a profit on them, unless the rate of interest fell below 3 per cent. The replanting cycle, for hard woods, in this rather cold climate, was as long as one hundred years.

Besides vegetables, milk, and wood, the land around the city will develop into an approximately circular region of grain-growing land, until a distance is reached where transport costs render its sale (to the city at the centre of the region) uneconomic. The staple grain in this region was rye, and all costs are expressed in terms of kilograms of rye. While it now sells at a lower price, the nutritive value of rye bread is not significantly different than that of wheat bread; many people, not only Germans, find rye bread more palatable.

The rye was carried to market in large wagons, containing 1.16 tonnes when they reached their destination — more when they began their journey, because a substantial amount of rye had to be used as fodder for horses on the way. Hay would have been too bulky and inconvenient a product to carry for fodder. Von Thünen used his own wagons and labour for transport, and also some of the men's wages were paid in rye. On a representative journey of 37 kilometres length, costs worked out at 2.7 kilograms of rye equivalent per ton-kilometre of delivered weight (lower than the median cost of wagon transport of 3.6 units given in the Table in Chapter 1). Von

Thünen estimated the maximum distance from the town at which grain could be grown at 230 kilometres. We must not simply multiply 230 by 2.7 to express the aggregate transport cost in terms of the price of rye. The town price would represent farm price plus some average transport cost. However Von Thünen calculated that at this distance of 230 kilometres transport costs would absorb two-thirds of the price received in the town, leaving the producer just enough to pay current costs, yielding no rent to land at this distance from the town.

Von Thünen then went on to illustrate this principle by an extremely prescient theoretical statement. "If potatoes were the only edible vegetable, arable farming would cease at seventy kilometres from the town"; and both the region and the town would have a considerably smaller population than with the existing rye economy.

More than two hundred kilometres from the market town (and in the absence of a navigable river) we will have a quite different type of rural economy, whose inhabitants will grow only enough rye (or other grain) for their own subsistence. Most of the land will be given over to grazing, to produce butter and cheese which can be transported, and animals which can be walked to market. Von Thunen obtained some transport charges on butter travelling a distance of 166 kilometres, and found that it incurred a transport charge as high as 7.5 kilograms rye/tonne kilometre. The reason for this very much higher charge may perhaps be found in the perishability of the load, which necessitated its being carried as rapidly as possible; but also the greater distance. Carters had to be paid for the unloaded return journey, and also apparently were reluctant to spend so much time away from home.

Still more distant zones were given over to the production of wool. At that time the price of a kilogram of scoured wool was ten times or more the price of a kilogram of rye, and it could therefore stand much greater transport costs. It was an equally remarkable achievement of Von Thünen's theoretical insight that he foresaw the development of wool production in Australia, as indeed took place, many years before the coming of railways.

Including its high transport cost, butter sold in the market town at about eleven times the price of the same weight of rye.

Even with the more moderate transport costs of the eighteenth and early nineteenth centuries, transport bias, or price and wage gradients, still prevailed. One of the most striking is given by Von Thünen himself. He gives a most interesting collection (Table 4) of average prices of rye in German markets over the period 1828–41, showing "transport bias", whereby grain prices fall with distance from the market — and with them wages and other costs expressed

Table 4. Rye Prices 1828-41 £/Tonne.

East and West Prussia	4.02
Posen	4.26
Silesia	4.55
Bradenburg and Pomerania	4.65
Saxony	5.07
Westphalia	5.84
Rhineland	6.30

in grain. Von Thünen took this consideration into account in calculating costs in the remote pastoral zone. Prices rose toward the western and more populous part of Germany, which was also nearer to the principal export market. Here, however, Von Thünen had a justifiable grievance. Britain, which had been a grain-exporting economy up to 1750, had become, with the rise both in population and in real incomes, a grain-importing country, subject to comparatively moderate tariffs, in the later eighteenth century. In 1815, the "Landlords' Parliament" made the Corn Laws more stringent.[24]

Germany was the principal source of exportable grain at this time. The effect of the Corn Laws was to create a great dispartiy in prices. During the period 1828–41, when the maximum German price of rye was only a little over £6/tonne, British buyers were paying £14/ tonne for wheat, and many of them were going hungry. Further analysis is required before we can judge the extent to which these adverse consequences fell upon German landowners and German labourers respectively. The relative movement of German wages and of German rents after Britain's sudden repeal of the Corn Laws in 1846 should provide interesting material for study.

In modern Indonesia, where transport is deficient and where there has been a growth since 1970 of timber exports (oil exports seem to have less effect) from Kalimantan (Borneo), a wage gradient has appeared[25] giving East Kalimantan three times the wage of Java (other than Jakarta): but prices there have also risen – in 1972 East Kalimantan prices were sixty-five per cent above Jakarta level, the regions of

24. They had included, since the seventeenth century, with a view to stabilizing internal prices, the device now known as the "variable levy", a deplorable ancient error which the European Common Market authorities have revived, under the impression that they have hit upon something ingenious and new.
25. H. W. Arndt and R. M. Sundrum, "Regional Price Disparities", *Bulletin of Indonesian Economic Studies* 85, no. 4 (July 1975), pp. 599–628.

Sulawesi (Celebes) ten—thirty per cent. Real incomes per head (measured at Jakarta prices, excluding oil revenues) in 1972, in thousands of rupiahs, ranged from 19 in Nusatenggara and 23 in Yogyakarta to 221 in East Kalimantan — 55 in Jakarta and only 25 in Sulawesi. These great differences in real income, affecting labour costs of handling and services, might in themselves be expected to contribute to the price differences. But the correlation between prices and *real* per head income is found to be "not high and may be spurious . . . the higher level of prices in most provinces outside Java has more to do with transport costs".

In 1971—72 average public works wages were only 124 rupiah/day in Java, outside Jakarta, 182 in the remote Eastern islands, 247 in Sulawesi, 330 in Sumatra, 350 in Jakarta City, and 439 in Kalimantan.

In Vietnam in 1937[26] there was more than a 2:1 difference between the south and north (southern wage for male labourers 0.61 piastres/ day as against 0.29). The piastre was then equivalent to 10 French francs).

Wide differences prevailed in China in the 1920s.[27] In Shanghai and Canton unskilled male wages were eight—nine Chinese dollars/month and skilled twenty (the Chinese dollar was then worth $US0.5). In provincial China unskilled male wages (except on the railways) were about half of this, and in "outer areas" about a quarter — likewise the wages of female silk reelers. For skilled men however the discrepancy was less.

One of the most extreme discrepancies reported is that[28] of Indian school teachers, always a lowly paid class, in 1931, ranging from forty-seven rupees/month in Bombay to twenty-five in Punjab and Madhya Pradesh to eighteen in Uttar Pradesh and eight in Bengal — with no great price differences.

A transport economy depending primarily upon wagons travelling along improved roads, as in the later eighteenth century, made possible the growth of quite large cities. But their growth was held in check by transport considerations. From information given by Arthur Young, it is possible to draw contours showing steadily rising prices as London was approached. This in turn necessitated considerably higher money wages (though perhaps not real wages) in London than elsewhere (Table 5); which factor in turn checked the growth of manufactures there.

Relative wages in Lancashire, initially so low, rose with improving transport, and they proved attractive to industrial employers,

26. *Monthly Labour Review,* July 1944.
27. *International Labour Review,* various issues.
28. Publication No. 1. (Poona: Gokhale Institute).

Table 5. Unskilled Urban Wages Pence/Day [1]

	London	Kent	Oxfordshire	Lancashire
1700-04	21.0	18.0	14.0	8.35
1735-9	23.7	18.0	14.0	12.0
1770	24.5	18.5	14.0	18.0
1785-9	25.0	21.5	16.0	19.7

1. E.W. Gilboy, *Wages in Eighteenth Century England* (Cambridge, Mass.: Cambridge University Press, 1934). Craftsmen's wages throughout were about fifty per cent higher, except in the last period in Lancashire, when the ratio fell.

particularly in weaving in the northern Lancashire towns. Spinning developed in southern Lancashire, to some extent in response to other factors, particularly access to sea transport.[29]

Gilboy quotes Arthur Young's classification (Table 6) of agricultural wages in 1772 according to distance from London. Adam Smith also made some observations (Table 7).[30]

Table 6.

Distance from London, miles	Under 20	20-60	60-110	110-170
Daily wage, pence	21.5	15.3	12.7	12.5

Table 7.

Wages pence/day		
London	18	
"Few miles distance"	14-15	
Edinburgh	10	
"Few miles distance"	8	
Scottish Lowlands generally	8	
Some parts of Highlands and Islands	6 (5 in winter)	
On the other hand, in the remote Shetland Islands, with a substantial income from fishing, unskilled wages were 10 pence/day		

29. J. Jewkes, "The Localization of the Cotton Industry" *Economic History* (supplement to *Economic Journal*) 1930–33, pp. 91–110.
30. Adam Smith, *The Wealth of Nations*, Everymans Library No. 412 (London: Dent, 1910), Book 1, Chaps. 8 and 10.

These money wage differences were partly but by no means entirely offset by price differences. Bread prices were much the same everywhere, but Young records meat costing a penny a pound more in London that it did elsewhere, and Gilboy shows some evidence of clothing (a labour-intensive product) costing less in the remoter rural areas.

Furthermore "House rent is almost double in London to what it is elsewhere. Fuel, to which sea coals belong in particular, is four, nay five times dearer than in the northern and some other parts of the Kingdom".[31]

High transport costs had a selective effect on manufacture as well as on agriculture. By the early eighteenth century Birmingham and Sheffield were already growing manufacturing towns — but their principal products were light high-value metal goods, such as pins and knives, which could stand the cost of pack-horse transport.

Boswell, accompanying Johnson on a visit to his native town of Lichfield, "found however two strange manufactures for so inland a place, [some one hundred kilometres from the sea] sail cloth and streamers for ships".[32] But this was in 1776, by which time road and canal transport were improving.

As in so many regional developments, change has been slow. Many of these regional differences in wages, rents, and prices, whose origin lay in the high transport costs of the past, persisted into the nineteenth and twentieth centuries; data are shown in Chapter 11, on regional incomes.

Generally speaking manufacture, as we understand the word, namely the continuous processing of goods for distribution to a large market, is absolutely dependent upon cheap transport.

Railway transport (mechanical road transport in the modern world) brings about the greatest *relative* reduction in the costs of transport of heavy and bulky goods. Its effects upon agriculture therefore are more immediate than upon industry; it becomes feasible to transport even comparatively low-valued crops away from the producing areas. From the proceeds of these sales the cultivator is able to buy numerous cheap manufactured goods, and to dispense with the high-priced products of the village weavers and other craftsmen, who are thus forced to seek urban employment, or remain persistently under-employed. We can see this tragic but unavoidable process occurring in England about the 1830s, in India about fifty years later, as the

31. Wenderhorn, *A View of England Towards the Close of the Eighteenth Century* (London: 1791), quoted in *Town and Country Planning* (January 1964).

32. Boswell, *Life of Johnson.*

railways spread, and we can see it happening in some parts of the world now.

Of equal importance, however, is the fact that, while subsistence agriculture had to produce all the local requirements of food and fibre, once modern transport has been introduced geographical specialization of agriculture rapidly follows, with consequent further increases in productivity.

In the decades just before the arrival of motor transport, it was reckoned in the United States that it was quite uneconomic for anyone much more than 100 kilometres from the railway to attempt to produce wheat. This would indeed be the case if transport costs were of the order of magnitude of 3.5 kilograms wheat/tonne kilometre, which transport costs would, in effect, use up a third of the crop in transporting it to the railway. Thorn[33] pointed out that there were 1.3 million hectares of good land in the American Great Plains which in 1920 were still more than 130 kilometres from the railway, entailing, quite apart from the question of cost, four to six days' time to make a round trip by horse wagon to the railway line. This area became cultivable with the advent of motor transport.

In Australia the economic limit was generally adjudged at a shorter distance, perhaps because the railways were state-owned, and the farmers were able to organize to bring stronger political pressure to bear than American farmers could exercise on the private railway companies. When the West Australian Railways were constructed the reasonable maximum distance over which a settler could be expected to carry his produce, particularly wheat, was considered to be about 12.5 miles.[34] The consequence was a close network of railway branches (many of which have since been abandoned, but are clearly discernible on contemporary maps) demarcating the "wheat belt".

33. World Population Conference 1954.
34. *Royal Commission on West Australian Government Railways*, p. 4, quoted in *Economic Record* (December 1963), p. 474.

3

Agricultural Land and Labour [1]

Other commodities and factors of production have values which change with demand but which, in the long run, cannot fall below the (full) costs of production. But land (with very rare exceptions) cannot be produced and has no cost of production. Its value must be determined by demand alone. To state the issue more precisely, there is a limited stock of agricultural land, whose price must rise or fall to the level at which those who (collectively) have to hold this stock, will be willing to do so.

The proprietors of other, reproducible capital assets may lease them out at a rent which is affected by demand, but which is primarily determined by their cost of production. With land however the situation is reversed. Demand determines the rent which can be obtained from the land, and what determines the price of the land is the capitalization of the rent.

Note however that the market (perhaps subject to substantial time lags) will capitalize the rent at a *real* rate of interest, which will be below the money rate of interest when prices are rising and above it when they are falling; because, unlike money loans, the proprietor will have his real asset unchanged at the end of the lease.

There are further qualifications. Particularly in a country such as Britain, there may be substantial fixtures, such as houses for the farmer and his employees, buildings for livestock, roads, drainage, hedges, and so on, and the land cannot be leased or sold without them. In many countries national or local taxation is imposed upon the revenue from land, with the price therefore representing the capitalized value of rent net of tax.

Under some circumstances, the reciprocal of the rate of interest, or the number of years' purchase of the rent represented by the price of the land, appears enormously high, more so in some countries and times than others. "The rent is not the full measure

1. A fuller account is given in C. Clark, *The Value of Agricultural Land* (London: Pergamon Press, 1973).

of the benefits of land holding", wrote a prominent nineteenth century English firm of estate agents, in their stately Victorian prose "and that they have fetched these large numbers of years' purchase in open competition in the public market shows that the amenties attached to land were much appreciated". These factors other than the capitalized rent include a valuation of the social prestige, political authority, sporting rights, and the like, conveyed by land ownership.

We have the simplest case of regional economic equilibrium where the only significant production is agricultural, and the only significant factors of production are land and labour, the amount of capital employed being insignificant. Both land and labour are immobile and confined to the region. Land, except for very small amounts, has no alternative use except for agriculture, and labour is in the same position, if we assume that there is no significant amount of alternative employment. (This latter assumption is crucial, as we shall shortly see.) Under these circumstances the rent, or price of land is found to rise with the quantity of labour input per hectare, with a slope (on a logarithmic scale) approaching one. This relationship cannot be said to represent the true marginal productivities of land and of labour; with an immobile, densely settled rural labour force, without alternative employment, the land owner is in a position of oligopsony (limited numbers of buyers in the market).

The suggestion that we are observing a false correlation, i.e., that the land with the best soil and climate attracts most labour, and at the same time is most highly priced, is confuted by a special analysis in the Philippines, where the ratio of price to population density is found to be the same for good- and poor-rainfall lands alike.

This situation however is immediately altered as soon as alternative employment becomes available, as is seen alike in nineteenth century England and present-day Italy. This principle was also illustrated for nineteenth century France by Leroy-Beaulieu, who obtained the paradoxical results that rent represented the lowest proportion of the product in the Department Nord, where the land was good, but there was also abundant alternative industrial employment, and rent took the highest proportion of the product in Cantal and Aveyron, poor mountain regions where there was little or no alternative employment.

A good deal of work has been done in various countries in fitting production functions for land, labour, capital, and the like, in agricultural output, generally of the Cobb-Douglas type. The use of the estimated marginal productivities of land and labour obtained from such functions to predict land rents and wages has achieved only limited success. Production functions represent no more than a preliminary approach to problems which should eventually be solved by linear programming. The latter however makes far higher demands both for detailed information, and for effort, skill, and computer time in analysis.

A thorough study using programming shows, that under conditions of peasant farming, how mistaken it is to assume a single marginal product for land, labour, or capital, and how dependent these variables are on the scale of the enterprise.[2] In a poor region in Greece for the average farm of 5.2 hectares the programmed marginal productivity of land was about three times the rent at which land was being leased, and for the smallest farms three times higher again, or more. Likewise, on the average farm, with a labour input of 1,334 man hours/hectare/ year, the marginal productivity of labour was less than half the wage currently payable. On the larger farms, on the other hand, with a labour input of 800 manhours/hectare/year, marginal productivity of labour was substantially above the wage rate.

Finally, regarding short-term capital, on the more highly capitalized farms the marginal productivity was closely adjusted to the rate of interest, whereas on the less capitalized farms the marginal productivity of capital was far higher.

In other words, peasant agriculture is in a state of extreme economic disequilibrium, because most of the smaller farmers lack access to money to buy land, and to short-term credit, both of which would show very high marginal productivities in their hands, if they could obtain them.

In the more advanced economies there is much more detail to be assembled and programming studies still have much further to go. The object of a programme should be to apply other inputs until the point of zero marginal return to land has been obtained; that is, optimal land use. In mixed or livestock farming, with a high capital input, both French and British results indicate that this is probably obtained with a land input of about twenty hectares/man-year. In advanced economies rents of agricultural land, including fixtures, appear to come to about twenty per cent of factor income in Europe, thirty to forty per cent in United States (about a third of which gross rent however will be absorbed in maintenance expenses and taxation).

2. G. I. Kitsopanides, *Parametric Programming: An Application to Greek Far-ming* (Thessaloniki: University of Thessaloniki, 1965). Kitsopanides's diagrams are shown in C. Clark, *ibid.*, p. 53.

4

Transport in Modern Economies

On this subject many large books could be written. This chapter sets out only to deal with the salient features which are likely to be related to the location of industry and population.

Demand for transport per unit of real national product (Table 8) is affected
1. by the country's geographical extent;
2. by the extent of its economic development — a simple agricultural society living largely in small regional economies will have little demand for transport;
3. by the relative importance of heavy industry and of light industry and services; but also
4. by the extent to which industrial production is concentrated, or decentralized to regional or branch plants.

The extraordinarily heavy demand for transport in Soviet Russia is noticeable. This is due not only to the geographical extent of the country and the predominance of heavy industry, but also to the deliberate policy of dispersal (for defence reasons) of many important heavy industries. Quite significant declines however are observable in the United States and France, and stationary requirements in United Kingdom and Japan.

Noticeable is the rapid rise as industrialization proceeds in India, a country of wide geographical extent where industries are largely centralized. During the 1970s transport demand has been rising eight per cent per year (about twice the rate of growth of real product) and the railways' capacity is strained.

The service industries, by their nature, require little or no transport of goods, and their increasing relative importance in the national incomes of all countries therefore exerts a downward pressure on the transport volume/national product ratios. It is better, if it is possible, to analyse the relationship of transport to the national product excluding services, that is, of goods and structures only. This can be done for United States of America whose national accounts present tables in the required form (Table 9).

Table 8. Transport volumes in tonne kilometres/$ of net national product expressed in $US of 1950 purchasing power.

Australia	1951-2	3.78
	1958-9	3.99
France[a]	1830	0.60
	1845-54	0.69
	1865-74	1.16
	1905-13	1.63
	1935-38	1.82
	1956-60	1.49
	1968	1.44
Germany	1955	2.91
India[b]	1900	0.35
	1928	0.70
	1945	0.76
	1950	1.01
	1970	1.88
Japan	1955	1.37
	1970	1.33
United Kingdom	1938	1.54
	1955	1.70
	1970-2	1.73
U.S.A.[a]	1924-9	4.68
	1940	4.55
	1955-9	4.15
	1968	3.57
U.S.S.R.	1913	3.00
	1937	7.46
	1956	10.87
	1965-9	12.54

Official estimates except for France, Toutain, J.-C., *Les Transports en France de 1830 a 1965* Econo et Soc. 1(8) Sept.-Oct. '67, pp. 3-306.

a. Per unit of gross national product

b. Including Pakistan before 1947

Measured in this way, transport requirements per unit of product are still seen to have fallen substantially since the 1920s, though now to have approximately stabilized. Transport charges per ton/mile, in relation to the price index for goods and structures (excluding services) showed a marked fall to 1968, with a subsequent rise.

ɔle 9. Transport Volumes and Cost in the United States.

		1929	1940	1950	1960	1968	1973
ꞏsport	Rail		412	628	595	769	858
me[a]	Road		62	173	285	396	505
illion	Inland waterways[c]		118	165	220	287	358
miles[b]	Oil pipeline		59	129	229	391	507
	Coastal shipping[d]		235	274	313	321	330
		840[e]	886	1367	1642	2164	2558
ꞏrage	Rail	1.088[f]	.870	1.263	1.370	1.293	1.632
ꞏge	Road		1.448	2.160	2.531	2.972	4.119
ꞏs/ton	Inland waterways		.096	.202	.194	.152	.172
	Oil pipeline		.383	.343	.336	.262	.285
	All Transport[g]		.595	.991	1.083	1.116	1.483
ꞏout of goods and structures luding services) $ billion ꞏ972 prices		187.9	204.1	327.5	426.1	602.0	703.3
ꞏe of goods and structures ꞏ2 base			.315	.605	.734	.850	1.062
ꞏ miles/$ goods and ꞏtures product at 1972 ꞏs		4.47	4.34	4.17	3.85	3.59	3.64
ꞏsport charge cents/ton — goods and structures ꞏ index			1.889	1.638	1.475	1.313	1.396

ꞏces: Statistical Abstract of the United States, *The National Income and Product Accounts of the United States*, Tables 1.3 1.5.

ꞏxcluding intra-city transport and air traffic

ꞏo convert to tonne/kilometres divide by 1.102 to convert American tons to metric, and multiply by 1.609 to convert miles ꞏo kilometres

ꞏncluding Great Lakes traffic

ꞏonnage only recorded; assumed average journey length, 1,500 miles

ꞏrom index of freight transportation output, *Historical Statistics of U.S.A. to 1957*, Series Q.14.

ꞏbid., Series Q.86

ꞏoastal shipping charges per ton mile assumed twice inland water-ways charge

In other words, the economy has been reducing its demands for transport per unit of product, even though transport has become relatively cheaper in terms of goods. This seems to indicate a substantial degree of decentralization of production, but also probably some reduction in the relative importance of heavy industry.

The average charges per ton/mile by the different forms of transport are of interest, with inland water transport being much the cheapest for those who are able to make use of it. Both these costs, and the cost by oil pipeline, have shown significant falls at a time when the general price level showed a substantial rise. Road transport continues to gain traffic relative to rail, in spite of its higher cost, mainly because of the avoidance of double handling of freight.

For countries in the early stages of growth Isomura cautiously speculated that the income elasticity of demand for transport was greater than one.[1] Wilfred Owen raised the estimate for income elasticity of demand for transport in developing countries to 2–3.[2] The figures for India however (Table 10) suggest an income elasticity of the order of magnitude of 5. Indian planners, both in government and in private business, have been taken by surprise at the rapidity of the increase in demand for transport and consequent heavy capital requirements. The concentration of Indian planning upon the development of heavy industries has accelerated this increase.

Little has been said about shipping charges. These remain largely unpublished and what information we do have shows extreme fluctuations with the business cycle. Also, as indicated in a previous chapter, the industry is highly cartellized, and acts very strongly as a discriminating monopoly, charging much higher rates for the more highly-valued products. Shipment of wool from Australia, for example, costs three or four times as much per ton as for lower-valued cargoes. Coastal shipping, which usually enjoys legislative protection against competition from foreign shipping companies, may be inordinately expensive. It often costs more to send goods from one Australian port to another than to send them to Europe. Jute mills in Sao Paulo in southern Brazil buying jute within their own country in the Amazon Valley find that it may cost twice as much to ship it for this journey as to ship it for three times the distance from India.[3] Coastal shipping in New Guinea is substantially more costly (about 2.2 kilograms wheat equivalent/tonne kilometre) than road transport.[4]

In developing countries, costs of sea-going shipping are usually very high. Quite apart from the question of cartellization, the ship-owners find that they have to use small ships and make frequent calls to pick up small consignments, because only in this way can adequate terminal facilities be developed. Bulk ship loads would be quite unmanageable in a port which had neither bulk handling or storage facilities, nor bulk transport for inland distribution.

It is on low-priced commodities, carried in large ships, that the lowest rates appear.

In shipbuilding, as in a number of other engineering works, and in ship operation, costs per unit fall with size, that is aggregate costs

1. Isomura, Japan Centre for Areal Development Research, United States– Japan Conference on Regional Development, 1971.
2. Wilfred Owen, *Ekistics* (Jan 1968).
3. S. Kuznets, W. E. Moore, and J. J. Spengler, *Economic Growth – Brazil, India, Japan* (Durham, N.C.: Duke University Press, 1955).
4. M. Ward, "The Rigo Road: A Study of the Economic Effects of New Road Construction" *New Guinea Research Bulletin*, 33 (Jan 1970).

Table 10. Goods Transport Billion Tonne Kilometres[a]

	Rail	Rail and Road	Tonne km/ Population[b]	Per Head National Income		
				Rupees of 1948-9 purchasing power[c]	Rupees of 1960-1 purchasing power[d]	Tonne km/rupee real income
India including Pakistan						
1900	11.4		38.8	199	221	.176
1909	15.0		47.9	217	241	.199
1913-4	25.0		78.8	233	259	.304
1928-9	35.2		101.5	260	289	.352
1939	37.0		92.5	264	293	.316
1945	46.0		108.0	255	283	.382
India excluding Pakistan						
1947	26.9		138.7	247.5	275	.504
1950-1	44.1	49.6	175.3	267.8	298	.589
1955-6	59.6	68.6	242.1		306.3	.790
1960-1	87.7	105.1	312.0		310.4	1.004
1965-6	116.9	151.0				
1970-1	127.4	175.3	324.0		345.8	.939

a Indian Institute of Public Opinion, Feb. 1956 and March-April 1972; other (water) transport, estimated at 6 billion tonne km in 1964-65, not included in the estimates.

b Rail only to 1945.

c M. Mukherjee, National Income of India: Trends and Structure (Calcutta: Statistical Publication Society, 1969), p. 61; interpolated from decennial averages; from 1950-51 from Central Statistical Organisation Estimates of National Income 1948-49 to 1961-62; conversion factor to 1960-1 prices (1.11) also from this source.

d From 1960-61 Central Statistical Organisation Estimates of National Income 1960-61 to 1969-70 and 1960-61 to 1971-72; earlier years from previous column multiplied by 1.11 (see Note c).

rise with size, but less rapidly. It is found that this relationship can be most conveniently expressed in the form

Aggregate Costs = a (Size)^b

where the exponent b is of course less than 1.

Estimates of these exponents for shipping are low (that is, great economies of size).[5]

Construction cost .6
Operating cost not fuel .4
Fuel .72

At the beginning of the 1970s, before the boom, grain traffic from Australia to Europe and Asia could be carried at 0.06 cents/tonne kilometre, and coal traffic to Europe at the following charges[6] (Table 11).

Table 11.

Size of ship '000 tons	U.S. $/ton
40	11
58	9
120	6

Note: The lowest figure represents only about 0.03 cents/ton kilometre.

The above figures suggest an exponent as low as 0.45; they refer however to a time when fuel represented a lower proportion of total cost. Most of the shipbuilding orders in recent years have been for very large ships; it has been estimated that raising the size from forty to eighty thousand tonnes shows a thirty per cent saving in cost per tonne constructed, not to mention savings in operation. There are, however, very few ports in the world which are capable of handling ships of seventy-five thousand tonnes, and in other ports the costs of deepening the harbours and providing sufficient stacking space for these very large ships, would be prohibitively expensive.

These developments seem to lead to an increased geographical concentration of industry.

5. Jansson and Schneerson, *Review of Economics and Statistics,* May 1975, p. 291.
6. *The Age* (Melbourne), 4 May 1978.

5

The Economies of Aggregation

To borrow the striking image posed by Valavanis,[1] if there were no transport costs, but there were economies of scale, production would then be carried on in a few large plants of optimum size, scattered at random over the map; if there were transport costs, but no economies of scale, production of every commodity would be carried on in the smallest possible units everywhere over the earth's habitable surface; however, qualifying both these propositions, agriculture's demand for land would mean that in either case non-agricultural activities would be concentrated into limited areas.

Valavanis has done great service in focussing our attention so dramatically on the fact that nearly all issues in the economics of location turn on the comparative pull of transport costs on one hand, and of economies of scale on the other, subject to agriculture's demand for land.

However, his analysis needs to be further modified in two respects. For "economies of scale" we should write "economies of aggregation"; and for "transport costs" we should write "distance costs".

When a business is selling or buying at a distance from the place where it is carried on, it has to consider not only transport costs, important though they may be for some heavy industries, comparatively light for others. There are a number of other less tangible costs which may rank heavily in business decisions. The salesmen, buyers, perhaps higher executives, have to incur expenses of travel and also, more important, loss of time in travelling, which might have been devoted to other business. With goods coming from a distance, there are also delays and uncertainties of delivery. These costs are greatly accentuated if the goods have to cross a national frontier, where there will be the expense and delay of customs, and the possibility of governmental restrictions being placed on the trade.

Lösch went so far as to say that American businessmen did not

1. In a review article on Lösch by S. Valavanis in the *American Economic Review* 45, no. 4 (September 1955), pp. 637–44.

properly understand their own interests in the exaggerated distances over which they attempted to sell.

"Economies of scale" have to be considered at both the macro and micro levels. At the macro level, as we now know, an important element in the economies of scale is the sub-division of processes, many of which may be transferred to specialized firms supplying components, for processing; and may even lead to a fall in the average size of firm. These considerations however are not what affect the decisions of the individual industrialist, who knows only the economies of scale within his own business — which may be highly significant. However the proximity of other firms which supply him with components and services, or process his output, is an important consideration with him; in other words, what are called "linkages", both forward and backward.

There is no doubt about the economies of scale to individual businesses, at any rate when we are considering the comparatively small businesses whose economies of scale help to lead to the formation of villages and towns.

We can illustrate this most clearly from the example of Japan, a country which, in respect of certain industries and services at any rate, is still in a state of transition, with numerous small businesses still surviving (Table 12). Some very interesting information is also available about the service industries (Table 13).

In the manufacturing industries in which small firms are still abundant, the economies of scale are apparent at every stage of the classification.

Table 12. Japanese Manufactures 1974.

Numbers employed per establishment	Gross value added ('000 yen/person)			
	3 or less	4-9	10-19	20 & over
Lumber and wood products	1224	2026	2619	2957
Furniture	1375	1944	2554	3188
Leather products	1218	2335	2934	2931
Fabricated metal products	1461	2497	2464	4394

Industries in which more than fifty per cent of all employment is in establishments with less than twenty workers.

Source: Japan Statistical Yearbook 1977, Table 125.

Table 13. Selected Japanese Service Industries 1975.

Annual sales per establishment (million yen)	Average Sales per Employee Million yen/year (approximately)							
	Under 1	1-3	3-5	5-10	10-30	30-50	50-100	100-300
Hotels and boarding houses	.5	1.2	1.8	2.2	3.8	4.6	5.1	6.2
Laundries	.7	1.5	2.3	3.0	3.4	3.3	3.9	5.2
Barbering	.7	1.5	2.2	2.6	3.5	4.1		
"Beautifying"	.7	1.4	2.0	2.4	3.2	3.8	4.0	4.6
Sporting facilities	.5	1.0	1.3	1.7	2.6	3.8	4.1	3.8
Recreation halls	.7	1.4	1.9	2.1	3.2	4.6	7.2	13.9
Automobile maintenance	.6	1.3	2.0	2.6	4.3	5.1	5.7	8.2
Machinery repair		1.1	1.8	2.0	3.7	4.7	5.0	7.5

Source: Japan Statistical Yearbook 1977, Table 59.

In the service industries the economies of scale, perhaps unexpectedly, are even more apparent, likewise the higher wages paid by the larger businesses. This latter increase however slows down at the highest levels. For retailing, the principal business of small urban settlements, the economies of scale are even more marked. These results go a long way towards explaining the relative decline of the smaller rural settlements in many countries.

"Economies of aggregation" however mean more than business's economies of scale. Quite apart from the obvious advantages to buyers in having competing suppliers close together, the individual business also usually sees a gain in proximity to its competitors. This important theorem, which commonsense at first might be disposed to reject, was demonstrated by Hotelling.[2]

Hotelling analyzed the simplest case, of a market with transport, or "distance" costs, directly proportional to distance; with only two competitors, no economies of scale, and required inputs equally available anywhere. The market was represented by a straight line. Potential consumers were considered to be distributed evenly over its whole length. Each competitor is free to set prices at whatever level he chooses, knowing however that this will affect the distance over which he is able to compete.

A possible illustration might be the competition between two ice cream vendors on a beach. Hotelling demonstrates, both by diagram and algebraically that both competitors stand to gain by moving from the ends towards the centre of the beach, until they meet in the middle — not the solution to maximize the welfare of the consumers.

Secondly, he shows how both competitors stand to gain from higher transport costs. Hotelling comments wryly on how frequently businessmen fail to recognize their own interests when they press public authorities for improved roads, and so on.

2. H. Hotelling, "Stability in Competition" *Economic Journal* 33, (1929), pp. 41–57.

6

The Pattern of Rural Settlements

"Smiths, carpenters, wheelwrights, and ploughwrights, masons and bricklayers, tanners, shoemakers and tailors, are people whose service the farmer has frequent occasion for", wrote Adam Smith. "Such artificers, too, stand occasionally in need of the assistance of one another, and as their residence is not, like that of the farmer, necessarily tied down to a precise spot, they naturally settle in the neighbourhood of one another, and thus form a small town or village".

The basic pattern of settlements of different sizes was the subject of a famous theorem published by Christaller in 1933.[1] His theorem was that there were seven types of settlements, distributed as follows (Table 14):

Writing when he did, Christaller assumed a farm and rural population relying for transport principally on horse-drawn vehicles, and bicycles.

Table 14.

		Approximate population '000	Average distance apart km	Deduced relative numbers
I	Marktort	1	7	729
II	Amtsort	2	12	243
III	Kreisstadt	4	21	81
IV	Bezirksstadt	10	36	27
V	Gaustadt	30	63	9
VI	Provinzstadt	100	110	3
VII	Landstadt	500	185	1

Note: The titles are left in German because they are almost untranslatable, except for *Ort* (place) and *Stadt* (town) — a somewhat arbitrary distinction: while *markt* indicates trading and *amt* official activities. The other prefixes represent steps in the German administrative hierarchy.

1. Walter Christaller, *Die Zentralen Orte in Sud Deutschland*.

They would not want to have to go far for the purchases of their staple necessaries. So he hypothecated a network of small villages, with limited shopping facilities, averaging only seven kilometres apart. The next stage of requirements was represented by the larger villages, with post office, police station, and various other facilities; and on the average one of these was needed for every three villages of lower order. Then as we go up the scale at each stage one town of higher order is required for each three of lower order. Consequently the relative numbers of the different types of settlements (3rd column) must rise in powers of three, from 1 to 729. The requirements of symmetrical placing also necessitate average distances apart (2nd column) rising proportionately to the square root of three, if we start from the initial assumption of villages seven kilometres apart.

On the face of it, one would conclude that this was an extraordinary piece of theoretical reasoning, which could bear little if any relation to reality. In fact, however, it was found to give a very precise description of the pattern of settlements in Swabia, a well-populated agricultural area in southern Germany, with some widely distributed small industries.

Lösch[2] set out to apply Christaller's principle in the United States, using the State of Iowa for his field work. Iowa is (by American standards) a fairly densely populated and successful agricultural state, on a level plain, without natural barriers.

Lösch classified the Iowa settlements in rather fewer orders; and set out to measure average distances between them. Average distance between towns of order (*n+1*) should, according to Christaller's theorem, exceed that between settlements of order *n* by a factor of the square root of three. Lösch found in Iowa, on the other hand, that this ratio was in the neighbourhood of two. Applying the square root rule, he concluded that on the average one settlement of higher order was required for each four, not three, of each lower order.

Taking as his starting point the actual number (819) of lowest order settlements in Iowa, Lösch found (Table 15) that the Christaller theorem, but with a factor of four, gave an excellent prediction of the numbers of higher-order settlements.

Another case of an unexpectedly good fit (using Christaller's factor of three) was found (Table 16) in modern Denmark.[3] The theoretical patterns were slightly altered to allow for the capital city.

2. W. H. Woglom, trans., *The Economics of Location* (New Haven: Yale University Press, 1954), p. 435.
3. Rallis, *Regional Science Association Proceedings*, 1962.

Table 15.

Population of Settlement	Numbers Calculated	Actual
180-1000		819
1-4000	205	204
4-20,000	51	51
10-60,000	13	12
60-200,000	3	3
200-800,000	1	

It may at first sight appear surprising that a modern motorized community should have preserved so precisely a pattern supposed to fit a horse and bicycle transport economy. Patterns of settlements however change with extraordinary slowness.[4]

In India, on the other hand, Berry,[5] working in the neighbourhood of Kanpur, finds (Table 17) only four orders of settlement size, and his proposed multiplying factor is seven not three or four.

Berry suggests as a generalization that Christaller's factor of three arises "where market conditions prevail and the urban hierarchy develops from the local level upwards by a process of progressive specialization occurring indigenously". He suggests that the factor of four arises "where development was externally induced from an overlay of long-distance trade routes" (probably the situation in Iowa). The factor of seven arises however, he suggests, when the system of centres has been established "for administrative convenience, in an areal division of powers". In every case however the basic geometry, on a uniform plain, will be "hierarchical hexagonal".

Double logarithmic diagrams relating the size of a settlement to the cumulated number of settlements at or above that size, that is, its "rank", are known as rank-size diagrams. For the larger cities, as will be shown in the next chapter, a straight-line relationship is often, though by no means always, found. But it is clear that the number of small settlements, and the total number of settlements, is finite, and the diagram therefore, as we descend the size co-ordinate, must at some point flatten its slope, and become horizontal.

The Christaller theorem however, whether we take the factor of

4. See the present writer's "The Stability of Village Populations", *Urban Studies* 12, no. 1, (1975), pp. 109–11, which traces the populations of villages in Gloucestershire from the sixteenth century to the twentieth (Diagram 1).
5. Private communication.

Table 16. Denmark.

Town rank	Number of inhabitants (thousands)	Number of towns		Distance between towns		Hinterland	
		Actual	Losch	Actual (km.)	Losch	Actual (sq.km.)	Losch (sq.km.)
7	0.25-1	458	486	9	9	70	70
6	1-5	147	162	16	16	210	210
5	5-20	43	54	27	27	580	630
4	20-30	13	18	52	47	1800	1890
3	30-100	5	6	70	81	5700	5670
2	100-1000	2	2	140	140	13500	17010
1	1000 +	1	1	275	240	43000	31030

Table 17. Kanpur District 1961.

| | Numbers | | Distances apart | |
	Theoretical	Actual	Theoretical	Actual
City	1	1	—	—
Districts	6	7	93	86
"Tahsils"	42	49	35	43
"Hats"	294	n.a.	12	
Villages		11239		

three or of four, does not indicate a straight line, but a curved relationship.

Christaller terminated his diagram in a peculiar manner by assuming no settlement of size less than one thousand population. This assumption can only be permitted for a densely populated countryside. In Diagram 1 for Gloucestershire villages the Christaller ratios are all shifted in the same proportion.

We will consider first the pattern of settlements in predominantly agricultural countries, or agricultural regions in industrial countries, before examining the pattern of larger towns.

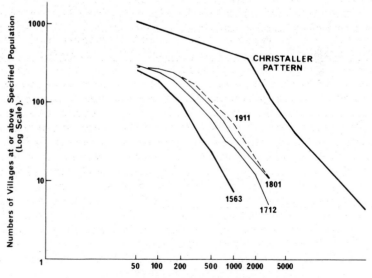

Diagram 1. Gloucestershire Villages.

Christaller's theorem (with a factor of four) is closely matched (Table 18, Diagram 2) by the national data for the agricultural economy of mid-nineteenth century France, less precisely by data from Japan and Italy.

Table 18. Distribution of Settlements in Rural Economies.

Cumulated numbers with population exceeding	Christaller Theorem Factor of 3	Factor of 4	France 1851	India 1961	Italy 1951	Japan 1898	Turkey 1940
500,000	1	1	1	12		2	1
400,000							
300,000						3	
250,000					11		
200,000				40		5	1
100,000	4	5	4	107	25	8	4
50,000			10	248	78	20	
30,000	13	21			160		
20,000			53	763	288	80	40
10,000	40	85	146	2353	789	233	97
5,000			417	2593		1314	
4,000	121	341	452				
3,000			1217		3574		
2,000	364	1365	2679	33300		9330	463
1,500			4773				
1,000	1093	5461	9196	98600	6634		
500			21151	217800	7482	13380	
400			25067				
300			29685				
200			33842				
100			36342				
All	1093	5461	36775	567400	7514	13997	

Sources: France: Statistique de la France 1855, Deuxieme Serie, Territoire et Population, p. 124.
India: Mitra, International Union for the Scientific Study of Population, 1967.
Italy: Chiassino, Annali dell' Instituto di Statistica, Vol. XXVI.
Japan: Sale, Journal of the Royal Statistical Society, April 1911.
Turkey: Sarc, International Statistical Institute, Brussels 1958.
Christaller, Die Zentralen Orte in Sud Deutschland, 1933.

We may look more closely (Table 19, Diagrams 3 and 4) at the pattern of settlements of the smallest size, expressing relative numbers of settlements above each size per thousand of the total number of settlements, thus placing all the data on the same vertical scale. The first question to be asked is to what extent population density deter-

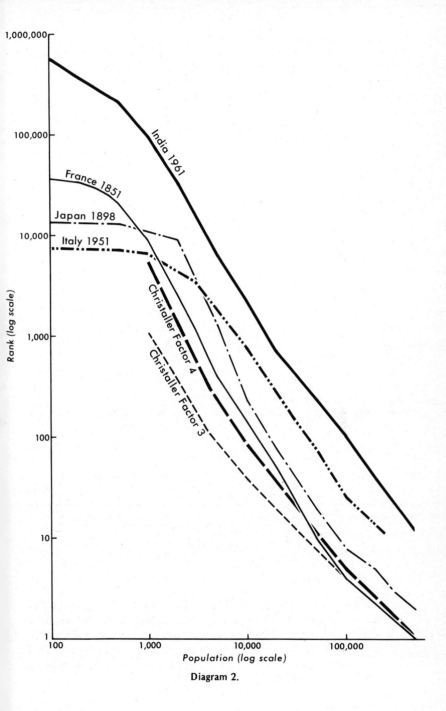

Diagram 2.

Table 19. Numbers per thousand of all small towns and villages at or above specified size.

		20	50	100	150	200	250	500	1000	1500	2000	2500	3000	4000	5000	100000
Japan	1898					1000		956	800		667				93	17
Christaller-Losch (factor 4)					1000				250					62		27
Oxford neighbourhood[b]	1951		960	920		710		288	164	106	68	54	46	30	22	16
	1961		960	920		710		320	188	132	92	60	50	40	28	18
Gloucestershire[c]	1563		895	662		326	222	84	24							
	1911		993	930		765	568	250	181		66					
India[d]						688		381	170		54		37		7	
China[e]							730	420	151	52	19	9				
Wisconsin[f]	1911		750	565		450		260	125		75			30	20	
England & Wales			1000	861			600	388	229							
Leicestershire[g] (interpolated)	1086	670	326	138	66	30	15	2								
Upper Volta[h]						640		310	120		30		10			
Queensland pastoral[i]	1933	928	860	561			275	148	80		37					
	1954		733	538			282	170	106		53					
agricultural	1933	900	821	498			170	72	30		12					
	1954		820	488			170	70	33		17					
Saskatchewan[j]	1951			858				182							16	
France[k] (depopulating areas)	1906			968			867	608[1]	203		54					
	1954			858			618	273[1]	238		59					

a. ~~Losch,~~ application of Christaller in Iowa (Losch, p. 4??). Theoretical distribution (which is very close to actual) interpolated to give figure for 10,000 population; minimum size surveyed at population 180.

b. Census. Berks, Bucks & Oxon counties excluding Greater London periphery and immediate neighbourhoods of Oxford and Reading.

c. Urban Studies (1975), pp. 109-111.

d. Jain World Population Conference (1965).

e. Gamble, *North China Villages*, p. 315; refers to 1920s; family numbers x 4.8 interpolated.

f. Brush, *Geographical Review* (July 1953).

g. Russell, *Journal of Economic History* (March 1964).

h. Geirard in *La developpements de la Hante Volta* ISEA Supplement 112 (1963).

i. Economic News July 1956 (1954 Census. The recent Census does not distinguish the settlements below 200 population).

j. Saskatchewan Royal Commission on Agriculture.

k. Sauvy and others, *Population*, October-December 1955, pp. 739-40. Data for 11 Departements.

l. 400 not 500.

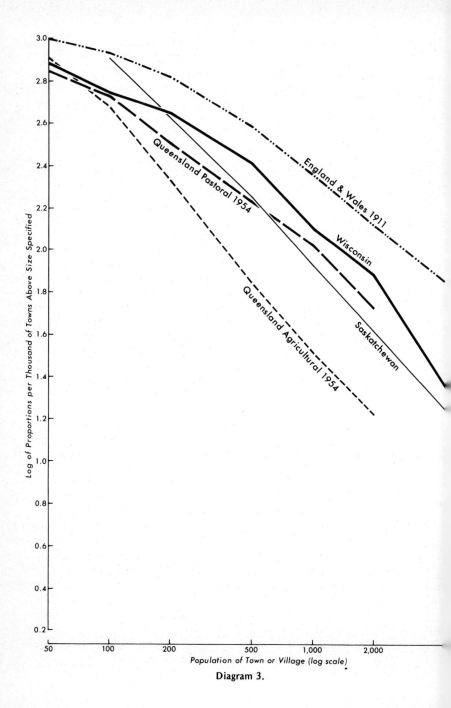

Diagram 3.

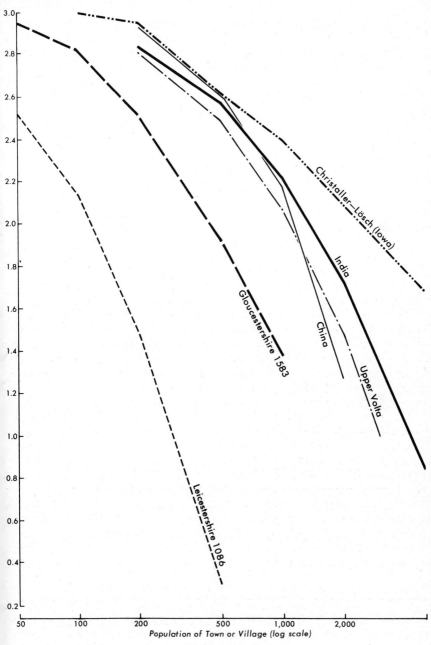

Diagram 4.

mines the pattern of settlement. In a striking comparison[6] between the State of Wisconsin, settled in the mid-nineteenth century, and southern England, settled more than a thousand years earlier, with a very much denser population, it was found that the actual pattern of settlement of the two regions was similar, but that the average size of towns, of any given order, was much greater in the more densely-populated country. Lower order centres were found to be thirteen kilometres apart in England and sixteen in Wisconsin, but with median populations of 5,100 and 400 respectively; and higher order centres thirty-four kilometres apart in both countries, with median populations of 2500 and 14000. The lowest orders of settlement, in districts not served by larger towns, were in both cases found to be about eight kilometres apart.

In Wisconsin "hamlets" usually provided only a general store and a primary school. "Villages" (100–1400 population) usually provided in addition tavern, petrol sales, auto and implement dealer, hardware, appliances, lumber, food, bank, auto repairs, truckers (livestock, milk, freight), post office, phone exchange, feed mill, church, high school, village council.[7]

It is interesting to compare the estimated threshold[8] populations (Table 20) for various functions in the densely populated low-income economy of southern Sri Lanka (Ceylon).

The data for a depopulating region in France in 1906 bear some resemblance to those for England and Wales of 1911; but by 1954 they had come to bear a surprising similarity to those for Wisconsin.

Table 20.

Secondary schools	2,137
Market places and village fairs	1,662
Dispensaries	1,277
Post Offices	950
Cooperative stores	663
Primary schools	660

6. J. E. Brush and H. E. Bracey, "Rural Service Centres in South-western Wisconsin and Southern England" *Geographical Review* (October 1955).
7. Quoted in D. R. Vining, *Economic Development and Cultural Change*, (1954–55), pp. 170–171.
8. P. Haggett and K. A. Gunawardena, "Determination of Population Thresholds for Settlement Functions by the Reed-Muench Method" *The Professional Geographer* 16, no. 4 (July 1964), p. 6.

Diagram 3 repeats, in effect, the Brush-Bracey comparison between England and Wisconsin. (We cannot here compare the Christaller pattern, because for most of our diagram we are below his assumed minimum population of 1,000.) With lower population densities, the whole relationship is shifted downward, that is, functions of a given order in the supposed hierarchy are performed by settlements with smaller population in the less densely populated country. A somewhat different pattern is shown by the data for Saskatchewan.

We come up against a paradox, however, when we examine the data for the pastoral and agricultural areas of Queensland. The pastoral are low-rainfall areas, with a very sparse population, yet they appear to show a pattern of larger settlements, for any given order in the hierarchy, than the agricultural areas. It may be that the agricultural areas were still preserving, in 1954, the old pattern of settlements appropriate to horse-drawn transport in an area of low-density agricultural population. The pastoral areas, on the other hand, probably became motorized earlier than the agricultural areas, with the disappearance of some of the very small settlements which originally arose in these sparsely populated areas.

Diagram 4 takes as its starting point the Christaller-Lösch distribution for Iowa, and compares it with a number of other distributions, for countries of varying density, but at a much lower level of economic development. Here we see not merely the shifting of the curve downwards, as for countries of lower densities, but a change in its shape. The curvature is markedly increased, meaning that relatively far fewer of the higher order settlements are required. This is to be expected in countries of low real incomes and with bad transport and communication. Many of the higher order functions cannot be afforded at all, and most of the necessary functions would be performed in the village itself, without seeking to trade with a larger settlement.

This principle is illustrated most clearly by data which we are fortunate to possess for an English county at the time of Doomsday Book. Even if, as some historians contend, the Doomsday Book populations are understated, through the omission of dependent relatives and others, the information on the relative numbers of settlements of different sizes still stands. Not only were there difficulties of transport and communication; but in mediaeval Europe, to a lesser extent in modern Africa, villagers may have felt some insecurity in travelling far from their own villages.

The villages in Gloucestershire can be seen (Diagram 1) making their gradual transformation between the sixteenth century and the early twentieth century (the date 1911 was chosen as that of the last Census before the beginning of the motor age). Intervening data for 1712 and 1801 show how gradually the change came, with each village showing little change in its relative position in the hierarchy, but with the shape of the curve changing, till it came to about the same as that shown in Diagram 3 for the whole of England and Wales. This change in shape of the curve meant that the larger villages slowly gained population relatively to the smaller, almost certainly due to the increasing number of higher-order functions, for which the larger villages were better suited.

There is also interesting evidence[9] of change in Indian village size with the larger villages growing faster (Table 21) from a study of 245 villages in a "backward district" in Karnataka (populations were given for 1971, and calculated back to 1941 from growth rates given).

Table 21. Indian Village Populations.

Number of villages	67	66	75	29	8
1941 average population	86	226	450	816	1405
% per year growth 1941-71	1.4	1.7	1.9	1.7	2.6

We can obtain a much fuller understanding of the pattern of rural settlements, for a present day high-income population, by listing the functions, economic and other, which each type of settlement actually performs. Such a study was undertaken on a really thorough scale by Berry, Barnum, and Tennant.[10] They chose for their survey an area in south western Iowa, a level land without mountains or other topographical breaks, uniformly inhabited by a fairly high-income farm population. They classified settlements in declining categories from the regional capital (Council Bluffs-Omaha), through cities, towns, "villages", and "hamlets". A "hamlet" is generally nothing more than a few businesses at a crossroad, sometimes only a single business, in every case (so the definition goes) less than ten businesses. A single trader may perform several functions, combining for example, a grocery store, petrol selling, and post office.

The essence of the analysis was to distinguish numbers of traders from numbers of functions performed. With increasing sizes of settlement, the number of functions performed increases, but the number of traders increases more rapidly, that is, there is an increased degree of competition.

9. V. M. Rao, *Essays in Honour of V.K.R.V. Rao* (New Delhi: Allied Publishers), p. 229.
10. B. J. L. Berry, Barnum, and Tennant, "Retail Location and Consumer Behaviour" (Papers from the Proceedings for the Regional Science Association, 1962). A more detailed account of this and other studies is given in C. Clark, *Population Growth and Land Use* beginning p. 302.

The most valuable discovery made in this study was that if we tabulate for each settlement the number of functions, and the number of traders, plotting the results on a semilogarithmic diagram, we obtain evidence of the number of traders increasing more rapidly than the number of functions, but with clearly distinguished breaks in the slopes, enabling us to categorize cities, towns, and villages (Diagram 5).

"Villages", thus defined, perform on the average some sixteen functions — though there is a wide range about this figure; as seen from Diagram 5, some perform more than twenty functions, some less than ten. Besides the elementary functions groceries, petrol

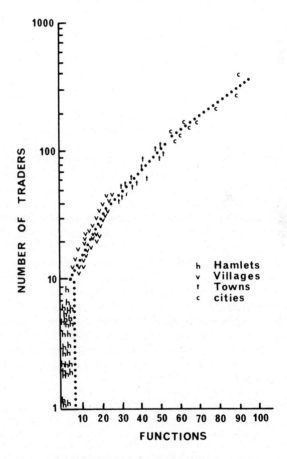

Diagram 5. Number of Traders and Functions.

selling, post office, already mentioned for "hamlets", the average village performs the social functions of providing a church, a hall for social gatherings, and a local council office, besides its economic functions of restaurant, tavern, hardware store, businesses related to selling farm requirements and dealing in farm products, and also (remember that this is a high income community) a hairdresser and beauty parlour.

"Town" functions are much more diversified. It is to "towns" that people have to look for such services as physician, dentist, pharmacist, veterinarian, undertaker, bank, furniture store, real estate agent, and a number of others. "Cities" perform up to ninety different functions of a more specialized nature; specialized shops such as clothing, shoes, jewellery, florists, new and used cars, and wines and spirits; and more specialized services such as medical specialists, lawyers, plumbers, trade union organizers, and amusement parlours.

While the numbers of functions and traders follow a closely defined pattern, as we see in the Diagram, the spacing of settlements was not so precise. Hamlets service, presumably, populations of only a few hundred. Villages might serve anything from five hundred to fifteen hundred population, with a service area anywhere from ten to a hundred square miles. Towns may serve between fifteen hundred and six thousand population and from ninety to three hundred square miles. A population of six thousand is estimated to be the "threshold" which calls for city services; cities may serve anything between six and thirty thousand population, and an area ranging from one thousand square miles down to only a little over one hundred square miles in a few cases. A regional population of one hundred thousand or more calls for the services of a regional metropolis.

An interesting conclusion is that the areas served by both towns and cities are approximately proportional to the populations which they serve. This means that, in areas of higher population density, there is *not* any apparent tendency to place towns or cities closer together. This confirms the results of the Brush-Bracey comparison mentioned above. With a denser population each village or town of any given order will be more populous, but their spatial pattern will not significantly alter.

Berry obtained a very interesting result when he applied the same method to a very different sort of rural area, namely the partially industrialized area of Illinois in the neighbourhood of Chicago.[11] While such an area has not needed "hamlets" it still differentiates its

---

11. B. J. L. Berry, Metropolitan Planning Guidelines: Commercial Structure in North East Illinois Planning Commission, p. 177.

trading centres into four types (neighbourhood, community, smaller regional, and major regional centres), but with some twenty functions performed even by the smallest centres. As before, the number of establishments rises faster than the number of functions (that is, increasing competition); though not so steeply as in Iowa.

This study also revealed an interesting case of "economic externalities". The number and locations of the major regional centres were, in effect, settled by the decisions of the principal chain stores. These attracted so many customers that most smaller retailers could not afford to locate except in proximity to them. So, Berry pointed out, the decisions of a few firms could determine the locations of some twenty thousand lesser retail and service businesses for many years into the future.

Berry and his co-workers may indeed have discovered a principle of general application. It is strikingly confirmed by a detailed historical study[12] of the business directories of San Diego County in 1890. The results are plotted on Diagram 6 (semi-logarithmic). Below ten

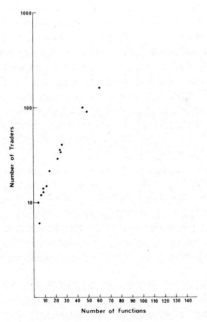

Diagram 6. San Diego County 1890.

12. Smolensky and Ratajczak, *Explorations in Entrepreneurial History*, Vol. 2, No. 2.

functions the curve climbs steeply, with slope then progressively diminishing.

Of the 137 functions performed by the capital city of San Diego, 76 performed by 1000 traders are also found in one or more of the country towns. The remaining 61 (914 traders) are unique to the capital city.

A relation similar to Berry's was also found[13] in a rural area in Australia, in the less-densely populated Darling Downs region in Queensland. In this case the settlements were classified by size of workforce, which bears some relation to the number of enterprises (Table 22). The number of functions, plotted against the logarithm of the workforce, gives a curve similar to Berry's.

Table 22.

	Number of settlements	Average work force	Average number of functions
Hamlets	45	6	8
Villages	27	32	29
Small towns	8	418	113
Large towns	2	2690	241
Small city	1	15310	437

A careful counting of functions was also made by Stiglbauer[14] who graded settlements in the predominantly agricultural province of Lower Austria (Table 23).

Table 23.

Average number of trade and manufacturing functions	Number of places
5	583
14	435
36	228
84	79
116	49
229	32

Note: The average area served (estimated approximately from the reciprocals of the second column) rises considerably less rapidly than the number of functions.

13. R. S. Dick, "A Definition of the Central Place Hierarchy of the Darling Downs, Queensland" *Queensland Geographical Journal* (December 1971), p. 30.
14. K. Stiglbauer, "Some Problems of Central Places at the Lowest Level in Austria" *Regional Sciences Association Papers* 18 (1967) pp. 52–55.

7
The Pattern of Urban Settlements

A considerable stir was caused in the economic world in the 1890s when Pareto announced his discovery of a law of distribution of incomes, namely that the logarithm of the number of incomes at or above an amount n was a linear function of the logarithm of n. This generalization contains some important truth and was a valuable discovery, but (1) the slope of the relationship is not always the 1.5 which Pareto believed it to be, but can vary widely; (2) the rule is obviously only applicable, as soon as we come to think of it, to the numbers of higher incomes – literally applied, it would mean an infinite number of small incomes.

An analagous law relating to the sizes of urban settlements (the non-linear relationship for rural settlements was dealt with in the previous chapter) attracted little attention when it was first discovered by Auerbach,[1] and it was in fact forgotten until rediscovered by Singer.[2] Singer's results were also neglected in a well-known book published by Zipf in 1940, which made the mistake, once again, of assuming a uniform slope of one, whereas Singer had already shown that the slopes could differ widely.

The slope of this rank-size relationship on double-log plotting does provide some measure of the degree of dispersal or centralization of urban populations. At the theoretical extremes, if all cities were of the same size, the rank-size diagram would be a vertical line; if all population were concentrated in one city it would be horizontal, that is, slopes of infinity and zero respectively. A slope of one represents some sort of median position, with higher slopes representing a greater and lower slopes a lesser degree of dispersal.

Diagram 7 shows the rank-size diagrams for three representative countries. The slopes are seen to be only approximately linear, with some significant deviations.

---

1. Dr A. Petermann, Geographischer Mitteilungen (Gotha: Haark, 1913).
2. H. W. Singer, "Courbe des populations: a Parallel to Pareto's law", *Economic Journal*, 46 (June 1936), pp. 254–63.

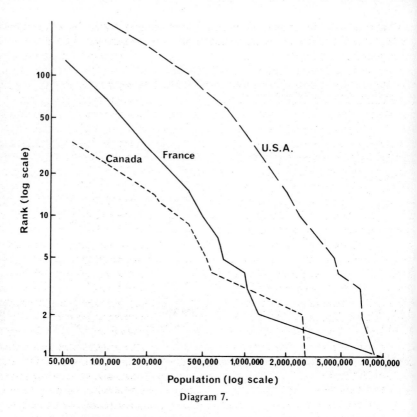

Diagram 7.

Rank-size diagrams for a number of countries are shown in Chapter 8 the present writer's *Population Growth and Land Use*. These and other results are summarized below.

Largely rural economies (including Bulgaria, Denmark even now, 1830 Netherlands, 1906 Australia) have continued to show a Christaller pattern; or a linear relationship, with a high degree of dispersal (slopes of 1.5 in early nineteenth century France, Germany and Sweden and modern Nigeria; 1.4 in 14th century England, Spain in 1900, India in 1921; 1.3 in Belgium in 1830 and 1.2 in China in 1936).

However it is clear that a number of the relationships may show a "bulge", as in the United States — in this case settlements with a population of about three-quarters of a million are relatively more numerous, and the population of the largest cities relatively less than was to be expected from a linear rank-size relation. Conversely, as in Canada, there may be a "kink", that is, a comparative deficiency of settlements about this size; or extreme cases such as France, where the primate city is out of all proportion larger than the linear relationship would indicate. The principal inflexions (bulges and kinks) are noted in Table 24.

Table 24. Inflexions of Rank-Size Relationship (points at which change appears approximately indicated).

BULGE		KINK	
(slope greater, i.e., comparative equality among larger cities)		(slope less, i.e., comparative inequality among larger cities)	
U.S.A.	(0.75 m.)	Canada	(48,000)
Belgium	(0.25 m.)	Brazil	(150,000)
Germany	(1.5 m.)	China	(1 m.)
Italy	(Turin)	India	(0.5 m.)
Netherlands	(700,000)	Japan	(0.5 m.)
Switzerland	(200,000)	U.K.	(0.5 m.)
U.S.S.R.	(100,000)	U.S.S.R.	(Kiev)
		Australia	(75,000)

EXCEPTIONALLY MARKED PRIMACIES
Jamaica
Argentine
Mexico
France
Greece

These results may indicate that the current pressures of economic forces are indicating some sort of optimal size of metropolitan area (whether or not private and social optima coincide is another matter) in the neighbourhood of three-quarters of a million for United States of America, and corresponding figures for other countries shown in Table 24.

The "kinks" are more difficult to explain. In these cases "oligarchies" of larger cities have formed — two in Canada and Brazil, four in India and Australia, which oligarchies appear to have been able, by economic competition, or perhaps by political pressure, to check the growth of cities of the next lower rank. (In the hierarchy of cities of Soviet Russia, is the relatively slow development of Kiev to be accounted for by political pressure?)

From oligarchy we pass to cases of "primacy", where the capital city is quite outstandingly larger than indicated by a linear rank-size relationship. We cannot explain these primacies without bringing in cultural and political considerations. At first sight, looking at France and Latin America, we might judge that it may be in the Latin tradition to seek, not only extreme political and administrative centralization, but also an intense desire for the cultural life of the capital city, and dislike of provincial culture. But on such an explanation, how to account for Italy and Spain? All that can be said is that these centralizing political and cultural tendencies prevail except when they are offset by strong forces making for regional differentiation, which in Italy were still a political reality until the nineteenth century, and in Spain where there is still strong cultural differentiation.

Much has been said about the abnormal growth of the capital cities of Latin American countries, which are still at a low level of general economic development. In this case it is fairly clear that the social optimum would be for dispersal to a number of cities of more moderate size. But the balance of private advantage is probably with the capital city, not only for the business man who may have many reasons for establishing there, but also for the poor peasant family who exchange their (perhaps more commodious) mud hut in the village for a squalid shanty on the outskirts of the capital city. Here, horrifying though their situation appears to us, they find some chance of securing employment, of obtaining some medical service and education for their children, chances of which are little or nothing for those remaining in the villages.

These considerations depend, of course, upon political factors. The inhabitants of the capital city find themselves enjoying ever increasing political strength. In Mexico City, now one of the most populous cities in the world, even the price of food is subsidized, at the expense of the rest of the country. With oil wealth, a really striking development of primacy has appeared in Iran, with nearly tenfold growth of the capital city since 1940 (Diagram 8).

The present pattern for the United States is clearly one of "bulge" or, as we may call it, counter-primacy. The population of the New York metropolitan area is much less than would be expected from the projection of a linear rank-size relationship (and is now declining). But it was not always so.[3] New York developed a marked primacy in the period 1830–50, then lost it, then recovered it about 1900, then by 1940 lost it again. These strange developments are perhaps connected with New York's position as the principal terminal for trans-Atlantic shipping, and the varying large waves of migrant inflow. Many migrants tend to settle in the port where they arrive.

We have now some indications of the sizes of cities, in some countries relatively favoured, in some relatively disfavoured, in the course of urban growth. But there is another factor which we must examine. Does the proximity of a larger city exercise a "shadowing" effect, slowing down growth? Alternatively, does it, through the

3. Vining, Economic Development and Cultural Change (1954–55), p. 133.

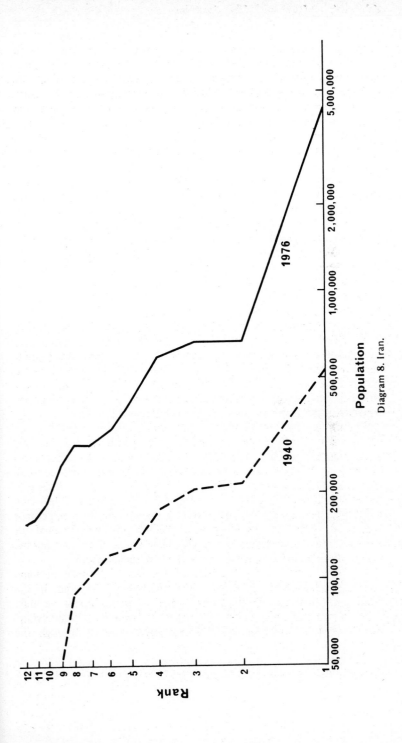

Population

Diagram 8. Iran.

existence of various economic complementarities, favour growth? The former appears to be the case.

For most countries data are too few for any sort of statistical analysis, but it is possible for the United States. The units measured are "metropolitan districts", which means not only the older cities within their arbitrarily demarcated municipal boundaries, but all adjacent urban areas deemed, on various criteria, to be essentially part of the same economic unit. These metropolitan areas are taken as now officially defined, though there are bound to be a few uncertainties — for instance, should northeastern New Jersey be regarded as an integral part of the New York metropolitan area? (It is not now, but was on some demarcations made in the past). There are difficulties in obtaining population estimates for comparable areas in the past, at a time when much of what is now suburbs was still agricultural land. Official estimates have been made for the larger metropolitan areas back to 1900.[4] For many of the smaller metropolitan areas only the 1900 population of the central city could be ascertained, with an approximate estimate added for the population of what now constitute the outlying parts of the metropolitan area.

The rates of growth vary very widely between cities. For this reason the results were analyzed (Table 25) by medians and not by means. The data are classified by distance from the next larger metropolitan area, but also cross-classified by the population attained by the metropolitan area in 1975 — on the face of it, the metropolitan areas which are large now are those which may be expected to have shown higher rates of growth in the past. Reading across the table horizontally

Table 25. Metropolitan Areas[1] Factors of Growth 1900-1975 in the United States. Median values (figures in brackets represent numbers of cases).

Distance from next larger metropolitan area kms.	Population in 1975			
	Under 0.25 million	0.25-0.5 million	0.5 million	Over 1 million
0-125	3.3 (12)	4.2 (19)	4.7 (15)	3.3 (9)
125-250			3.6 (9)	
250-375	4.3 (13)	6.1 (26)	7.9 (8)	4.4 (8)
over 375				6.2 (12)

1. Excluding New York, Chicago, and Los Angeles.

4. *The Growth of Metropolitan Districts in the United States 1900–1940* (United States Bureau of Census, 1947).

shows that, other things being equal, the highest rates of growth have generally been attained by metropolitan areas now in the half to one million neighbourhood — a conclusion already drawn from the bulge in the rank-size diagram.

Reading the table vertically we see, with one exception, that rates of growth are indeed higher in cities more distant from competitors.

A critic might object that a further variable ought to be analyzed out, to take account of the fact that in the United States many of the most rapidly growing metropolitan areas are in the west and south, and these also happen to be distant from their competitors. The suggestion is that cities in the west and south would still have grown rapidly, even if they had been nearer to competitors. Theoretically this is possible, but it does not seem probable.

8

The Optimum Size of City

The interesting kinks and bulges shown in different countries in the rank-size diagrams of urban settlements suggest the possibility that certain city sizes may represent an optimum more attractive to population than other-sized cities – and conversely that some other sizes are relatively unattractive. It is also clear however that it will take a very long time before significant changes become apparent in the shape of the urban size-distribution pattern, particularly when the rate of general population growth is slow.

The comparative attractiveness of cities of sizes specified in the previous chapter – for example, three-quarters of a million in the United States – represents however only the private optimum, from choices made by individual decisions. Whether this also constitutes the social optimum is another question. The social optimum may differ from the private if there are significant economic externalities. Economic externalities were long ago defined by Pigou, in precise terms, as follows: when "One person A, in the course of rendering some service for which payment is made to a second person B incidentally also renders services or dis-services to other persons, of such a sort that payment cannot be extracted from the benefitted parties, or compensation enforced on behalf of the injured parties."[1]

Where externalities prevail the market, by definition, cannot secure adjustment, and action by public authority is necessary. It is not however always direct action that is necessary; public authorities can sometimes "internalize" an externality by taxes, subsidies, or similar devices, still leaving decisions with individual businesses, but encouraging them in the required direction.

Economies of aggregation are clearly the principal factor in the growth of cities. The productivity of manufacturing labour in United States cities has been analyzed[2] and shows a rise of 6 per cent for each doubling of city size – rather less than might have been expected.

1. A. Pigou, *Wealth and Welfare* (London: Macmillan, 1920).
2. L. Sveikauskas, "The Productivity of Cities", *Quarterly Journal of Economics* 89, no. 30 (August 1975), pp. 393–413.

This is a crude productivity figure, calculated before taking into
account capital inputs, both private and public, per unit of labour.
If these are higher in the larger cities, the total productivity gain
will be still smaller.

Developing the concept of economic externalities, we can define
the duty of public authorities as the provision of "public goods".
This is a technical term which has to be carefully defined. At first
sight, an adequate supply of food and clothing might be considered
"public goods". But we do not look to public authorities to provide
them, in other than the most exceptional circumstances – we buy
them for ourselves. Even if we are in poverty, we look to public
authorities to provide us with money to buy them, not to provide
them direct. "Public goods" – look back to the definition of
economic externalities – are only those where "payment cannot
be extracted from the benefitted parties". Conversely, "public goods"
include the removal of harmful economic externalities. In colloquial
language, public goods are those in the provision of which it is
impossible to prevent free-loading. Outstanding examples are the
provision of national defence, the prevention of crime, the checking
of infectious diseases, and the like. "Cannot be exacted" includes
cases such as charging tolls on roads, which in practice is only possible
on a few long distance highways, and the like. Traffic congestion
(see further in Chapter 17) is an obvious harmful economic externality
– it is neither legal nor practicable to go up to the driver of the next
vehicle and ask him to get off the road – this is certainly a field for
action by public authorities. Likewise air and water pollution.

Town and country planning, properly conducted, should have as
their object the mitigation of traffic congestion, but primarily the
preservation of beauty and order in landscape and townscape, which
they have so often failed to do. These are objects which should benefit
all and for which payment cannot be exacted.

More will be said in Chapter 14 on some of the aberrations of
town planning.

Decisions about a social optimum are clearly required in the
planning of "New Towns".

New Towns are not a new idea. In the ancient world a prominent
and successful example of Alexandria, named after the great ruler
who planned it. In medieval England Salisbury, with its famous
cathedral, was designed as a new town to replace "Old Sarum",
a short distance away, where there were difficulties with the
water supply. Not far away Devizes (Latin *Divisia*) was also planned
as a new town. Washington, Canberra, and Brasilia have all been
designed as new towns to act as centres of government. In each of
these cases however, planners seem to have had very uncertain,

if any, ideas about the optimum population towards which the new towns should ultimately grow. Washington has now swollen into a metropolitan area of over three million people and many would agree that this is much too large.

Planning a new town as a site for central government certainly relieves pressure on land and other resources in the older capital city. It is also intended to free politicians and officials from the larger city's sectional pressures. But there is the converse danger, that the rulers will become too detached from circumstances of ordinary life. Canada may have been wiser in constructing a capital out of an existing small industrial town, while not encouraging it to grow too large. An interesting compromise was the construction of New Delhi, begun in 1911, situated about five miles away from the old capital, and in a position to share many of its facilities.

Regarding new towns in modern times, the world should be very grateful to Britain for the numerous experiments which have been conducted, principally for showing the rest of the world what not to do. Most of the British new towns have been designed too small, and too close to London.

The idea of new towns in Britain began in the 1890s with the social reformer Ebenezer Howard. He observed that most of the inhabitants of London, and of other large cities, were living in crowded tenements or houses, without gardens or open spaces. He saw no prospect of being able to provide these on the existing pattern of the cities, and concluded that the right action would be to build new "garden cities". These however were not to be at any great distance from the old cities, and were not to be self-contained. They were to be "satellite cities" (how harmful this concept has ultimately proved to be!) separated from the old capital city by a "green belt". Most of the inhabitants of a satellite city were indeed to find local employment, but would have to proceed (by steam train) occasionally to the central city for the more specialized medical and cultural services. The "green belt" was to be kept open for agriculture and recreation, and also (a nice touch) as a site for homes for rehabilitation of alcoholics, in whom nineteenth century London abounded.

The fatal fault in this idea was that, even in the age of steam trains, still more of motorized transport, overwhelming economic and political pressures were bound to build up to develop industrial and residential settlements along the main routes between the capital city and the satellites. An increasing proportion of the inhabitants of the satellite cities would come to work and to do other business in the capital city, thus adding to transport and traffic problems. And no farmer was anxious to cultivate land in the "green belt", which soon came to be known among town planners as the "weed belt", because most people believed that it was destined soon to be built over.

This idea was first taken up, not by public authorities, but by two large and wealthy private employers with social consciences, seeking to improve the lot of their own employees by building "garden suburbs" — Canbury on what were then the outskirts of Birmingham, and Lever a little further from the centre of Liverpool. To obviate travel costs their large factories (producing chocolate and soap, respectively) were placed in the garden suburbs, but designed not to emit smoke and to harmonize as much as possible with their surroundings.

The idea of complete "garden cities" was also first developed by two private companies, at Letchworth in 1912 and Welwyn in 1920 (the latter was later taken over by a public authority). Letchworth was far enough from London to discourage all but a very few of the inhabitants from travelling daily to work in London, and satisfactory local employment gradually developed. After some decades it turned out that the venture had made a very large profit, and there was an unedifying dispute over its distribution. For Welwyn however, only twenty miles from London, the situation was quite different. A large proportion of the inhabitants worked in London, and the project ran into financial difficulties.

Nothing further happened in this field until 1946, when the Attlee Labour Government legislated for public funds to start a number of new towns, mostly fairly close to London, but some in other parts of Great Britain. An exception to the general plan for low density garden cities was Cumbernauld in Scotland, designed at very high density (most families living in apartments) but with a view to every home being within walking distances of the city centre. To the lack of gardens, it was thought, there should be no objection in the Scottish climate.

From the beginning of this policy, and up to this stage, there was a clearly expressed policy that the optimum size of city, towards which each should aim, and on which plans should be based, was a population of about fifty thousand. The most thorough research has failed to discover how this figure originated. It seems to have been an intuitive judgement in the early days, on someone's part, and is almost certainly too small. British administrators, rather late in the day, must seem to have recognized this. Most recent plans for new towns, unlikely now to be fulfilled, in view of the prospective fall in population, at Milton Keynes, half way between London and Birmingham, and a proposed new town on the Humber Estuary, envisage an ultimate population between two hundred and fifty and four hundred thousand.

In considering an urban optimum we may first look at the cost of providing municipal services and administration. These costs may be partly "internalized", in the form of higher or lower levels of municipal taxes or rates. But only to a limited degree. These charges fall on inhabitants other than those making location decisions; and a large part of municipal costs may be met by central government grants.

Two early studies (Table 26) show costs rising almost uniformly with the size of city in the United States, and an optimal size of one to one hundred and fifty thousand in England. Lomax made adjustments where he could to allow for the quality of the services provided, which Ogden only did in respect of education and police. He found what appeared to be a better education service in the smaller towns, and many fewer policy per ten thousand population – perhaps they were less necessary.

With or without these adjustments for the quality of services, it is however impossible to reconcile these conclusions with those developed more recently.

Hirsch[3] confined himself to the St. Louis neighbourhood, and analyzed costs of municipalities with populations ranging from a few hundred to nearly a million. For education, police, and refuse collection he found no significant relation to size of city. Fire service did however show a significant optimum at about one hundred thousand population. Increases above this minimum cost for cities at optimum population level, in dollars per head of population, were 1.2 at a population of one thousand, 3.6 at a population of three hundred thousand, and 15.9 at a population of half a million. One may speculate about the social and economic factors associated with greater risk of fire damage in large cities.

Scot and Feder[4] and Brazier[5] also find few significant relationships; though what they do find, in some cases, are diseconomies of scale. Brazier set out to analyze costs, holding constant population density, rate of growth, employment, and inter-government subsidies, and found little or no relation to the size of city, but did find another significant variable, namely median family income. With the other variables held constant, each form of municipal expenditure did show

3. Hirsch, "Expenditure Implications of Metropolitan Growth and Consolidation", Review of Economics and Statistics 41, no. 3 (August 1959), pp. 232–241.
4. S. Scot and E. L. Feder, *Factors Associated with Variations in Municipal Expenditure Levels* (Berkeley: University of California, Bureau of Public Administration 1957).
5. H. E. Brazier, "City Expenditures in the United States" *National Bureau of Economic Research, Occasional Paper No. 66* (1959).

Table 26. Costs per head (or per child) in United States cities, 1930 and English cities 1930-36.[1]

Population of city	Costs of municipal services in English cities £ per head per year 1930-36[2]	Population of city	Costs in $ per head of population for:							
			Police per 10,000 population	Pupils per teacher	Costs of education $ per child	Hospitals and institutions	Public health	Public recreations	Libraries	Courts and police
Under 7,500	8.16	Under 30,000	29	22	73	1.5	0.5	0.9	0.4	0.1
75-100,000	8.02	30- 50,000	31	22	77	1.4	0.6	1.0	0.4	0.1
100-150,000	7.91	50- 100,000	33	25	79	1.7	0.9	1.2	0.6	0.1
150-300,000	8.41	100- 300,000	43	24	97	4.6	1.6	1.9	0.7	0.2
Over 300,000	9.84	300- 600,000	45	29	94	4.7	1.4	2.3	0.9	0.4
		600-1,000,000	55	29	102	4.8	1.5	2.0	0.7	0.6

1. Ogburn, *Social Characteristics of Cities*, 1937.
2. Lomax, *Journal of the Royal Statistical Society*, 1943.

a positive elasticity in relation to income, the lowest being 0.30 for fire protection, and the highest 0.56 for police. Part of the difference between Ogden and Hirsch may be explained by the fact that the latter took a geographically homogeneous region, whereas in Ogden's wider survey there may have been great differences in salary scales between regions.

A Canadian study[6] (confined to Ontario municipalities), standardized for variables other than population, gives erratic results for the (probably few) larger cities. Current expenditure per head (excluding education, and capital charges) shows a district rise at one hundred thousand population, in all services except water supply, whose cost fell from $11.7 per head (in 1961) in the smallest towns to a minimum of $7.0 with one hundred and fifty thousand population, above that again rising.

An analysis of school accounts[7] found that costs per pupil no longer decreased after the size of primary school rose above three hundred pupils (corresponding to a population of only approximately twenty-five hundred). The threshold was claimed to be seven hundred for a high school, still however corresponding to only a comparatively small population. Attempts in rural and outer suburban areas to raise school numbers to optimum size by provision of additional transport led to the conclusion that the cost of such transport outweighed the gain.

In high schools, with their more specialized teaching and other facilities, economies of scale are indeed more important. Riew considers that $200 per pupil year can be saved by raising pupil numbers from two to seventeen hundred.[8] But a much lower estimate is made by Osborn after analyzing the 1966 data from the State of Missouri standardized for a number of other variables.[9] Cost savings in dollars per pupil year were as follows:—

Size Change	200–500	500–1000	1000–1500	1500–2000	2000–2244
	13	17	11	6	1

If high school education for say five years becomes universal the high school population will be about one-twelfth of the total

6. R. G. Bodkin and D. W. Conklin, "Scale and Other Determinants of Municipal Government Expenditures in Ontario: A Quantitative Analysis" *International Economic Review* 12, no. 3 (Oct. 1971), p. 476.
7. J. S. McLure, *Effect of Population Sparsity of School Cost* (New York: Columbia University, 1947).
8. J. Riew, "Scale Economies in Public Schools" *Review of Economics and Statistics* 54, no. 1 (February 1972), p. 100.
9. D. D. Osborn, "Economies of Size Associated with Public High Schools" Review of Economics and Statistics (Feb. 1970), p. 115.

population, and the optimum sized school of fifteen hundred would serve a population of eighteen thousand.

Many educators, while admitting some economic advantage to larger schools, consider that this is more than counterbalanced by the greater personal attention which each pupil can receive in a smaller school. Some more recent figures do show marked rises in costs with size of city (Table 27).[10]

Table 27. Municipal Expenses (Stone) £/person/year 1956-7.

	Fire	Police
London	.75	
Other metropolitan areas	.50	1.85
Other large towns	.45	1.75
Small towns	.40	1.55

Smaller towns in lower-income countries appear to show much greater comparative advantage. This is nearly 3:1, according to an Italian estimate of capital costs (Table 28).

Table 28. Social Costs '000 Lire for One Worker Plus One Dependent.

Town below	30,000	123
Town	30-200,000	194
Town over	200,000	357

Source: Informazione Svimez, 1957, p. 438.

Substantial difference was also shown by an Indian estimate.[11] The authors defined as public capital costs housing (whether publicly or privately provided) at the modest rate of 5.5 square metres/person, water, roads, schools, public hospital, medical service, police buildings, and bus and rail transport in the metropolitan area. Marginal capital costs for one additional manufacturing worker with average dependency ratio they found to be twenty-nine thousand rupees in Bombay and for a small town (Nasik) seventeen thousand rupees (at prices of the 1960s).

These calculations (as also in Italy) must have been affected by the estimated lower labour costs and land prices in the smaller towns.

10. P. A. Stone, *Town Planning Review* (October 1959).
11. G. S. and A. P. Kulkarni, Gokhale Institute, Poona, private communication.

But considering that the net productivity of an Indian manufacturing worker at that time was only in the order of magnitude of two thousand rupees/year, the Indian figures represent large capital investments.

World Health Organization estimates, covering minimum hygienic requirements, show water supply costs (in dollars of 1978 purchasing power per additional person served) at fifty to one hundred and fifty urban as against thirty to fifty rural.[12] Water closets, with their high water consumption, may approach six hundred in costs, but hygienic use of earth closets or other "alternative sanitation technologies" imposes a cost of up to one hundred for urban population as against forty for rural or urban fringe population.

Capital costs in Australia were also estimated to be substantially higher in Sydney than for the same population increase (assumed half a million) distributed among country towns.[13] Per head costs (excluding land) (at prices of about 1970) of water headworks and distribution, sewerage, roads, bridges, public transport, and flood control were estimated at $912 and $672 respectively. Of the difference $214 represented sewerage and $61 roads, with some minor costs differing in Sydney's favour.

It is not of course implied that per head costs of public services are lower in sparsely populated regions – indeed they are substantially higher. In a survey carried out in Queensland it was possible to compare costs over regions with an extremely wide range of population densities. An attempt was made to include capital as well as current costs, at a time when capital costs had not been distorted by recent large changes in the value of money. It is seen that costs were lowest in an agricultural area (Darling Downs) with fairly high (by Australian standards) population density, rather than in the metropolitan area (Table 29). The opposite tendency is shown in the education column. This reflects the absence of high schools in the remoter areas.

Table 29. State and Municipal Expenditure in Certain Queensland Regions. (*Economic News*, Dec. 1940) £/head.

	Population '000	Persons /km²	Education	Hospital	Police	Municipal	TOTAL
Far West	5.45	.12	1.21	1.93	1.84	4.17	9.15
S.W.	12.1	.36	1.27	1.76	1.55	3.80	8.38
Maranoa	16.8	1.24	1.43	1.72	1.17	3.61	7.93
Darling Downs	108.8	10.3	1.64	.72	.54	2.25	5.15
Moreton	448	13.4	1.53	.76	.53	2.96	5.77

12. Y. Rovani, *Finance and Development* (International Monetary Fund and World Bank, March 1979), p. 15.
13. *Report of the Committee of Commonwealth and State Officials on Decentralization, 1972.*

Some interesting more recent figures are available from Japan[14] relating to public expenditure in 1959–61. They apparently do not include local government expenditure and it is not clear whether they include capital expenditure. These also show (Table 30) fairly high costs in the most sparsely inhabited region, falling to rise to a very high figure in the Tokyo (Kanto) region (probably due to payments for general national administration, which were excluded in the Queensland comparison).

Table 30.

Region	Population density '000/km^2	Treasury expenditure 1959-61 '000 yen/person/year
Hokkaido	2.7	39.0
Tohoku	5.9	23.2
Chubu	9.2	23.1
Shikoku	9.9	17.0
Chugoku	10.6	21.7
Kyushu	15.6	19.8
Kanto	77.7	117.2

An early attempt to analyze the economic functions of a city in relation to its size was made by the present writer.[15] The object was to express employment in various services, not as a proportion of all employment, but in relation to regional incomes. Some data on regional incomes were at that time available for the United States and Canada; the analysis also covered British and Australian data, for which only indirect indications of regional income were available. The basic concept was that, to an increasing degree, the function of cities was to provide services rather than manufactures, but that the smaller towns were less able to provide the more specialized services to their own and the surrounding region's inhabitants, who thus either had to do without them, or to "import" them from larger towns. The general conclusion reached was that at a population level somewhat between one and two hundred thousand the city became capable of providing a fairly full range of services, excluding only a

14. M. Chisholm, *Geography and Economics* (London: Bell, 1966), p. 219, based on data privately communicated by Professor K. Murata, Chuo University (Population densities were approximately estimated from map provided).
15. C. Clark, "The Economic Functions of a City in Relation to its Size" *Econometrica* 13, no. 2 (April 1945).

few most specialized, to its inhabitants and those of the surrounding region. Such cities however, on the evidence then available — likewise now — did not appear sufficiently attractive to manufacture, and it was thought that a size approaching half a million might be necessary so to attract. This matter will be reconsidered later after we have examined the comparative "economic potential" of regions.

A much more accurate and detailed study was prepared by Neutze on data from New Zealand.[16] The principal results in a summary diagram were given in the present writer's *Population Growth and Land Use* (p. 334). In New Zealand much detailed information about incomes and employment is available for regions, which are fairly sharply demarcated geographically. The smallest regional capital has a population only a little over twenty thousand. The degree of regional self-sufficiency in the provision of manufactures and services measured by employment per unit of income, was of the order of magnitude of seventy per cent for the regions with central cities below 50,000 population; for manufacture, of the order of magnitude of forty per cent in these regions, consisting mostly of materials-oriented manufactures. Self-sufficiency in services was found to be almost complete for cities over two hundred thousand population (see Chapter 12 for fuller information).

A Russian planner,[17] thinking in economic terms, found cities in the fifty to two hundred thousand population range the most efficient, though optimum size varied with the city's function. The economy of a town[18] improved up to two hundred to two hundred and fifty thousand population, above which point infrastructure became more expensive.

Then however, regrettably, Abrasimov went on to propose satellite towns twenty-fifty to fifty kilometres away from the parent town, with populations of about sixty-five thousand.

A recent study[19] considers optima and desirable upper limits for city size in the light of pollution, health, crime, income, and leisure. On the non-economic criteria, for the advanced countries, the author finds the optima at two to three hundred thousand population and the upper limit 0.5 million. For developing countries the corresponding figures are three to five hundred thousand, and six hundred thousand.

16. Neutze (Thesis deposited in the Bodleian Library, and unpublished elsewhere).
17. Davidovich, quoted in Chauncey Harris, *Cities of the Soviet Union*, p. 46.
18. Abrasimov, Secretary, Union of Soviet Architects, *Pravda* (Moskva), 6 June 1960.
19. Paul Bairoch, *Taille des villes, conditions de vie et developpement economique* (Paris: Ecole des Hautes Etudes en Sciences Sociales, 1977). Conclusions summarized in Population, May–June 1979, p. 732.

The economic criteria, particularly employment, productivity and saving indicate slightly higher figures, but seem to disappear after the city has reached 0.5 million in the advanced and seven hundred thousand in the developing countries — with the indication that the latter figure will fall with development, and that a limit of six hundred thousand should be the object of policy.

The great growth of cities beyond these limits throughout the world is described by Bairoch in a trenchant phrase as "a form of disorder of the mechanisms of growth in a living body", which is the medical description of a cancer.

Washington, New Delhi, Canberra, Brasilia are all new towns built specifically to serve as national capitals, and the capital city of a large and wealthy country will inevitably become large. Experience of these cities has been mixed, with some good features. Japanese ideas on this subject are of interest.

The official National Land Agency published a proposal[20] to move the political capital from Tokyo, with its smog and congestion. No specific site was proposed, but it was stipulated that it should be more than one hundred but less than 250 kilometres from Tokyo. The planned population was 550,000. Later a more specific proposal was abandoned with the fall from power of its sponsor Prime Minister Tanaka — he had omitted to impose a moratorium on land purchases in the area and considerable speculation was taking place.

Proposals were also made[21] to enlarge the existing city of Morioka, to the north of Tokyo, which might become the political capital, or might be devoted to "education, research, medical service, culture, communication and distribution". It was to be a city of "mountain, forest, water", of which the Japanese have so keen an appreciation, housing a million population in a great square of twenty kilometre sides, served by a trunk road flanked by five hundred to one thousand metres of grassland and vegetable farms, with three kilometres of riverside recreational area in the city centre with one kilometre of green zone at right angles to it. All residential blocks were to be "characterized by slope, hill, pond and river, each facing Mount Iwate". All blocks to be linked by monorail (maximum distance from home to station, two kilometres) "automatically driven and free".

In considering the disadvantageous externalities of large cities we must look at some of the less quantifiable. Traffic congestion and the economic cost and fatigue which arise from it, will be considered in a later chapter. Noise, over-crowding, air and water

20. *Nihon Keizai Shimbun* (Tokyo), 18 February 1975 (English Edition).
21. Suzuki, 4th International Symposium on Regional Development, Japan Centre for Area Development Research, 1972), p. 17.

pollution are features of many large cities. They may be found in smaller towns too; but the problems of dealing with them are aggravated in a large metropolitan area.

Wordsworth, it is true, discerned an unearthly beauty in London seen at dawn from Westminster Bridge on a summer morning in 1802, when it was still a comparatively small city, "open unto the fields and to the sky". Later he saw the darker side of city life when he wrote (in "The Recluse"):

> He truly is alone
> He of the multitude whose eyes are doomed
> To hold a vacant commerce day by day
> With objects wanting life, repelling love.

Technocrats and town planners need to be reminded that there is in almost all men this profound desire for some contact with other forms of life, either animal or plant. It remains none the less urgent for all our inability to give a rational explanation of it.

Belloc, in his wonderful book of reflections and stories disguised as a yachting handbook, *The Cruise of the Nona,* gives perhaps the best account of the social and political disadvantages of great cities, in a style which will never be imitated. It might be better, he thinks, to be a citizen of a small country because "in a great kingdom you must suffer a capital city, which will be a sink of crime. Your rulers will grow rich by deceit — for a very large community can always be deceived; nothing about you will be real, and the mass of your fellow-citizens will be desperately poor. For it is the nature of large communities to separate into strata and for the mass to grow indigent."

Economic poverty now may not be so desperate as it was in Belloc's day, but it is possible that social divisions have become even more accentuated. In the country, or in a moderately sized town, it is true that some people may be very poor. But rich and poor do at least share a few common local interests. In the larger cities, social divisions deepen; the richer and the poorer suburbs tend to get further and further apart.

That income inequalities are greater in larger cities can be demonstrated on a thorough analysis[22] of United States cities in 1970. The regional Gini coefficients (measures of inequality) were standardized for factors tending to reduce inequality (average per head income, proportion of labour force under twenty-five) and factors tending to increase it (proportions of blacks, of non-manual workers, and of female heads of families, population increase, and location in

---

22. J. E. Long, D. W. Rasmusse, and C. T. Haworth, "Income Inequality and City Size" *Review of Economics and Statistics* 59, no. 2 (May 1977), p. 245.

the southern states). After these factors have been eliminated we are left with the true and significant effects of city size as follows:

	Male Earners	Family Incomes
Constant in Gini coefficient	.397	.297
Addition for each thousand of city population	.00024	.00029

(Family incomes show less inequality than individual earnings because of the effects of aggregation.)

Further, even with given incomes, numbers in need may be greater. Examination of eighteen different public opinion surveys taken between 1946 and 1969 (no time trend was found in the results) gave the following relative values for the minimum incomes required for a family of four to "get along".[23]

Farm and rural	83
Town below 50,000 population	98
Town 50,000–500,000	104
Town 50,000–100,000	110
Over 1,000,000	119

There is also very little doubt that political apathy is widespread in very large cities. Even if the rulers do not "grow rich by deceit", as they do in many of the world's large cities, genuine democratic local government becomes difficult, and city administration tends to fall into the hands of bureaucrats and technocrats.

As a factor in the growth of very large cities, we must not underestimate the influence of thinkers. "One man with ideas counts for as much as a hundred who merely have interests", said John Stuart Mill. Unfortunately the three leading thinkers in this field have all been pulling in the wrong direction — so much do they love Paris, Athens, and Tokyo respectively, that they are urging their indefinite extension.

It is with the deepest regret that I have to reproach Gottman, Doxiadis, and Tange for the harm which they have been doing. But the plans for the further enlargement of Paris, which French politicians disguise unconvincingly under the title of a "New Towns" policy, are a small thing compared with the other aspirations. Doxiadis[24] looked forward to a world concentrating its inhabitants in cities modelled on "Ecumenopolis" which, so far as his drawing can be interpreted, will have a diameter of about seven hundred kilometres and which, while twenty-seven per cent of its area is open space and forty per

23. Massachusetts Institute of Technology and Harvard Joint Centre for Urban Studies, Rainwater Paper, No. 10.
24. C. A. Doxiades, "Ekistics and Regional Science" *Regional Science Association Proceedings* 10 (1963), p. 43.

cent comparatively lightly built up, nevertheless appears set to house nearly four hundred million people.

In Japan, even as it is now, forty-five per cent of the entire population lives in the narrow congested zone between Tokyo and Osaka. Not only independent town planners, but the government Economic Planning Agency itself, happily borrow the word "megalopolis" from Gottman's writings, and predict that soon seventy per cent of the entire population of Japan will be living in this zone. Professor Ichimura of the University of Osaka has the courage to criticize these proposals. Writing in terse and forceful English, he points out that:

> Living conditions will deteriorate. This urbanization process implies many new problems. These problems seem to be changing the Japanese socio-economic structure. For instance, Japanese people did not commit crimes in the countryside; they are very moral people. Now in urban areas young men and young girls do commit crimes three times as often as those in the countryside. The Japanese suicide rate is the highest in the world, and is particularly high in big cities. In Japan those who most commit suicide are the young generation, who are brought up in the country, and move to the big cities where they have few friends, and have to work hard. They are often mentally maladjusted.[25]

Greater incidence of crime appears to be one of the outstanding unfavourable externalities of larger cities. We have a direct indication from data for England and Wales (Table 31).

Table 31. Crime in England and Wales 1965.

Population of Town	Rates per thousand population		Detection rates %
	Major crimes	All crimes	
London	15.7	33.8	21.4
Other over 400,000	13.7	33.3	42.0
200-400,000	8.7	33.3	41.0
100-200,000	7.4	28.0	46.9
Below 10,000	5.8	25.4	50.7
Counties	5.1	17.5	45.7
England & Wales	7.9	23.7	39.2

Source: McClintock and Avison, *Crime in England and Wales.*

25. Ichimura, *The Japanese Economy, 1968* (Osaka: Institute of Social and Economic Research, Osaka University).

In the United States, where the data are more abundant, they have been subjected (Table 32) to more detailed analysis.[26] A most elaborate multiple regression was used to analyze out other social and economic factors, which happened to be associated with the size of city. Aggravating crime were unemployment, overcrowding, numbers of males not living with their families, and (believe it or not) high summer temperatures. A factor mitigating the crime rate was the proportion of aged and children in the population who, after all, are the least capable or likely to commit crime. There were also regional variables, crime being worst in the south, followed by the west.

ɔle **32.** United States City Crime Rates 1970

ulation ‚ ('000)	Homicide	Rape	Crude Index (average 100) Robbery	Assault	Burglary	Larceny	Auto theft
ɔ - 250	85	74	62	85	80	89	61
ɔ - 500	94	89	67	95	94	91	75
ɔ-1000	100	96	91	96	102	104	120
◦0-2500	118	134	152	112	116	115	128
◦0-9000	133	154	252	134	126	115	171
⸗ 9000 ⱳ York)	138	106	470	178	156	157	200
			Index as function of size of city only				
ɔ - 250	96	92	94	101	94	103	73
ɔ - 500	96	96	96	96	97	98	86
ɔ-1000	99	98	104	99	105	108	117
ɔ-2500	110	121	102	104	102	98	119
ɔ-9000	107	66	117	107	103	80	119
York	98	65	137	134	136	118	108

Finally there are ethnic variables, with the proportion of non-whites aggravating the crime index (except for the Japanese), and foreign-born citizens and their children, who reduce the crime index.

It is seen that the crude figures have to be substantially modified. But even on the revised figures the cities of below half a million population still make a better showing on the average, for all crimes except larceny. Above one million population there is no general picture. New York heads four but not all of the columns.

It is possible to bring these diverse index about optimum population of cities to a conclusion? The evidence indicates that some large towns will be needed, to be sufficiently attractive to industrialists, and at the same time to give labour access to a sufficient diversity of

26. Annual Report, National Bureau of Economic Research, 1973, p. 100.

possible employments. Statistical testing[27] shows "quite clearly that diversity of employment is associated with the absolute size of the [regional] work force". The question of accessibility to employment will be dealt with more thoroughly in the next chapter. But, to state the case by its opposite, men do not like working in a town where there are few alternative opportunities for employment for themselves and their families, other than in one or two large concerns, whose economic future may be unstable.

Thijsse[28] of the International School of Social Science at The Hague, advanced an extremely bold and original proposal (Diagram 9) for the best pattern of urban settlements for an advanced motorized

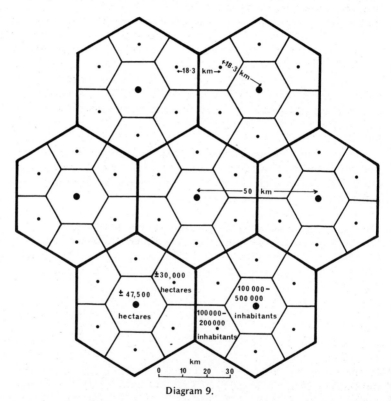

Diagram 9.

27. M. Chisholm and J. Oeppen, *The Changing Pattern of Employment: Regional Specialization and Industrialization in Britain* (London: Croom Helm, 1973), p. 54.
28. J. P. Thijsse, "A Rural Pattern for the Future in the Netherlands" *Regional Science Association*, 10 (1963).

community. He begins with the assumption of a dense rural population such as the Dutch, all of whom have the use of at least motorcycle transport. The old pattern of villages has become redundant. The rural areas should be served by towns of ten to twenty thousand inhabitants at a calculated optimum average distance apart of 18.3 kilometres. The larger towns might be anywhere in the one to four hundred thousand size range, at an average distance apart of fifty kilometres. The whole should be arranged in the pattern of hexagons which, as can be seen (and shown mathematically) minimizes the amount of travel required.

Shortly afterwards[29] Thijsse revised his plan on the assumption that even motorcycle transport would soon be obsolete and that one should look forward to every rural family having one or more cars. Under these circumstances the average distance apart of service centres could be raised to twenty-five kilometres, and their size to twenty to twenty-five thousand population.

It was expected that rural workers (except perhaps those in charge of livestock) would mostly live in such service centres, to which the maximum length of journey would be fourteen kilometres, or twenty-five to thirty minutes. Distance between towns would remain fifty kilometres.

For the much less dense rural populations found in many parts of the world, the populations of the service centres would of course be lower; but their average distance apart (if we can go on the Brush—Bracey comparison, quoted above) might be made the same.

Thijsse pointed out that the three northeastern provinces of the Netherlands (Friesland, Groningen, and Drenthe) contained three full sized towns, as they should on this diagram, but no fewer than two hundred villages, when they should have had only twenty-five. The application of Thijsse's theory to an old settled area would certainly cause much disturbance.

But a unique opportunity of applying it was lost. About the only place in the world where a large area of agricultural land has been created by reclamation is in the Netherlands *polders,* from the reclamation of the Zuyder Zee. The Dutch Government insisted on providing the northeast Polder with a pattern of villages suited to the horse and bicycle age, numbering eleven in all, when three, on Thijsse's plan, would have sufficed. In fact most of these villages turned out to be economic failures. The next polder reclaimed (East Flevoland) should have had, on Thijsse's plan, one town and two villages. The original plan provided for one town and ten villages,

29. J. P. Thijsse, "Second Thoughts About a Rural Pattern for the Future of the Netherlands" *Regional Science Association,* 20 (1967), p. 69.

later revised to one town and four villages — "gradually the government plans are taking the right direction", Thijsse commented.

But what is the position for a densely populated, poor country, whose rural inhabitants do not have cars or motor cycles, or expect to do so until some time into the distant future? For such a community Thijsse proposed that something like the existing pattern of villages should be for the present preserved, selecting however those ultimately designed to become the main centres, some twenty kilometres or so apart, with a gradual transfer of functions to them; while in the lesser villages, so far as possible, all buildings should be of a temporary nature.

People are assumed to be willing to walk a maximum of 2.5 kilometres so that the villages could be five kilometres apart.

These ideas appear to have had some following in Germany. It has been suggested[30] that an optimum dispersion might be in regions of about four hundred thousand population, with one hundred thousand in the central city. Regarding the smaller centres, an official statement,[31] more courageous than usual, indicates that a population of twenty thousand and a "breathing area" of fifteen kilometres radius must be regarded as the minima for successful industrial development.

For a fully motorized economy, with large farms (average about five hundred hectares) and low population density, such as the American Middle West, Clawson[32] proposes towns with five thousand population, each serving its own and some five thousand farm population, eighty kilometres apart, with a road grid of 2x4 miles. Country people would face a maximum journey of forty kilometres only if provided with axial roads; making a series of right angle turns on a rectangular road grid would double the length of journey. For each eight of these towns there should be a larger centre providing more specialized services, including county government.

It is interesting that Berry (see Chapter 6), after working in India, suggested a factor of seven for the relative numbers of towns of successive orders, when the pattern was imposed by authority, as against the factors of three and four considered by Christaller and Lösch under market development.

We come back to the important question of access to land for recreation purposes. It is the land nearest the cities which should be

30. Klemmer, *Der Volkswirt*, No. 3, (1968), pp. 29–31. Quoted in Niesing, *Seminar fur Wirschaftspolitik und Strukurforschung*, Kiel University Discussion Paper No. 3 (1970).
31. *Bundesminister fur Wirtschaft*, 1969.
32. M. Clawson, "Factors and Forces Affecting the Optimum Future rural settlement Pattern in the United States", *Economic Geography* 42 (October 1966), pp. 283–93.

designated for the purpose, which is by no means always the case today.

It is clear that, even after all possible steps have been taken to decentralize to smaller and more dispersed cities, a modern urban population, fully supplied with cars, cannot expect to enjoy its recreation by leisurely driving around uncongested countryside, as a small car-owning minority could do in the past. They will have to be forced out of their cars, for their own good as well as their neighbours'. Much of the countryside should be provided with footpaths.

These provisions are applicable even for a very dense population as in the Netherlands.

The resourceful Thijsse is again at hand, in his 1967 paper,[33] with symmetrical drawings providing for cities only fifty kilometres apart, and preserving over 69 per cent of the land for agriculture, which admittedly are very severe assumptions when we are planning for the use of land for recreation. The Dutch planning authorities[34] look forward to a dense and highly motorized population in the year 2000 AD. The uses planned for the country's total area of 36150 square kilometres are as follows (Table 33).

Table 33

Major urban areas (excluding parks)	8.6%
Parks within urban areas	3.8%
National and regional parks	25.5%
'Scenic corridors' (tree-planted) linking parks	4.5%
Agriculture	57.6%

They look forward to a gross density of about 4,500 persons/square kilometre in urban areas, inclusive of urban parks. A hexagonal area of land near each city is to be reserved for woodland and recreation, the most distant lands being left for agriculture. The sturdy Dutch assume, as Thijsse indicates, that people will walk for recreation, and that on some occasions as many as eighty per cent of the urban population will want to be out in the open at the same time. In a modern city they will indeed drive out into the woodlands (at the average rate of three persons per car) before they start walking.

33. Thijsse, "Second Thoughts About A Rural Pattern for the Future of the Netherlands" *Regional Science Association* 20 (1967).
34. See Buchanan, "Towards the Netherlands 2000: the Dutch National Plan", *Economic Geography* 45, no. 3 (July 1969), pp. 259–74.

The amount of parking space so required, which might at first sight be feared to be inordinate, is in fact shown to be trivial.

Two of Thijsse's plans are selected for more detailed examination (Table 34) — one sufficient (on our assumed rate of four thousand persons per square kilometre) to house a population of over a million, the other for a smaller city.

Table 34.

	Plan 2D	Plan 2E
Whole area of hexagon to cover city and six villages km^2	2,020	2,020
Agricultural area km^2	1,230	1,230
Urban area km^2	260	82
Recreation area km^2	530	708
Population of city (at 4,000 persons/km^2)	1,040,000	328,000
Maximum number using recreation area at any one time	830,000	262,000
Number of cars in recreation area	277,000	87,000
Parking space* required km^2	5.5	1.7
Percent of recreation area required for parking space	1.04	0.24
Maximum number of persons per hectare of recreation area	16	4

* At 200 cars/acre, i.e. 500 cars/hectare or 50,000 cars/km^2.

We should all be grateful to the Dutch for setting us an example of how to make best use of a limited area of land. Even Amsterdam has an area of nine square kilometres of (artificially planted) woodland for recreation purposes. On fine Sundays as many as one hundred people per hectare may be found there; and Thijsse points out that at this degree of crowding "it is not pleasant any more". He suggests an upper limit of fifty persons per hectare. The number of people per unit of recreational land available on the above calculations, even on the busiest day, comes nowhere near this limit.

This chapter has dealt principally with the externalities of city size. The central economic question, of the ability of cities of different sizes to provide their inhabitants, and those of the surrounding regions, with an adequate range of services, will have to be considered in a later chapter.

9

The Location of Manufacture

The sequence in which knowledge has become available was first information (mainly from census sources) of employments in various activities by regions, cities, towns and villages; then, considerably later, information began to become available about regional and city incomes; later studies still began to show how regional incomes (and consequently regional employments) were generated and their levels determined by local needs and by inter-regional trade, with the latter having multiplier effects. A theoretical treatise based on complete knowledge would begin at the latter end, and then proceed to analyze regional incomes and employments. But, in the still imperfect state of our knowledge it is considered better to proceed in the opposite direction — with one important exception, namely examining first the principal available information about the location of manufacture, which is subject to special forces, and which is also a controlling factor in the location of other employments (Chapter 9). Then employments are analyzed in outline for some regions, but also (statistically) for large numbers of smaller towns, for which we cannot yet expect to have income data, and where some interesting relationships are obtained (Chapter 10). Information on regional incomes is then reviewed (Chapter 11) before proceeding to analyze the interregional trade, multipliers, etc., which determine them (Chapter 12).

There is no universally recognized classification of economic activities. In the past, when much the largest proportion of the labour force was engaged in agriculture, it was understandable that the title "primary production" should be given to it. It also seemed rational to include in this category the lesser forms of production directly from natural resources, forestry, fishing, and hunting; and also mining and quarrying, though these are sometimes included with manufacture, because of their capital-intensive nature; but we should certainly include them with primary production if we are analyzing economic activities in relation to their location.

The location of primary production is, by its nature, completely determined by the location of the natural resources on which it draws; subject to the consideration however that it cannot be undertaken (mining in particular) if transport costs to its markets are excessive in relation to the value of its product.

The term "secondary production" came to be applied to manufacture. Although widely used, "manufacture" is not an easy word to define (certainly it cannot be defined in terms of its literal meaning of "hand-made"). The best definition seems to be that it refers to continuous processes, carried out on a substantial scale, transforming commodities for sale to customers over a wide area. "Transforming" must be defined so as not to include transport or trading. The above definition also rules out activities such as building, construction, and civil engineering, which may be said to transform materials, but whose product, by its nature, must be located in one spot, and cannot be sold to customers elsewhere.

It was only comparatively recently that economists became aware that there was a large remaining sector of the economy, which for convenience was called "tertiary" and which now, in advanced economies, represents some 75 per cent of all employment. An alternative definition is to call this sector "service industries", in the sense that they supply services rather than transforming goods, although it is rather difficult to apply this category to building or other construction. A further distinction is sometimes made between those industries which handle goods (construction, goods transport, storage, wholesale and retail trade) and what might be called service industries proper — such as government, education, health, entertainment, and the like — though none of them can in fact be carried on without the use of a certain amount of material goods also.

Subject to some qualifications, the products of primary and secondary industry can be transported and stored. The all-important consideration about tertiary products, from the point of view of location analysis, is that, with a few exceptions, they cannot. It is true that a building can, in a sense, be "stored", though it is unusual to construct it before it is wanted. The values produced by transport and wholesale trade (to a lesser extent by retail trade) can also be incorporated in goods which are stored and transported. But, with these qualifications, the products of tertiary industry must be consumed at the time and also — this is what now most concerns us — at the place where they are supplied.

Several attempts have recently been made to describe a new category of "quaternary" products i.e. the provision of information, as distinct from the performance of services. It is an interesting theoretical idea, and there seems to be little doubt that activities providing information are increasing in relative importance — but quite impossible to apply in practice. To begin with, the production of books, newspapers, and other periodicals would have to be separated out from the secondary sector — and then how can we decide how much of these represent information, and how much entertainment? In every business and government department, part of the effort of those working is devoted to providing information, and part to making decisions and performing services, the combined functions often being within the duties of one man. Separation would be impossible.

The phrase "service industries" conveys the suggestion of services rendered direct to customers, such as entertainment or hairdressing. More careful analysis shows that, besides transport of goods and wholesale trade, a large part of the remaining output of the service industries consists of "intermediate products", that is, services provided to other businesses, rather than directly to the consumer. This is true, for instance, of most of the output of some professional industries such as accounting and law, and some of the output of passenger transport.

But, again with a few qualifications, the truth holds that the products of service industries have to be used at the place where they are supplied. This is not quite the same thing as saying that they can only be supplied to local residents. There are some activities performed in a limited number of centres, which render service to people at a distance, such as government, defence, and universities, and also the services supplied by seaports and other major transport centres. It is true that people can travel to a distant city for specialized medical services, and the like. But it remains true that tertiary industries, defined broadly, must depend on the local market, subject to the qualification that there may be a few "export" services.

Conversely, the local demand for tertiary services has to be provided by local tertiary industries, or left unsatisfied — the possibility of importing them from other regions is very limited.

Except in a subsistence agricultural society, primary production is generally producing for sale away from its own region, as also is most secondary production. As we shall see, a region must have enough primary, secondary, and "export" tertiary production (sometimes supplemented by government transfers, or by drawing on capital) to pay for the goods and services which it needs to import; and certain patterns of employment must ensue. We now look more closely at manufacture.

Some primary products are exceptionally difficult to transport, either because they are unusually heavy or bulky in relation to their value (for example, metal ores, log timber) or perishable (milk, sugar cane). Manufactures processing such materials therefore have the strongest incentive to locate as near as possible to where the materials are produced, (or, in some cases, landed from ships). This group of industries (now not of great relative importance) is known as "materials-oriented".

While some primary products are exceptionally bulky or perishable, this is also true of certain manufactures. Their producers therefore have strong incentives to locate near to where they will be sold. This is true, for instance, of bricks and concrete goods. Examples of perishable products are ice-cream and newspapers, though one is surprised at the distances over which these are sometimes transported. Further examples of goods which are bulky in relation to their value are beer and soft drinks, which again however are sometimes transported over surprisingly long distances. The anomalous distribution of beer, in some cases, may be explained by monopolistic trade conditions; most soft drinks are produced locally. This group of industries, less precisely defined than the "materials-oriented", is described as "market-oriented". They also constitute a small proportion of all manufacturing production. The great majority of manufactures do not have their location determined for them either by supplies of materials or by markets, and are conveniently described as "footloose".

Classifications for Australia and New Zealand (Table 35) show the greater relative importance of both materials-oriented and market-oriented industries in the less centrally situated regions (some comparable figures for USA are given below).[1]

Table 35. Percentages of All Manufacturing Employment.

	New Zealand	Queensland	All Australia
Materials-oriented	24	24	11
Market-oriented	25	34	29
Footloose	51	38	60

A clear picture of market-oriented industries in USA is provided by large-scale sample Census results showing, by detailed classification of industries, the distance over which their products were shipped in 1963 and 1967.[2] (Certain obviously market-oriented industries and one materials-oriented were omitted from the survey — fluid milk, bakeries, ice, primary forest products, newspapers, printing, engraving, typesetting, readymix concrete.)

1. G. J. R. Linge, "The Economic Concentration and Dispersion of Manufacturing in New Zealand" *Economic Geography* 36, no. 4 (1960), and private communication. Australian data refer to 1961–62.
2. L. W. Weiss, The Geographic Size of Markets for Manufacturing" *Review of Economics and Statistics* 54, no. 3 (August 1972), pp. 245–57.

Average distance below 100 miles — ice-cream,[3] soft-drinks.

Average distance 100–199 miles — animal feed, mattresses, containers (metal and other), cement, brick and tile, other structural clay products, concrete and gypsum products, cut stone, special dies, tools and moulds, scrap metal.

Average distances 200–299 miles — beer, flavouring syrups, soybean oil, tobacoo stemming, felt, prefabricated buildings, envelopes (not stationery), die-cut paper, industrial gases, asphalt felts, glass containers, refractories, ground minerals, coke, iron and steel primary products, castings and forgings, nonferrous metal castings and forgings, metal kegs, fabricated boiler plate, miscellaneous metal, storage batteries.

The industries supplying over greater distances are enumerated in Table 36.

Table 36. Numbers of Other Industries Classified by Average Distance Shipment of Products.

Miles	
300-399	47
400-499	57
500-599	45
600-699	38
700-799	28
800-899	11
900-999	3
1,000 & over	5

The next distinction which has to be made is between those manufacturing industries which do, and those which do not have to face international competition. Most countries, at most times, have shielded their manufacturing industries from the full force of international competition by tariff protection, sometimes by direct regulation of imports. If we exclude such protected industries from consideration, as well as materials-oriented and market-oriented industries, we find that "footloose" manufactures, which are able to compete internationally, occupy a surprisingly limited area of the earth's surface. Even within major industrial countries there are large areas which have little manufacturing employment beyond local market-oriented

3. Weiss adds, "The 0.2 per cent of ice-cream that was shipped more than fifteen hundred miles must have been very special brands or flavours".

industries. In western Europe, where manufacture (as we now define it) began, most such competitive manufacture has lain along an "axis" (a favourite word with geographers) running from central Scotland, through the English North Country, Midlands, and south east, the Low Countries, north-eastern France, the Rhine-Ruhr basins, southern Germany, Switzerland to northern Italy, with an offshoot to Denmark and Sweden.

In the United States, most competitive manufactures originally located in New England spread along the Chicago–Connecticut axis. It took a long time for the concentration along this axis to be reduced (Table 37).

Up to 1929 some three-quarters of all manufacturing growth was concentrated on the "Axis" – a striking figure. Growth outside the axis appeared first in California and Texas and in various outlying regions. After 1947 fresh strong growth appeared in Florida, with acceleration in California and Texas; and the South reversed its comparative decline.

"Market-oriented" industries were defined and measured by Fuchs.[4] It is sometimes believed that the growth of industry in California and Texas, and most of all in Florida (well known as a retirement centre), has been in market-oriented industries. Analyzing employment gains in comparison with the United States average, Fuchs finds no great changes in the relative importance of market-oriented industries, with marked declines in California and Texas, but some increase in Florida. He is right in concluding that market-oriented industries have not been the main factor of change. The new locations have genuinely attracted "footloose" industries.

Before we go into the causes of the concentrations of manufacture in a limited number of locations, we may observe that there are remarkable difficulties in the way of any new industrial region being able to break into the competitive world market.

The "economies of aggregation" (to be further analyzed below), which the established manufacturing regions enjoy, can however be counteracted by competitors with much lower relative wages. (Note that this refers to *money* wages, which are what concern the industrialist – low money wages sometimes go with relatively high real wages). The world's first substantial development of competitive international export industry was probably the cotton trade in late eighteenth century Lancashire. Economic historians have made much of other factors – availability of sea and river transport, water power from streams, humid climate suitable for spinning. But these were in varying degrees also available elsewhere. The remarkably low wages

4. *Review of Economics and Statistics* 1962.

Table 37. U.S. Manufacturing Employment[1] Percentage Distributions.

	Manufacturing employment	Increments of manufacturing employment				Percentage of all manufacturing employment in market-oriented industries
	1967	1899-1914	1914-29	1929-47	1947-67	1954
"Axis"[2]	51.8	70.8	75.4	57.2	26.7	10.2
South[3]	19.3	10.4	14.4	12.5	27.8	12.4
California	8.2	3.0	8.8	6.7	18.1	13.2
New England[4]	5.6	9.9	−1.6	2.5	0.3	7.1
Texas	3.4	2.3	4.1	3.4	7.2	18.6
Florida	1.5	0.9	0.5	0.2	4.1	32.2
Rest USA	10.2	0.7	8.2	18.0	15.9	15.9
U.S. Total						11.4

1. United States Census of Manufactures and Fuchs, *Review of Economics and Statistics* (May 1962)
2. From Connecticut westwards to Illinois and Wisconsin
3. Excluding Florida and Texas
4. Excluding Connecticut

in Lancashire before industrialization (noted previously) must have played an important part.

The outstanding example of a competitior's starting from nothing and successfully breaking into world export markets for manufacture is, of course, Japan. (The present writer must confess to a personal interest because his father, in 1890, was one of the first foreign merchants to come to Japan to buy textiles and other goods for the Australian market, on which deal he made a substantial profit.) Money wages in nineteenth century Japan, by European standards, were very low. But even so, Japan probably would not have succeeded so rapidly had it not been for the accidental factor that the Japanese currency at that time was based on silver, which underwent a considerable depreciation in terms of major world currencies in the 1890s. This lowered money wages, from the point of view of international competition, without affecting real wages.

But what makes the story still more interesting is that in modern Japan most manufacture is still concentrated in a very limited zone between Tokyo and Osaka along the southern coast of the main island. Most of the rest of Japan is now depopulating.

In India, on the other hand, low money wages and exchange devaluation have so far had very limited success in promoting manufacture for export — perhaps owing to the attraction of the large, very highly protected internal market. That such a factor is probably at work is shown[4] by a regression analysis of manufactured exports per head from forty-five developing countries (manufactures being defined to exclude those predominantly resource-based, or to any substantial degree market-oriented because of high transport costs). Exports were significantly correlated with "openness of market". This was measured by the incremental import/consumption ratio for manufactured goods. Direct information on tariff levels was not available for all countries, and in any case imports are often restricted by means other than tariffs; but so far as the tariff information goes, it gives a similar result.

Other factors benefiting developing countries' exports of manufactures were found to be population (a larger population yielding economies of scale), and population density (that is, comparative scarcity of agricultural land).

Russia has developed into an economy with a large manufacturing sector under government direction and located (perhaps for strategic reasons) over widely dispersed areas — but it remains to be seen

4. T. K. Morrison, "Manufactured Exports and Protection in Developing Countries: A Cross-Country Analysis" *Economic Development and Cultural Change* 25 (1976), p. 154.

whether these industries are capable of competing in international markets.

Recent successful newcomers to the international market for manufactures — Taiwan, South Korea, Hong Kong, Singapore, in many ways close copies of the Japanese process of development, some 60 years later — have done so on the basis of initially low money wages, though once export markets have been developed these have risen rapidly.

Leaving aside the totally unskilled, whose wages are always relatively very low in developing countries, median wages in 1957 (South Korea in 1967)[5] for twenty specified skilled and semi-skilled operations, converted into United States currency at current rates of exchange, were:

	U.S. cents/hour
Singapore	27.4
Hong Kong	21.0
Taiwan	14.7
Korea	13.0

For Japan in 1957 (still in the process of recovery; it has since risen very rapidly) the figure was only 19.4; for Britain it was 48.5.

The wide regional divergences of wages, which used to prevail in the past, with the maximum in capital cities, probably had some effect in bringing manufacturing employment to outlying regions. Conversely, the greater equalization of wages for modern mobile populations, aggravated, as Lösch pointed out, by the irrational tendency of trade unions and governmental wage-fixing authorities to negotiate uniform wages for the whole country, is acting to discourage manufacturing employment in outlying regions.

The problem of why industry has developed in certain regions was originally analyzed by methods of remarkable crudity. First on the scene were the geographers, who proposed that the industrialization of any region depended on the availability of supplies of coal and iron ore, regarded as basic materials of modern industry. They neglected the obvious fact that a country which lacked coal and iron ore, but which could produce other goods successfully, could without difficulty import all the steel and other materials which it needed.

Economists originally showed a quite undue preoccupation with the problems of heavy industries, particularly steel, a commodity which seems to exercise some occult fascination over economists as well as over politicians. Such industries are faced with high transport

5. *Yearbook of Labour Statistics, 1958,* International Labour Office Table 20; and Bank of Korea, *Report of Wage Survey* (1967).

costs per unit value of goods transported, both for obtaining materials, and in carrying their products to market. Weber devised an extraordinary theorem to which far too much attention has been paid — interesting in the case of steel, but in no other case — whereby the optimum location of a steel plant could be decided by constructing a device with pulleys and weights attached, representing the comparative location and distance of its sources of materials, and the destination of its products. It is believed that this method was used once, at any rate, to decide the location of a steel plant at Gary, on the lake shore just east of Chicago.

Steel however is probably unique in that, unlike material-oriented and market-oriented industries, it faces high transport costs both on its inputs and on its output, while yielding great economies of scale in production, so that large plants have to be designed. For most industries however transport costs represent a very small proportion of the value of their output, or input of materials, and all such reasoning falls to the ground.

We must divert our minds from the simple issue of transport costs to the much more important matter of "distance costs", of which transport costs are only one component. Both in purchasing inputs and in selling outputs substantial elements in the costs of doing business arise out of the distances from which they come or to which they go. Journeys have to be made, and considerable time and effort expended, by salesmen, and by buyers, and sometimes by higher executives whose time is still more valuable. When goods have to be transported over a distance there may be uncertainties about delivery which can disrupt the orderly organization of production. These difficulties are accentuated when the goods have to cross a national frontier, having to face not only tariffs, customs formalities, and delays, but also the possibility of the trade sometimes being interrupted by import restrictions. These are all additional difficulties, in comparison with a business which can engage its managerial and other labour, purchase its material inputs, and sell its output, all in its immediate neighbourhood. There is no doubt about the economies of aggregation, indeed even location near one's competitors, as we saw in Chapter 5. We come to the important generalization that — subject to certain limits, which we will consider later — population attracts population.

Lösch extended this principle to an extraordinary degree. The successful industrial regions of modern Europe, he contended, were on the whole those which had already attained a high density of agricultural population in the eighteenth century. But it is, on the whole, true. Maps are available comparing what approximate information we have about population densities in 18th century Europe with those of the present time and also the extent to which current population growth is related to existing population density.[6]

The same conclusion was reached from a more detailed historical study (Table 38) of forty-four rural districts in England classified according to their initial agricultural population density, which was shown to bear a strong positive relation to their growth of non-agricultural employment in the subsequent century.

Table 38. Quartiles of Rural Districts Arranged in Descending Order of Males Engaged in Agriculture Per 100 Acres in 1831*

Men per 100 acres, 1831	Medians % change, 1831-1931	
	Nos. engaged in agriculture	Nos. engaged in non-agricultural activities
5.3	−42	+42
4.3	−42	+45
3.5	−32	+18
2.5	−35	+ 2

*The selection of districts for this study was made difficult by frequent boundary changes, and it was impossible to carry it beyond 1931.

Districts subject to mining development, or sites of government installations, were excluded.

The most densely populated districts showed a little above-average rate of loss of agricultural population, but greatly above-average gain in other employment.

There is one important exception to Lösch's generalization. This is southern Italy. This region has suffered certain adverse political factors, mentioned above; but there has been an economic disadvantage as well. This is distance from the principal markets and sources of supply.

We come back to the question of "distance costs". It is impossible to do what we should like to do, to analyze distance costs separately for each business, or even for each type of business, although we know that such costs greatly vary between businesses. Further, we need information about the capacity of each region to supply the various categories of inputs and to purchase outputs; but it will be a long time before the development of regional input-output tables enables us to do anything like this. At the present time the only information which we can use is the aggregate income of regions.

6. *Population Growth and Land Use* maps on pp. 289, 290, and 300.

This has to serve as the best available indication of a region's capacity both to supply inputs and to purchase outputs. But it is considerably better than no information at all.

The device used for measuring the comparative attraction of any location, in relation to surrounding regions, is that of "economic potential". The concept of potential is borrowed from physics; in practical electrical work it is called "voltage"; the theoretical definition of the potential or voltage at any one point is the summation of the electrical charges which surround it, each divided by its distance from the point in question. The first device suggested by the physicist J. Q. Stewart,[7] was to estimate the "economic potential" of any point by summing the populations of the regions accessible to it, each divided by its distance from the point in question. (On the evidence from freight movements within Britain however it has been suggested[8] that a better fit might be obtained with the exponent for distance the −2.5 power rather than the simple reciprocal.)

This method was further developed by Professor Chauncey Harris[9] in Chicago, including a special study for agricultural populations, to estimate economic potential from the point of view of a manufacturer of farm machinery (this potential was indeed at its highest in the Chicago neighbourhood).

The potential method was later refined by using regional incomes instead of populations, and dividing by "distance costs".

In estimating "distance costs", it is immediately apparent that it will not do to make them simply proportional to distance. If we do this, transactions in one's own region or immediate neighbourhood, which may constitute a large proportion of all business, will show low or zero distance costs, and consequently almost infinite potential. But there are distance costs even in doing business with the firm next door. Our estimates must therefore include a substantial minimum or terminal charge even for one's own region, plus further factors for distance, with yet further allowances for crossing international borders, as explained above.

Calculating potential on a population basis, Beverly Duncan analyzed manufacturing location, taking the 1950 percentage of the labour force in manufacture in one hundred non-metropolitan "economic areas" (as defined by the Census Bureau), standardizing for

7. J. Q. Stewart, "Empirical mathematical rules concerning the distributors and equilibrium of population". *Geographical Review*, 37 (July 1947), pp. 461–85.
8. M. Chisholm and P. O'Sullivan, *Freight Flows and Spatial Aspects of the British Economy* (1954).
9. Chauncey Harris, Annals of the Association of American Geographers (December 1954).

city size, and also using two other explanatory variables in addition to potential.[10] "Processing" industries were distinguished, on a definition wider than materials-oriented, including all non-durable consumption goods as well as wood products and primary metals: this group is seen to be less responsive to potential, and to the two other explanatory factors, than are the truly footloose "fabricating" industries.

The following (Table 39) multiple regressions were obtained:

Elkan, working in New Zealand, developed what was equivalent to the potential method, but used what were in effect reciprocals of potential, which he called "market distance indexes".[11] The quantity of manufacture in a region was measured as the ratio of its value added to that of the region's primary industry. He analyzed (Table 40) data for the states of Australia, the provinces of Canada, and the two islands of New Zealand, distinguishing the metropolitan areas from the rest of the regions by their proportions of total retail sales.

Table 39. Explanatory Variables.

	Potential	Distance from competing metropolitan centre	Extent of urbanization within "Economic area"
"Processing" industries	−.03*	−.24	.17*
"Fabricating" industries	.63	−.13*	.33
All manufacture	.29	−.36	.32

*Values not significant at 5% level

Both Australia and Canada (Diagrams 10 and 11) yielded interesting results. As "distance index" increases (that is, potential falls) the amount of manufacture in relation to primary production falls, but in the remotest regions (West Australia and British Columbia) it rises again. In the remotest regions the "natural protection" afforded to local industries by the high transport costs faced by their competitors outweighs the disadvantages which they face. This is by no means the case only for market-oriented industries. Extreme distances also

10. Beverley Duncan, "Population Distribution and Manufacturing Activity: the Nonmetropolitan US in 1950" *Regional Science Association Papers*, 5 (1959), p. 95.
11. P. G. Elkan, New Zealand Institute of Economic Research Technical Memorandum No. 8 (1965) and "Estimating New Zealand's Manufacturing Output in a Common Market with Australia" *Journal of Development Studies* 4, no. 2 (Jan. 1968).

Table 40. Manufacturing Output as Percentage of Primary Output 1958-62.

	AUSTRALIA						NEW ZEALAND	
	New South Wales	Victoria	South Australia	Tasmania	Queensland	West Australia	North Island	South Island
Materials-oriented industries	56	42	25	68	26	14	43	28
Market-oriented industries	33	31	22	24	15	18	30	23
Footloose industries	124	147	89	43	31	44	66	48

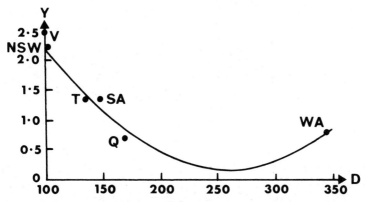

Diagram 10. The Industrialisation ratio related to the market distance index, Australia.

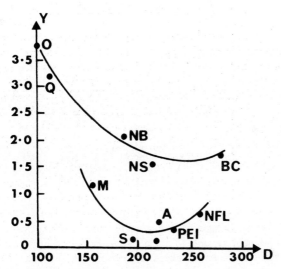

Diagram 11. The Industrialisation ratio related to the market distance index, Canada.

benefited industries usually classified as footloose, particularly metal products.

In Canada the five provinces which have "good land communications within Canada, good sea connections with external markets, and which lie opposite industrialized regions of the United States" were distinguished from those who do not possess these advantages. But both groups show a similarly curved relationship.

Elkan reached the pessimistic conclusion that if New Zealand were to form an economic union with Australia — a proposal frequently discussed — it would not reach the upward position on the curve enjoyed by West Australia. New Zealand's North Island would lose about half of its net manufacturing output (expressed as a proportion of net primary output) and the South Island about a third. These conclusions have, of course, been disputed in both countries. The recent marked fall in New Zealand money wages in relation to Australia might have been expected to have altered the prospect considerably. And indeed this has been the case. Since Elkan wrote, with the gradual reduction of tariffs on trade in manufactures between the two countries, employment in manufacture in New Zealand has risen substantially relative to Australia, though relatively less in the South Island. The New Zealand experience is an interesting illustration of how relative lack of potential can be overcome by changes in relative wages — which, internationally, may come about fairly easily — they are more difficult to obtain between regions within a country.

A potential analysis for the United States based on regional incomes, with some allowances for international trade,[12] shows a general correspondence between manufacturing location and potential over a five hundred-fold range of values for the manufacture/primary production ratio.

Two other features are apparent. The first are the higher than expected values for the New England states, owing to the long persistence of locations established when these states were the principal manufacturing centre.

The other is the growth of manufacture on the Pacific Coast, in spite of its comparatively low potential, perhaps because of its extreme distance advantage (discussed above in the cases of Canada and Australia).

A study by Berry for India, based on populations, showed the great relative advantages of the already developed centres, Calcutta, Bombay, and Madras, and to a less extent Delhi, and their immediate surroundings.[13] A belt of moderately high potential however stretches westward from Madras to the Kerala Coast.

A more thorough study was made covering the whole of Western Europe, based on the income data for 103 regions, taking into account also potential trade with other parts of the world.[14] Potentials were

12. See map in *Population Growth and Land Use* p. 296.
13. B. J. L. Berry, "Interdependency of Spatial Structure and Spatial Behaviour: A General Field Formulation" Regional Science Association Proceedings, Vol. 21.
14. C. Clark, Wilson and Bradley, Industrial Location and Economic Potential in Western Europe *Regional Studies* 3, no. 2 (1969), pp. 197–212.

calculated on the transport costs of ten tons of goods, with a minimum distance charge of $28, and allowing for extra charges incurred in loading or unloading at seaports or in crossing frontiers. (The goods whose transport costs were recorded were glassware, a fairly highly rated commodity; this makes some allowance for elements other than average transport cost in distance costs, discussed above.) Potentials were calculated first before the initiation of the Common Market then on varying assumptions about the extent of the Common Market, finally on the containerization of shipping cargoes. The Common Market, together with some shipping improvements, is having striking effects. Potential has been raised all round, but in place of the former separated centres of high potential there is now one clearly marked maximum zone covering the Low Countries, most of West Germany, and northeastern France. The three thousand contour now covers a rectangular block of England, but excludes the north and southwest. The daigram continues to show economic adversity for southern Italy, Scotland, and Ireland — with little prospect of these disadvantages being offset by substantially lower money wage rates to enable them to compete.

It now remains to test the effects of such economic potential on manufacturing location. Great variance was to be expected between regions, for many reasons, including actions by governments attempting to attract manufacturing industry to distressed regions. To obtain a general view, regions were grouped (Table 41) in five quintiles of potential, and increases in manufacturing employment measured per thousand population, distinguishing the most rapidly expanding branches of industry, such as engineering and chemicals.

Table 41. Increases in Employment in Manufacturing Industries in Western Europe, Per nnum and Per Thousand Total Population.

Regions grouped according to onomic potential	Expanding Industries		All Industries (net)	
	1950-60	1960-65	1950-60	1960-65
owest quintile	0.36	0.52	0.47	0.44
econd quintile	0.65	0.73	0.74	0.59
hird quintile	1.11	1.98	1.06	1.85
ourth & Fifth quintiles	1.69	1.66	1.53	1.99

It is clear that potential attracts. But, after 1960, the two highest quintiles proved less attractive to expanding industries than the third quintile. The declining industries (such as textiles) also showed the most rapid decreases in the higher potential quintiles.

So we may free ourselves from the fear that all the industry of Europe will ultimately concentrate in a small central zone.

We may speculate on the factors now reducing the attraction to industry of the highest potential zones — air and water pollution, general deterioration of the environment — but probably the strongest factors are shortages of certain types of required labour, and traffic congestion, affecting goods movements as well as personal travel.

An interesting German study,[15] confined to newly established manufacturing plants, classified them to "congested areas" (over a half a million population and five hundred persons/square kilometre throughout), "major city regions" (over one hundred and fifty thousand population and one thousand persons/square kilometre, "industrialized (rural) zones" (manufacturing workers more than twenty per cent of urban population), and remaining rural areas. As much as fifty-five per cent of the new employment went to the last-named. Congested areas (including West Berlin) received twenty-nine per cent, major city regions nine per cent, and industrialized rural zones seven per cent. The industries still most attracted to congested and major city zones were basic metals (not fabricated metals), with sixty-four per cent of all employment (probably due to availability of coal), printing sixty-three per cent, aircraft fifty per cent, and electrical and electronic products fifty per cent. Industries showing more than the average attraction to rural areas (including "industrialized rural zones"), some of them declining industries apparently in search of cheaper labour, including shoes (ninety-four per cent), musical instruments and toys (eighty-five per cent), clothing (eighty-four per cent), leather (eighty-three per cent), textiles (seventy-eight per cent), wood and wood products (seventy-eight per cent). But except for printing and basic metals no industry showed a figure below fifty per cent.

We are now approaching some of the less quantifiable aspects of manufacturing location. New and fast-growing industries appear "in the older and larger and more sophisticated industrial centres, where the work skills are highest, risk capital easiest to obtain . . . specialised laboratories . . . technical specialists".[16]

But later, in their more mature stages, industries find themselves constrained to seek cheaper labour, sometimes in "languishing

15. *Seminar fur Wirtschafts Politik and Strukturforschung,* Kiel University Discussion Paper Nos. 4 (1970) and 8 (1973).
16. W. R. Thompson in H. Bryce, ed., *Small Cities in Transition* (1976).

farm centres with underemployed hinterlands"; able to escape congestion, and, in USA at any rate, inordinately high municipal taxation on real property.

In a most extensive study of manufacturing location in a large area of southeast England, enclosed approximately by lines running Harwich–Banbury–Poole, excluding Greater London, economic potential was measured and found to have a *negative* effect (due perhaps to labour shortages, congestion, and other repulsive factors).[17] Total population within a fifteen kilometre radius proved to be an attractive factor – there was a general labour shortage constraint (this was in the 1960s), especially of female labour, and one factor driving firms out of Greater London was the increasing shortage of skilled labour there. There was a tendency for industry to prefer small and medium sized towns to the larger centres, and a curious "radial" tendency (meaning that a firm previously situated in northwest London would tend to seek a new site in a north-westerly direction). No significant effect was found for the price of industrial land. Proximity to radial roads had little significance. It is sometimes said that location decisions have been made in an arbitrary uneconomic manner by the preferences of the manager and his family for certain areas with "residential image". This was found rarely to be the case, and then only for small firms – larger businesses apparently cannot afford the luxury of such preferences.

A different conclusion is reached[18] however in an analysis of the locations in Canada of branch plants of United States firms, which are heavily biassed to the western side of Toronto. Analysis in relation to the location of the head office in the United States of America indicates that "convenience of executives" plays an important part. But this perhaps may be considered as an example of the intangible elements, mentioned above, in "distance costs".

The British Government has long been attempting to move industry into the depressed regions. The Managing Director of Crosfield Electronics eloquently stated[19] the case for his firm remaining in London. Of his output, eighty per cent went for export, in the face of tough international competition, shipped by airfreight; and it was likewise necessary that the firm should be easily accessible for visits by foreign customers, also arriving by air. Fulfilling an order might involve urgently chasing suppliers. most of whom were in London, of any out of some six thousand specialized components.

17. Keeble and Hauser, *Spatial Correlates of Industrial Growth in Outer South East England,* Report to Social Science Reserach Council (1970).
18. D. M. Ray, *Market Potential and Economic Shadow* (Chicago: Department of Geography, University of Chicago, 1965).
19. Letter to *The Times* (London), 22 December 1962.

Of his staff, twenty-six per cent were professional engineers or physicists, who would decline to move to the north of England, who could easily find alternative employment in or near London, and who valued its technical institutions and cultural life. It made no sense to talk of training unemployed men in the north to become physicists.

Manufacturers required by government orders to locate in depressed regions found as one of their principal difficulties the complaints by the graduate staff about having to live in "a cultural desert".[20]

The preferences, not so much of managers as of men with scarce professional skills, do now play an important part in location. The present writer once asked the head of an American firm why he was located in southern California, and he replied that this was not his choice, but southern California was where so many engineers and physicists preferred to live, and he could not do without them. An employer in Munich said that for similar reasons (more agreeable surroundings, and access to the Alps) he was better able to attract professional labour than were employers in northern German cities.

But in England now it is not always a matter of London.[21] "There is a significant and growing amount of non-central location by high-threshold specialist services". These were however located for preference in adjacent high-income towns such as Beaconsfield and Windsor, rather than Slough.

20. Federation of British Industries Conference, Brighton, 24–26 November 1960.
21. R. K. Schiller, "Location Trends of Spatial Services" *Regional Studies* 5 (April 1971).

10

Regional Employment

We have attempted to recount the simpler trade and services functions performed by smaller settlements, proceeding progressively to the larger settlements for the performance of more specialized functions; and we have seen how most manufactures, and many trade and service functions, gain from "economies of aggregation", that is, proximity to a variety of other businesses, including even their competitors.

We may now seek to quantify information about the expected employment structure of settlements of various sizes. Such information is important for purposes of both private business and public administration.

This we must do against a background of the great and growing importance of the service industries (broadly defined, including commerce and transport) as against both manufacture and primary production, now occupying some seventy per cent of the labour force in the United States (more in some regions), and approaching this figure elsewhere.

Table 42 shows labour force distribution for a number of countries, and the changes which have taken place since the 1930s. The classification is *industrial* not *occupational*, describing the service performed by the business rather than the nature of the work performed by the individual, for example, the repairman in a department store would be classified under commerce, not under construction.

Surprising is the comparatively low figure for manufacturing employment in Japan, now one of the world's leading industrial exporters, and the figure has not increased since 1970; the reason appears to be that Japan is largely engaged in new industries with comparatively low labour requirements, while Germany, Italy, and Britain have more antiquated industrial structures.

In studying the regional distribution of employments we may begin at the very lowest level, in the poverty-stricken Indian state of Bihar, where the proportions of the labour force engaged in primary

Table 42. Industrial Distribution of the Labour Force.

Classifications (in some cases omitting unemployed and workers of industry unspecified)	Agriculture[a]	Mines & quarries	Manufacture[b]	Construction	Transport & communication	Commerce & finance	Other services
1970-71							
Australia	7.4	1.5	24.9	7.9	7.1	25.8	25.4
Canada	7.9	1.6	23.0	6.3	7.6	20.9	32.7
France[c]	9.6	1.0	28.6	10.0	6.2	20.8[e]	23.8
Germany[c]	4.5	1.8	41.7	8.1	5.7	15.3	22.9
Italy	14.2	0.6	34.3	11.3	5.6	15.9	18.1
Japan[c]	10.1	0.5	29.4	8.6	6.9	24.4	20.1
U.K.	2.9	1.6	34.6	7.0	6.6	16.0	31.3
U.S.A.	4.3	0.6	27.1	6.1	5.0	23.2	33.7
1930-36[d]							
Australia	24.7	2.3	19.1	6.9	8.8	18.2	20.0
Canada	32.6	1.9	19.5	6.8	8.2	12.9	18.1
France	24.7	2.0	29.8	4.3	6.0	15.6	17.6
Germany	16.9	2.7	37.5	7.2	5.6	13.0	17.1
Italy	40.3	0.8	25.5	6.2	4.4	8.3	14.5
Japan	35.8	1.3	21.3	4.3	4.1	21.8	11.8
U.K.[f]	5.9	6.1	35.0	5.4	8.0	16.0	23.6
U.S.A.	22.6	2.3	24.2	6.4	9.1	15.7	19.7

a. Including forestry fishing and hunting

b. Including electricity gas and water

c. In these countries exceptional numbers of female workers were shown in agriculture, Census categories apparently so describing farmers' wives; elsewhere the numbers shown were small; these exceptional figures therefore have been excluded from the calculations.

d. Female workers recorded for agriculture omitted throughout (See Note c)

e. Including hotels and restaurants

f. Excluding Northern Ireland

production (Table 43) are the highest found anywhere, moreover still rising in all but a few districts, approaching what appears to be the absolute maximum figure of ninety per cent.[1]

Table 43. Bihar: Percentage of Labour Force in Primary Activities (Including Mining).

	1951	1971
Patna (district containing State capital)	68.6	74.0
3 partially industrialized districts (average) . .	78.2	72.9
Next 3 districts in ascending order of primary employment (average)	74.4	83.0
Next 5 districts in ascending order of primary employment (average)	80.7	87.6
Next 5 districts in ascending order of primary employment (average)	86.4	89.1

Indian manufacture shows some tendency to concentrate in the larger cities, though not too marked.[2] The percentages of the labour force occupied in manufacture (including handicrafts) showed medians rising from 27.1 for cities of fifty to sixty thousand population to 35.1 for cities over three hundred thousand. But there is great variance between cities.

A further examination of Indian regional employment will be made in the next chapter, also that of Brazil, a developing country at a considerably more advanced level.

Ascending the income scale, we now turn to the situation in southern Italy (Table 44). In 1861 it was as industrialized as the North.[3] The decline in the manufacturing proportion of the labour force in the south (see Chapter 8 regarding some of the political factors hastening this decline) did not lead to a reflux into agriculture, but to some increase in service employment (perhaps concealing some disguised unemployment). Since 1936 service employment in the south has risen parallel to that in the north, but with a difference, now declining. Analysis of the difference (until 1965 about four per cent of the labour force) shows that it is explained by lower employment in the South in commerce (other than retail food trading), finance, and hotels, and restaurants.

1. K. R. G. Nair, South Campus, University of Delhi, private communication.
2. G. E. Stoner Jnr, "A Comparative Analysis of Urban Economic Bases: the Employment Structure of Indian Cities 1951–61", *Economic Geography* 44, no. 1 (Jan. 1968), pp. 71–82.
3. Saraceno, World Population Conference 1954 (Rome), and official figures.

Table 44. Italian Labour Force Percentage Distribution.

		Labour force (millions)	Agriculture, forestry, fishing	Manufacture, mining, and construction	Servic
1861	South	5.6	57.0	30.5	12.9
	North	8.9	57.0	26.0	17.0
1936	South	5.8	57.0	27.5	15.9
	North	12.5	44.0	37.0	19.0
1965	South	6.03	37.6	30.7	31.8
	North	13.44	20.0	43.7	36.2
1975	South	5.76	27.4	33.1	39.5
	North	13.23	10.4	48.4	41.2

Japan publishes data (Table 45) on an occupational basis, but "Production and Labouring" gives an approximate measure of employment in manufacturing and construction. The proportions are high throughout, but falling. Tokyo and Osaka, the two principal metropolitan areas, have larger proportions of their labour force engaged in services and less in manufacture, than does the third metropolitan area Nagoya.

Table 45. Japanese Employment*

	Tokyo Area		Osaka Area		Nagoya Area		Rest of Japan	
	1955	1970	1955	1970	1955	1970	1955	197
All employment other than primary production and mining (millions)	5.16	11.01	3.86	7.36	2.05	3.88	11.97	19.
Percentage of above represented by "Production and Labouring"	38.6	34.8	42.7	40.9	49.3	47.4	40.1	40.

* Official figures summarized in Nihon Keizai Shimbun (English language edition) 7 August 1973.

Britain (Table 46) also has a high but declining proportion engaged in manufacture, with a concentration in the west Midlands, centred on Birmingham, and in Yorkshire. But on the whole the distribution of manufacturing employment is surprisingly uniform.

We now turn to the question of how these industrial and service employments may be expected to be distributed between settlements of various sizes, beginning with the smaller urban settlements. An Australian study may be taken as a base.

Table 46. Percentages* of Labour Force in Manufacture. United Kingdom.

	1948	1975
United Kingdom	39.6	30.9
Regions:		
North	33.7	34.1
Yorkshire and Humberside	47.1	34.7
East Midlands	42.8	37.6
East Anglia	32.7	26.9
South East	34.0	24.7
South West	30.3	28.9
West Midlands	54.9	43.6
Northwest	49.5	32.0
Wales	27.7	29.1
Scotland	37.2	29.2
Northern Ireland	43.0	28.1

* 1975 from Regional Statistics 1977 Tables 8.2 and 8.3. 1948 from Deane, "Regional Variations in United Kingdom Incomes from Employment, 1948". *Journal of the Royal Statistical Society* 116, no. 2 (1953). Not however strictly comparable owing to (i) exclusion of self-employed which might have raised the percentages in manufacture by up to two points, and (ii) certain boundary changes.

Canberra, designated as the national capital of Australia because of the implacable rivalry between Sydney and Melbourne, is an artificially planned city, starting on vacant land in the 1920s, but growing rapidly. Initially the labour force consisted mainly of government office staffs, with a minimum of service employments, but the latter naturally increased in relative importance as time went on, and the total population of the city increased. The National Capital Development Commission needed estimates of the probable composition of industry and labour force as the city grew by stages up to a predicted population of 200,000 (though it now appears that this figure is unlikely to be reached in the foreseeable future).

For the preparation of such estimates the Commission consulted Dr Linge, of the Australian National University Department of Human Geography. The natural basis for such an estimate was the employment structure of other small towns of various sizes, and in studying these Dr Linge made the important discovery that, as total population of the town varies, the *proportion* of the labour force in each industry showed an approximate linear relationship with the *logarithm* of the town's total population. Some of these relationships were positively sloped (relative importance increasing with size of town), including manufacture and the more specialized services; but it is clear that these must have been offset by some negative slopes (declining relative importance) for industries such as retailing and construction, which are the predominant functions of the smaller settlements.

Drawing such semi-logarithmic diagrams it was possible to obtain (Table 47) comparative results for three countries, standardized to three sizes of town, with additional figures for very small towns in Britain. The United States figures were confined to the more recently settled western states to avoid the possibility of distortion by ancient patterns persisting in the east. Linge's projections for Canberra with a population of 200,000 and for the proposed Japanese development[4] of a new political capital (described in Chapter 8) with a population of 500,000 are also shown.

The figures from France are from a presentation at the 1965 World Population Conference by Paul Carrère for a new town to be planned around a metallurgical complex near Marseilles (these plans have apparently been abandoned — in any case the new town would not have had much chance of independent economic existence when the first planning step was to design a six-lane highway to Marseilles, no great distance away). However Carrère performed a very useful exercise in analyzing employment in various trades as a function of size of town, omitting presumably the smallest towns and villages. He followed various service and manufacturing employments as they rose with rising size of town in more or less direct proportion to population, until a break appeared in the series, from which he concluded that the manufacture or service in question was beginning to sell its products outside the town. (This method might be very useful in analyzing the "export base" of regions, considered in the next chapter — but other economists have found it very difficult to apply). In this way he hoped to obtain the *minimum* employments in various industries required by any substantial new town.

Carrère's figures have been converted from his per thousand population base to percentage of labour force (labour force assumed 40 per cent of population).

Manufacture (excluding repair services) for local demand he put at only 6 per cent of labour force (some tailoring, printing, etc.) and

4. *Nihon Keizai Shimbun* (Tokyo), 18 February 1975 (English Edition).

LABOUR FORCE	Australia 5,000	Australia 10,000	Australia 50,000	Australia 80,000[b]	U.S.A.[c] 1960 5,000	U.S.A.[c] 1960 10,000	U.S.A.[c] 1960 50,000	Gt. Britain 1951 1,000	Gt. Britain 1951 5,000	Gt. Britain 1951 10,000	Gt. Britain 1951 50,000	Japan 283,000	France proposed new town
Public utilities	1.7	1.9	2.5	2.6	1.8	1.8	1.7	2.1	2.2	2.2	2.2	0.4	0.7
Building & construction	11.3	10.6	8.9	8.0	6.5	6.7	7.1	9.8	8.3	7.5	5.9	12.7	5.0
Transport	6.9	6.8	6.6	6.5	3.8	3.9	4.2	7.2	7.4	7.5	7.8	6.4	4.0
Communications	2.6	2.2	1.5	1.2	1.6	1.6	1.6		1.8	1.7	1.4		2.0
Finance & business services	2.5	2.4	2.1	1.9	4.5	5.0	6.2					4.6	2.0
Wholesale trade	3.0	3.2	3.5	3.5	3.5	3.7	4.4	2.9	2.8	3.0	3.3	5.3	2.7
Retail trade — food	14.4	13.4	11.0	10.0	3.0	2.9	2.6	7.6	6.0	5.3	3.7		
Retail trade — other					13.8	13.3	12.1	7.2	6.8	6.7	6.4	12.7	7.8
Garages & service stations[a]	2.6	2.2	1.3	1.0	1.8	1.8	1.7	2.3	1.8	1.7	1.3		0.8
Public authorities	4.2	3.7	2.4		5.1	5.2	5.6	5.6	5.4	5.5	5.5	30.0	6.2
Regional & social welfare	0.5	0.5	0.6	2.5									
Health & hospitals	4.4	3.9	2.8	2.6	7.6	7.6	7.7	9.2	8.1	8.0	7.1		
Education	3.1	3.0	2.7	2.6	6.2	6.2	6.0	6.1	4.5	4.4	3.1		
Hotel & catering	4.2	3.8	2.9	2.6	3.8	3.6	3.3						2.0
Private domestic service	0.9	0.8	0.7					4.1	2.5	2.4	1.2		
Other personal services	2.8	2.4	1.7		9.3	9.0	8.2	3.2	3.2	3.2	3.1		2.2
Services & public utilities not separately specified													6.3
TOTAL OF ABOVE	65.1	60.8	51.2	45.0	72.3	72.3	72.4		60.8	59.1	52.0		39.0
Manufacture and mining	8.0[d]				16.3	16.7	17.6	14.7	26.2	30.0	40.6	12.3[e]	

a. "Repair Services" in U.S.A.
b. Linge's projection for Canberra
c. Western States
d. Linge's estimate
3. Of which 4.0 for printing and publishing

all employment for local needs (including these small manufactures) at 45.75 per cent of labour force, leaving the other 54.25 per cent to work in "export" manufacture. He further assumed — unrealistically — that these proportions would persist as population increased.

He qualified the construction proportion (low in comparison with other countries) by adding that each addition of one thousand to the population of the town should, at the time, add seven hundred to construction employment. Thus a town of twenty thousand population (eight thousand labour force) would be expected to have a regular construction employment of only four hundred, but this figure would rise to seven hundred and fifty (9.4 per cent of the labour force) so long as total population was growing by five hundred, or 2.5 per cent per year.

It is interesting to see how many proportions decline with increasing size of city — the movements of several series in the United States of America however conflict with those for Britain and Australia. The distribution of manufacturing employment by size of town in the western United States is much more uniform.

While some towns and regions are exceptionally dependent on manufacture, the manufacturing proportion of the labour force generally goes on increasing with size of city until we come to the largest cities, where, as we saw from the Japanese and British data governmental, trading, and other service functions acquire greater relative importance.

In a highly original study of cities in France (excluding Paris) above forty thousand population Rochefort[5] enumerated how many functions each city fulfilled out of a list of over one hundred specialized services — a shorter list was used for cities under one hundred thousand population. Included in the lists were the less common types of commercial services, banks, lawyers, public administration, higher education, medical specialists, cultural and sporting facilities.

The conclusions[6] are striking. There is an approximately linear relationship between the populations of cities and the number of functions which they perform, except for those which are pulled over to the right of the diagrams. These appear to be prominent manufacturing cities or large seaports. Such manufacturing or transport functions, it might be said, cause them to become "over-populated" in relation to the service functions which they perform.

Similar explanations apply to the smaller towns. The divergence of Nice is accounted for by its business as a holiday centre, Grenoble

5. Rochefort, World Population Conference 1965 (Belgrade), Paper WPC/WP/74.
6. See Diagrams in *Population Growth and Land Use* p. 336.

as a university town, Rouen and Le Havre as seaports, and Brest and Toulon as naval bases.

The population deviations to the right of the diagrams represent not only the workers in manufacture, seaports etc., and their dependents, but also large numbers in local service industries providing for them. This question will be dealt with in the next chapter.

11

Regional Income Differences

The large regional wage and price discrepancies observed in the 18th (and earlier) centuries (Chapter 2), a function of transport costs, were only gradually reduced, probably more rapidly in Britain than elsewhere. In 1904 the British Government conducted an extensive survey into wages and prices (the principal object being to study what was then called the "cost of living") which yielded regional results (Table 48).[1] Rents in London differed greatly from those elsewhere, but other prices had become nearly uniform, with no great differences in the wages of urban workers.

Table 48. U.K. Regions 1904.

	WAGES	RENT	PRICES
London	100	100	100
North	86	62	97
Yorkshire	84	56	94
Lancashire-Cheshire	87	54	92
Midlands	85	51	93
East	76	50	98
South	80	61	102
Wales	86	60	96
Scotland	83	69	102
Ireland	84	50	97

Regional studies of residential rents in Britain (and in some other countries) have now lost all meaning through extensive governmental rent control. But the London differential for commercial rents remains high (Table 49).

1. British Government Command Paper 3864, 1908. The wage comparisons apparently exclude agricultural wages.

Table 49. British Regional Differentials.

Distance from Central London (miles)	Average 1970 salary £ /week	£ /worker/year	
		Rent	Rates
0	25.0	1,200	102
Up to 14	22.5	307	23
18 - 74	20.7	225	15
110-120 (Birmingham, Bristol)	22.3	187	19
184-186 (Leeds, Manchester)	17.5	217	29
269 (Newcastle)	15.6	207	16

By 1970–75 full-time weekly earnings of adult males in Greater London were seven per cent above the national average for manual and fourteen per cent for non-manual workers.[2] For the southeastern region, excluding Greater London, the differences from the national average were inappreciable.

Somewhat surprisingly however there was a considerable gradient[3] in the salaries of top grade female clerical workers (where there may have been a labour shortage). These were matched by great differences in rents of office space (assumed requirements per workers 150 square feet) and municipal rates (1971–72).

Wider differences prevailed in nineteenth century France.[4] In 1853, after the beginning of the Railway Age, Paris wages for four grades of skilled men averaged 4.3 francs/day, more than twice the average for other capitals of Departments; the same ratio still prevailed in 1885: by 1938 it was still 1.64, but by 1947 had fallen to 1.27. Data for modern France (as for most countries) suffer from aggregation, that is, failure to distinguish the varying proportions of skilled workers, which tend to be higher in the capital cities, and so the regional wage relativity is exaggerated.[5] Subject to this effect, the ratios between the rest of France (all areas, not only departmental capitals) and the Paris region were 1.35 for male and 1.41 for female manual workers; for non-manual workers, surprisingly, the ratios were lower, at 1.25 and 1.39 respectively. For male manual workers the lowest paid region was the mountain region of Limousin (ratio to Paris 1.63): for female wage earners, Languedoc (ratio 1.56).

2. N. W. H. Simon *Regional Studies* 11, p. 90.
3. R. K. Hall, "The Movement of Offices from Central London" Regional Studies 6 (Dec. 1972), p. 67. 385–92.
4. Meuriot, *Des Agglomerations Urbaines* quoting De Foville, and *Etudes et Conjoncture*, (Feb. 1948).
5. *Etudes et Conjoncture* (Nov. 1965), p. 67.

In the United States of America as in other modern industrial countries of high mobility, differences of money wages (and to some extent of prices too) between cities still remain and, in view of the greater distances, rather more than in Europe. Hoover has classified wages in the United States by three classes of skill, three classes of city size, and four regions.[6] Between cities over one million and less than a quarter million the maximum difference was some fifteen per cent (and usually much less). The low-wage Southern region (after standardizing for size of cities) was twenty per cent below the national average for the unskilled, but only five per cent below for skilled and clerical workers.

Even in Brazil, where distances are great and one might have expected lower mobility, wage data, if properly classified into homogeneous skill levels, show that it is only for low or moderately-skilled workers that real earnings are lower in the poorer regions.[7]

So far we have made some examination of regional differences in wages, which may be extensive in simpler economies with no adequate transport, but decline in more modern societies of greater human mobility; and of the employment patterns in settlements of various sizes. These latter give us a clear pattern of the progressive concentration of specialized functions, both manufacturing and service, with increasing size of city.

From census and other records abundant information is available on regional employments. Measuring regional incomes is not so easy. In some cases we may find that we still have to use regional employment figures as a substitute for income information.

In the United States of America official estimates of regional incomes began in 1940, the data being carried back to 1929.[8] Less precise estimates back to 1919 are now available with some nineteenth century information.[9] The units have been states — comprehensive official estimates of incomes in metropolitan and other regions within states were not prepared until recently. These estimates cover not only wage and salary earnings, but also incomes from business and property. Later incomes from social welfare payments were also analyzed.

It is necessary to record incomes by residence rather than by origin. That is to say, a large company will record its wages and salaries locally, but its distributed profits will be classified according to the

6. E. M. Hoover, *Introduction to Regional Economics* New York: Knopf, 1974, p. 170.
7. Carnoy and Katz, "Explaining Differentials in Earning among Large Brazilian Cities" *Urban Studies*, 8, 1 (1971), p. 35.
8. *Survey of Current Business,* October 1940.
9. *Economic Development and Cultural Change,* July 1958.

residences of the shareholders, who may be a long way away, while its undistributed profits will not appear in the regional income classifications at all.

Further minor adjustments in the United States official figures are now made, in respect of people who work in one region and reside in another.

It was some time before other countries followed the United States in preparing estimates of regional incomes; and these are mostly for rather broadly defined regions. However a limited number of private estimates have been made for smaller regions and individual cities.

There were a few other early developments. In Canada the Rowell-Sirois Commission on Federal Finance prepared estimates of provincial incomes in the 1920s. The German Statistical Office in the 1930s prepared and published in *Statistisches Jahrbuch* regional income estimates going back to 1913. Sweden and Norway published incomplete figures based on tax assessments.

We now come to the important generalization that regional development must, by its nature, be uneven. A massive survey of all the information available about regional incomes in different countries was undertaken by Williamson.[10] To summarize, his results are that at the lowest economic levels we find fairly uniformly distributed poverty; that economic growth appears in a limited number of regions only, with increasing regional inequalities; until at a later stage this process is reversed (by increasing mobility) and regional inequalities (for which Williamson designed an ingenious special measure) decrease.

To put it in concrete terms, as in America during recent decades, per head income in the poorer southern states has risen considerably more rapidly than in the richer states. Paradoxically, this does not necessarily mean that productivity per worker in any of the sectors, agriculture, industry, or services, has risen more rapidly in the south than in the north, the main factors at work have been changes in the relative numbers of agricultural and industrial workers, and also the out-migration of many of the poorer families, thus increasing the average per head income of those who remained, and raising the southern states' average rates of growth per head above the national average.

Williamson develops the index of regional divergences of income, weighted according to the population of each region as follows:

---

10. Williamson, *Economic Development and Cultural Change* (July 1965), Part 2. Detailed information for each country by regions is given in an appendix to Williamson's article.

Where f_i is population of region i
       n is national population
       y_i is income per head in region i
       y is national average income per head
Then v_w (weighted measure of inequality) is defined as

$$\sqrt{\sum (y_i-\bar{y})^2 \, f_i/n} \; /\bar{y}$$

This shows a strong general tendency (Table 50) for regional differences to be at their least in the advanced countries, and at their

Table 50. Value of Divergence Index by Countries Grouped Approximately According to Per Head Income.

Australia	0.058	Puerto Rico	0.520
New Zealand	0.063		
Canada	0.192	Group III average	0.335
United Kingdom	0.141		
U.S.A.	0.182	Brazil	0.700
Sweden	0.200	Italy	0.360
		Spain	0.415
Group I average	0.139	Colombia	0.541
		Greece	0.302
Finland	0.331		
France	0.283	Group IV average	0.464
West Germany	0.205		
Netherlands	0.131	Yugoslavia	0.340
Norway	0.309	Japan	0.244
Group II average	0.252		
		Group V average	0.292
Ireland	0.268		
Chile	0.327	Philippines	0.556
Austria	0.225	India	0.275

greatest in the poorest countries. There seems to be a subsidiary tendency for regional differences to be greater in countries of large geographical extent (though Puerto Rico is a striking exception).

Williamson also undertook the interesting exercise of measuring *intrastate* (i.e., between counties) inequalities in the United States in 1950 and 1960, which were found to range from 0.06 in Connecticut to 0.38 in Mississippi and Kentucky, and to show a significant negative correlation with state average income. The average inequality index fell more than ten per cent in the decade 1950–60.

Some minor additions are possible. For Indonesia in 1972 an index of 0.522 has been calculated.[11] For two more advanced Asian countries a more recent (1971) figure for the Philippines (calculated on recorded family expenditures, which always exceed stated incomes) shows a heavy fall to 0.289.[12] Malaysia in 1970 showed a figure of

11. Data from H. Esmara, "Regional Income Disparities" *Bulletin of Indonesian Economic Studies* 11, no. 1 (March 1975), p. 46.
12. Data from Bureau of Statistics, *Family Income and Expenditure*, 1971.

0.271.[13] Data are available for Portugal from which can be calculated indexes of 0.323 for 1953 rising to 0.385 for 1963.[14] Portugal in this decade was a rapidly growing economy, with real product per head of labour force rising sixty per cent in ten years. An uptodate figure has been added for United Kingdom (included in Table 51).[15] Recent changes in regional inequalities, to the extent that they are measured by unemployment figures, show inequality declining in Germany, Netherlands, Sweden and United Kingdom, stationary in Australia, Canada, and France, and rising in the United States of America.[16]

ble 51. Changes in Regional Inequality Coefficients.

A			Norway	1939	.424	Netherlands	1938	.302
	1840	.279		1952,			1950-59	.131
	1880	.355		1957-60	.309			
	1900	.322				Sweden	1920	.440
	1929	.369	United	1937	.116		1930	.539
	1940	.331	Kingdom [1]	1959-60	.141		1950-61	.200
	1950-61	.182		1974-75	.129			
¹ada²	1890	.099	Italy	1928	.313			
	1910	.130		1938	.345			
	1926	.176		1951-60	.360			
	1940	.220						
	1950-61	.192	Germany	Old Territory		Present W. German Territory		
zil³	1872	.925		1900	.220		.160	
	1900	.727		1913	.226		.165	
	1939	.502		1928	.186		.136	
	1950-59	.700		1936	.196		.148	
	1968	.589		1950-60			.205	

There appears to be a misprint in Williamson's historical table (p. 25).

Additional figures for 1890 and 1910 calculated from data of gross product and labour force given by Green, *Economic Development and Cultural Change*, July 1969, p. 583.

Approximate regional data for 1872 and 1900 from M. Buescu, 7th International Economic History Conference, Edinburgh, 1978, and the 1968 figures calculated from data of factor cost national product per head by provinces in *Anuario Statistico* 1971.

Interesting conclusions are reached however when Williamson examines the trend of the v_w coefficient over time. It is found to be rising in India, Japan, and Yugoslavia, stable in Australia, France, Italy, and the United Kingdom, falling in Brazil, Canada, Finland, West Germany, Netherlands, Norway, Spain, Sweden, and the United States.

A selection only of Williamson's results is given in Table 51; with

13. Data from Mid-Term Review of the Second Malaysia Plan.
14. Abreu, *O Crescimento Regional am Portugal* (1969). Calculations based on regional labour forces of 1950 and 1960 rather than on total population.
15. From the pretax personal incomes (*Regional Statistics*, 1977, Table 13.3; per head of total population for regions, distinguishing metropolitan counties.
16. Unpublished OECD study.

some additions, and with the averages for the 1950s from Table 50 included for comparison. These results refer to various dates in the 1950s. For some countries more than one year's data were available and an average was taken. For further use by other researchers full data are given by Williamson in a long appendix.

Some figures for the worst recession years of the 1930s show increases, mainly explained by the anomalously low incomes of agricultural regions at that time.

The basic theorem, of regional inequalities first increasing and later decreasing with rising incomes, appears to be established with some qualifications. Canada's period of rapid growth after 1890 was marked by increasing inequalities. Brazil had a past structure of extreme inequalities, gradually reducing, with a relapse in the 1950s.

The United States movements were not regular. In a later study Williamson analyzed changes in the United States coefficient since 1840, to separate out the effect of the impoverishment of the southern states after the Civil War, and their gradual recovery after 1900.[17] Using a different measure, he shows the change (Table 52) in the coefficient of inequality.

Table 52. Changes in U.S. Inequality Coefficient.

	1840-1880	1880-1900	1900-1929	1929-1950	1950-1970
Northern States	−.041	−.010	+.012	−.024	.000
All United States of America		−.010	−.050	−.066	−.018

Williamson's paper analyzes the contributions to these variances from agricultural and non-agricultural productivities, and the composition of output. Increasing regional inequalities among the northern states in the 1900–29 period are noticeable.

17. Williamson, Seventh International Economic History Conference, Edinburgh, 1978.

12

Regional Accounts and Multipliers

We must begin with a requirement so obvious that most people fail to see it. As various forms of non-agricultural employment grow, agriculture must be productive enough to feed and to supply certain raw materials to those so employed (except for any small quantities of minerals or manufactured goods produced which can be sold outside the region to pay for imported food). Further, as incomes and population rise, there will also be a strongly increased demand for imported goods and services; these also will have to be paid for in the main by exports of agricultural products. So increased agricultural productivity is seen to be, in most cases, an unavoidably necessary condition for general economic growth. This has been shown to be the case nationally for developing countries;[1] and it is true also for regions.

An outstanding example was the economic development of late 19th century Japan. In this case however the quantity of non-agricultural development, arising from a given increase in agricultural productivity, was found to be substantially greater than in other countries at a similar stage of development. This was probably mainly due to two factors: (i) Japan's unusually low income elasticity of demand for food – a reflexion of Japanese social customs and (ii) the existence of a good transport and trading network, increasing, at any given level of agriculturel income, the demand for non-agricultural products.

Nakayama showed that some of the earlier figures of agricultural output were understated, and rates of growth therefore overstated;[2] but the information appears to have been reasonably accurate after 1888, and Nakayama's attempt to disapprove the whole theory of prior development was shown to be entirely mistaken.[3]

1. M. R. Haswell and C. Clark, *Economics of Subsistence Agriculture* Chapter 13.
2. Nakayama, *Agricultural Production and the Economic Development of Japan 1873–1922* (Princeton: 1966).
3. Y. Hayami and S. Yamada, in *Agriculture and Economic Growth: Japan's Experience* ed. K. Ohkawa and B. F. Johnston (Tokyo: Tokyo University Press, 1969) and C. Clark's review of Nakayama *Journal of Agricultural Economics* 18, no. 3 (Sept. 1967).

The method developed in *Economics of Subsistence Agriculture* was to take the non-agricultural proportion of the labour force as the measure of economic development, the dependent variable; and as the explanatory variable agricultural output (plus "agriculture-substitutes") per head of agricultural labour force. For this purpose "agriculture-substitutes" consist of any output of forestry, mineral, or manufactured products capable of being exported.

It was found, over a wide range of countries and conditions, that the dependent variable showed a linear relation to the *logarithm* of the explanatory variable; that is, agricultural productivity has to improve at an increasing rate to provide for each succeeding increase in non-agricultural employment. This analysis, of course, is not applicable to advanced countries. A regional analysis on these lines has been attempted for two developing countries. India and Brazil.

Brazil has an extensive statistical system and publishes a large *Anuario Statistico do Brasil*; the 1970 census data on labour force, showing agricultural numbers and proportion in each state were obtained from the 1974 edition; and these can be related to state data of factor cost domestic product by sectors (1968 data from the 1971 *Anuario* were used). The fully industrialized regions of Rio de Janeiro, Sao Paulo, Guanabara, and Federal District were omitted; but the remaining states still show a wide range of values.

Unfortunately the factor cost product data by states only give "industry" as a single entry, followed by services, whereas it would be better to have figures excluding small scale and local market-oriented industries. Taking it to represent "agriculture-substitute" thus somewhat overstates it. But even so, as will be seen from the Table, it does not represent a large addition to agricultural income in the poorer states. The differences between them are principally due to differences in agricultural productivity.

In Table 53 the states are ranged in order of size of the explanatory variable.

For India regional information is available for "registered", meaning comparatively large-scale, manufacture, with output probably saleable outside the region, and for mining, from Central Statistical Office estimates. For convenient in calculation regional per head product is measured relative to the Indian average, and agricultural and manufacturing output expressed in the same units.

These data (Table 54) differ from the Brazilian and international results. Up to the productivity level of Rajasthan (12 per cent below the Indian average) the advance is slow; but beyond that something like linear growth appears (with exceptionally high non-agricultural employment in Kerala).

In more advanced economies wide regional differences in per head

Table 53. Brazilian Regions.

	Agricultural labour force '000	Product/million cruzeiros		Product per head of agricultural labour force '000 cruzeiros	Agricultural percentage of labour force
		Agriculture	Industry		
Piahi	346	169	21	.55	71.3
Maranhao	763	416	60	.62	78.4
Bahia	1437	1209	291	1.04	62.4
Paraiba	437	402	75	1.09	64.7
Alagoas	323	370	82	1.09	66.9
Para	347	198	185	1.10	56.0
Ceara	749	680	141	1.10	56.0
Sergipe	162	161	28	1.17	60.9
Mato Grosso	298	316	44	1.20	60.2
Rio Grande do Norte	241	294	61	1.47	58.8
Pernambuco	765	692	446	1.49	50.8
Amazonas	162	164	91	1.58	60.0
Goias	524	847	65	1.74	60.4
Parana	1439	2101	480	1.79	63.2
Espirito Santo	240	374	68	1.85	52.4
Minas Gerais	1717	2131	1446	2.08	49.6
Santa Caterina	452	705	453	2.56	51.2
Rio Grande do Sul	1045	2201	1134	3.19	46.1

agricultural product are still found. The determination of regional non-farm employment by the level of agricultural (plus substitute) productivity, as found in India and Brazil, becomes less firm with the increasing volume of interregional trade (industrial workers selling their output and buying their food across the regional border). But we now have to ask to what extent low regional agricultural productivity affects the regional level of non-farm productivity and incomes.

In Italy, where regional differences are outstanding, this relationship clearly holds.[4] The four agriculturally poorest regions (Molise, Basilicata, Marche, and Calabria) with 1970 annual gross product per agricultural worker of less than one million lire also have non-agricultural productivities well below average, less than 2.5 million lire gross products per non-agricultural worker. Campania however (the region around Naples) now has both agricultural and non-agricultural productivities above national average.

In Mexico[5] however the differences were less marked; Table 55 classifies regions by their agricultural productivity.

The diagram for Italy shows curvature – as incomes rise, the agricultural/non-agricultural differences lessen. A similar diagram[6]

4. Data from ISTAT, Conti Economici Territoriali, Annuario di Statistichi del labore e dell' emigrazione.
5. De Navarrete *Ceres* (Sept–Oct. 1971).
6. Compiled from *Statistisches Jahrbuch fur der B. R. Deutschland.*

Table 54. Indian Regions.

	(1) Net domestic product per head (Indian average = 100) 1962-3	(2)[d] PRODUCT Agriculture, forestry, fishing	(3)[d] Mining and manufacture[a]	(4) PRODUCT PER HEAD OF AGRICULTURAL POPULATION[b] Agriculture, forestry, fishing	(5) Mining and manufacture	(6) Percentage of male labour force in agriculture[c] 1961 Census
Andhra Pradesh	103.0	59.6	3.7	88.8	5.5	67.1
Assam	106.4	63.8	8.9	83.4	11.6	76.5
Bihar	70.7	34.5	9.3	44.5	12.0	77.5
Gujarat	125.9	56.6	15.4	90.3	24.6	62.7
Haryana	116.2	69.3	6.5	104.2	9.8	66.5
Jammu and Kashmir	81.4	46.8	1.3	62.0	1.7	75.5
Kerala	92.4	45.1	6.0	97.8	13.0	46.1
Madhya Pradesh	85.4	49.2	4.2	63.6	5.4	77.3
Maharashtra	130.8	48.1	25.2	77.8	40.8	61.8
Mysore	99.7	52.6	6.9	75.8	9.9	69.4
Orissa	79.6	46.6	4.2	60.8	5.5	76.7
Punjab	128.4	72.5	5.6	126.1	9.7	57.5
Rajasthan	88.1	54.0	3.0	72.7	4.0	74.3
Tamil Nadu	111.3	48.6	10.0	81.7	16.8	59.5
Uttar Pradesh	78.7	46.1	3.0	62.8	4.1	73.4
West Bengal	128.0	50.1	24.9	87.0	43.2	57.6

a. "Registered", i.e. large-scale manufacture only

b. Columns 2 and 3 divided by Column 6/100

c. Males only because it is clear that there are great differences between states in recording female labour

d. Same unit as for Column 1

Table 55. Product per worker (All Mexico = 1) 1960.

	Agriculture	Other industries
Mexico City	1.5	1.2
Regions of high agricultural productivity	2.3	1.1
Regions of medium agricultural· productivity	1.4	1.0
Regions of low agricultural productivity	0.6	0.8

for the German Lander in 1970 shows non-agricultural productivities (about forty per cent above Italian in purchasing power) by regions all within the range 25,000–29,000 marks gross product/worker/year, with no significant relation to agricultural productivities, which in the lowest region (Bavaria) stood at only 6,770 marks (equivalent to only 1,040,000 lire in Italy).

For France, with a greater abundance of regional subdivisions, similar results were obtained also for 1970, with non-agricultural productivities showing a very high degree of regional uniformity (except for Paris), in face of wide regional difference in agricultural productivity, ranging from 6,700 francs/farm family/year in Limousin to 29,800 in Picardy.[7]

Attempts to construct regional accounts may be of varying degrees of refinement. The most difficult step is to ascertain the amounts of commodities and services imported from and exported to other regions, as well as internationally. In modern interdependent regions, in close proximity, these may represent a very large proportion of the region's total income or output. Other items which have to go into regional accounts are transactions of all kinds with the central government, taxation, and various forms of public expenditure, and also if possible, capital movements.

In a simple economy, with inadequate transport, a poor and isolated region may supply most of its own small requirements, with a comparatively low dependency on interregional or international trade. On the other hand, in advanced countries with modern transport and social organization, the poorer and more isolated regions often show a very high rate of dependency on interregional trade, being able to import many of their services as well as commodity requirements, and being themselves engaged in some form of specialized

7. INSEE Regional Estimates.

agricultural or mining production, supplemented in some cases by social service payments from the central government.

But as the population and productivity of a region increase, and its capital city becomes larger, its relative dependence on international and interregional aid decreases. We come to the interesting conclusion, supported by the evidence, that the least relative dependence on interregional trade is found in regions such as the New York metropolitan area, with its very large population and regional product. As will be seen however in this Chapter, the same is not true of Paris.

As we saw in Chapter 1, at the lowest stage of economic development a society with only primitive means of transport is necessarily bound to subsistence agriculture. The farmer who might be able to produce more would be unable to sell it, so there is practically no interregional trade. As transport begins to improve, but is still costly in real terms, farmers produce beyond their own consumption, but sell mostly in the towns and villages of their own region, in exchange for handicrafts and services. It is only at a further stage of the development of transport, and also of agricultural productivity, that they sell significant amounts outside their region. It is also clear, that from the nature of the case, that such sales will have to be of specialized agricultural products. The immediate needs of the region will call for a diversity of agricultural products; but to succeed in competitive interregional trade, with transport costs still high, specialization of output will be necessary.

The next step is the beginning of manufacture, producing goods for transport to distant markets, and thus "footloose", rather than market-oriented or materials-oriented industries bound to their own region. Such manufactures are all to some degree dependent on economies of scale, more important for some than for others, but necessary in all cases. Interregional sales are therefore (with few exceptions) a necessary condition for the development of manufacture; and these in turn are dependent on reduced transport costs. This is why manufacture, in anything like the sense we understand it, only began about the end of the eighteenth century, and then largely dependent upon sea and canal transport. We have noted the principal factors which attracted it, density of population in the first instance, subject to more refined analysis as "economic potential"; and also, where available, low rates of money wages (which are not necessarily the same thing as low real wages).

We have seen how the various service industries, and manufactures, apportion themselves to settlements of different size, and have some understanding of their reasons for so doing. But we now have to face the more fundamental question — how did such employment originate, if we may so put it, before it began to apportion itself to different cities? The answer of course is perfectly clear, so far as the service industries are concerned. They arose to meet local demand — that is the nature of services. The only exception to the above rule is in the case of a few service industries whose nature it is to serve a much wider field than their own region, such as military bases designed to defend the whole country, large sea ports serving far beyond their own region, universities attracting other than regional students, and a few others. In other words, we have to carry the problem further back.

A few manufactures also, on the market-oriented kind, are also evoked by local demand. But this is as far as we can go. It certainly will not do to attempt to explain the whole of economic development in terms of demand changes. We find ourselves confronted with the whole problem of general economic development, a review of which is certainly not the function of this book, except in so far as it has regional aspects. Suffice it to say, on the general problem of economic growth, that we have now moved far away from simple theories of determination by the rate of capital accumulation — capital stock is a necessary but certainly by no means a sufficient condition for economic growth; and in any case, under many circumstances, a country or region can obtain its capital from outside. It is now clear that many factors other than economics lie at the base of the problem, including social psychology and political structures. Kuznets adverted to the Marxian proposition that political systems were nothing but a superstructure on economic conditions. The truth, he contended, was the exact opposite, namely that political structures had lagged, for very long periods, in adapting themselves to changed economic conditions, thereby seriously injuring economic growth.

So we must look at the basic economic growth of a region in terms of supply factors, coming back to local demand when we are analyzing service employment (and also employment in market-oriented manufactures).

We see that interregional trade forms, to an increasing degree, an integral part of the process of general economic development.

An economically self-contained region — the irrational objective of some — is only possible at very low economic levels. The same of course is true of a country isolated from international trade. Dislike of foreigners, even to the extent of trading with them, has deep psychological roots; and similar dislikes, in a milder form, sometimes appear in respect of interregional trade.

One of the few economists who combines his subject with profound psychological studies is Everett Hagen.[8] Though his psychological studies are difficult of comprehension by those who have not studied the subject (and may be disputed by adherents of rival schools of psychology), he has reached some very interesting conclusions when applying himself to economic history and economics. It was he who first showed the economic advantages of a rising population, not only owing to the wider spreading of "economic indivisibilities", or overhead costs of various kinds, both public and private, but also through a more subtle factor, to which he applied the curious phrase "absolving a country from the consequences", of errors in investment, both private and public.[9] Such errors are bound to occur; but with an advancing population it is comparatively easy to find some economic use for the misplaced investment; with a stationary or declining population much less so. A similar line of reasoning was followed by Keynes when he published *The End of Laissez-Faire* in 1926. At that time population decline appeared to be in prospect. But Keynes deduced that government regulation of investment would therefore be necessary, being (at that time) under the impression that governments always made right decisions. Later Keynes inverted his conclusions, and declared himself in favour of population growth as the necessary condition for flourishing private investment.[10] Hagen also made a most unusual study of the introducers of industrial innovations in late eighteenth-century England, a critical period of economic growth. Almost all, he found, were of "dissenting" religions (that is, Protestants who nevertheless rejected the established Church of England). Under the legislation then in force such men were excluded from politics, public administration, the universities, the armed forces, and various other callings. Thus economic considerations alone might have partially explained their increased tendency to devote themselves to business and technology; but Hagen also traces some stimulating psychological effects arising from such exclusions.

He also brings in psychological principles in analyzing economic development in Colombia. What was striking here was the extraordinary lead taken by a single province, Antioquia, and that a fairly remote one, without any exceptional endowment of natural resources. He gives what appears to the non-specialist to be a very

8. Everett Hagen, *On the Theory of Social Change; How Economic Growth Begins* A Study for Massachusetts Institute of Technology, (The Dorsey Series in Anthropology and Sociology (1962).
9. Everett Hagen in a paper at the 1953 Conference of the International Association for Research in Income and Wealth, not published at the time.
10. J. M. Keynes, "Some Economic Consequences of Declining Population" (Galton Lecture) *Eugenics Review* 10 n.s. (1937–38), p. 13.

able and thorough account of the psychological and social factors at work.

Setting aside for the moment the question of population density and economic potential, a region with low-productivity agriculture, where wages are low, is thus seen to be – as we know is the case – by no means always able to achieve manufacturing development, attractive though the low money wages may be to industiralists when other things are equal.

With all the above conditions in mind, we can now look at the possibilities for regional development, in the early stages. In some cases there is a successful mining development, or extensive export of a specialized agricultural product. We cannot expect substantial manufacturing production, for markets outside the region, to appear until a later stage; and in most cases, only to develop gradually. There will be an increased demand for locally-produced services and market-oriented manufactures.

Lösch quotes a study by Isenberg of the industries covering local demand in Germany.[11] (This study was published in 1941, and presumably refers to the 1933 Census; this Census recorded the unemployed, in great numbers in 1933, according to their normal employment.) He analyzed employment in one agricultural region, in a leading industrial region, and in one region (Württemberg) of industry dispersed throughout an agricultural area. Isenberg however confined his studies (Table 56) to the category "Industry and Handicrafts", employing 13.2 million out of a labour force of 27.9 million (the latter redefined to exclude women members of farm families). In addition there were 6.0 million engaged in commerce and transport, 1.3 million in domestic and 2.7 million in other services; but Lösch considers that these latter employments were fairly evenly distributed in proportion to population.

Table 56. Regional Employment per thousand population 1933.

	East Prussia	Wurttemberg	Ruhr	Germany
Services (distribution assumed uniform)				151
Industry and handicrafts:				
Building	30	32	26	38
Other for local sale	30	32	39	32
For district sale	26	30	31	24
Total local and district sale including services	237	245	247	245
Sale in distant markets	13	150	165	113

11. Lösch, *The Economics of Location*, pp. 373–74.

Reckoned per thousand population (labour force, as redefined above, constituting 42.3 per cent of population) the totals of non-agricultural employment were shown in Table 56.

The uniformity of the numbers working for local and district markets, at some fifty-eight per cent of the labour force, is remarkable. A study in France showed that in seven regional centres with a labour force under one hundred thousand, seventy per cent of the labour force, on the average, is engaged in supplying regional and local needs, after we have excluded Le Havre, Brest, and Toulon (seaport and naval bases), where the proportion is only fifty-seven per cent, and also excluding the eight smaller manufacturing centres, where the proportion is sixty-six per cent.[12]

For the larger cities there is no systematic variation with size of city. For Nice the proportion is seventy per cent and for Marseilles, in spite of its function as a seaport, sixty-eight per cent but otherwise the proportions range from fifty-two to sixty-four per cent (Paris fifty-four per cent).

Even with the aid of such elaborate tabulations as are quoted in Chapter 9, about the distances over which manufactured goods are transported, it is very difficult to judge how much of the manufacture of any particular region is for local and how much for interregional or international sale. In the early stages of development regional manufacture will consist primarily of the production of bulky or perishable goods for the local market, more so if the region is remote and facing high transport costs. With economic advance and improving transport these will decline in relative importance.

In more advanced economies, of course, regions develop "export bases" besides agriculture and mining, some forms of manufacture, some services of the kinds which are capable of being exported across the regional border, and also sometimes, in the modern world, a net balance of central government social welfare payments over taxation.

But first we may consider the extent to which regions can provide themselves with a full range of services, particularly if they lack large towns with their specialized service functions.

The present writer, in an early study, made use of the information then available, namely for the United States and Canadian regional income figures, and some roughly constructed estimates for Britain and Australia, for comparison with regional employment in various service industries.[13] Assuming, in effect, that service requirements

12. *Population* (March–April 1965).
13. C. Clark, "The Economic Functions of a City in Relation to its Size" *Econometrica* 13, no. 2 (April 1945).

per unit of income (not per unit of population) were approximately the same for all regions, the figures of regional service employment per unit of regional income thus gave some idea of the extent to which a region could satisfy its needs for services, or whether it would have to have some of its needs met from outside the region. The interesting result was obtained that once the central city had attained a population of some one hundred and fifty thousand, the region was able to provide for itself most of its service requirements. This conclusion may still stand. It appeared that manufacture, on the other hand, might require larger cities.

Measured by its proportion of the labour force, manufacture as a percentage of metropolitan area employment in the United States of America at that time showed extreme diversity, ranging from 55.9 per cent in Flint, Michigan to 7.2 per cent in Miami, Florida. By 1970 however these had been modified to 48.5 per cent and 14.8 per cent respectively.

This idea of critical size of town received partial confirmation from a study of New Zealand in the 1950s.[14] New Zealand provides an excellent field for such a study, being a country with a high-income homogenous population, with only slight interregional income differences, and with regions in most cases clearly marked off by mountains and sea (Table 57).

le 57. N.Z. Regional incomes produced per unit of total regional income.

	Median of 6 smaller regions	Dunedin	Christchurch	Wellington-Hutt	Auckland
Population of central city '000	9-33	99	186	223	362
sport and nunication	0.0794	0.0926	0.0820	0.0993	0.0813
esale and trade	0.1283	0.1342	0.1619	0.1731	0.1486
ice	0.0073	0.0096	0.0090	0.0131	0.0089
e industries domestic service)	0.1195	0.1359	0.1299	0.1300	0.1155
facture (exc. ary products ssing)	0.0986	0.1788	0.2063	0.2185	0.2037

14. From G. M. Neutze's thesis deposited in the Bodleian Library, Oxford, 1960. Some of the data were also published by Neutze, *New Zealand Geographer* (Oct. 1961).

While based on employment figures, the results are stated in the form of regional incomes produced. In so far as manufacturing and service industries may have higher product per man-year in the larger centres, the differences in *employment* will be somewhat greater than the differences shown in the table.

Data are available for ten regions. For the six smaller regions with central cities ranging in size from nine thousand (Blenheim and Greymouth) to thirty three thousand (Invercargill, in the far south) the data are aggregated and shown as a median.

The inability of the smaller cities to provide a full range of services, still less of manufactures, is apparent; and Dunedin falls short of the three larger cities in manufacture. In employment in finance Wellington apparently gains some advantage from its position as political capital.

Building (which depends principally on the region's rate of growth) and domestic service, are services which by their nature cannot be imported interregionally. The supply of the latter is fairly uniform, as also of the services of public administration (except for Wellington) and public utilities.

We are now approaching the problem of interregional exports and imports, and the balance between them, but we still have a long way to go. It will be apparent that we may seek, on the one hand, actual estimates of trade in goods (and services) crossing regional borders — a difficult and costly piece of research, of which we still have only a limited number of results — and, on the other hand, a large quantity of information on what *might* represent regional exports, in the form of "export-base" industries. The Indian and Brazilian results quoted above are a particularly crude but interesting example of the latter type of information.

But in a very populous and wealthy region the ratio may turn again, with the region's own demand for manufactured goods of a type which, if produced in a smaller region, would have been exported. (This is no more than an extension of the principle regarding international trade, which generally represents a smaller proportion of national product in larger than in smaller national economies.) In the New York Metropolitan Region in the 1950s, with sixteen million high-income population, sales within the region represent something approaching half all manufacturing output.[15]

Recent work by the United States Department of Commerce has resulted in a massive body of information extending the income data

15. Regional Plan Association, quoted in R. Vernon and E. M. Hoover, eds., *Anatomy of a Metropolis* (Cambridge, Mass.: Harvard University Press, 1959).

by states down to county level.[16] For our present purposes however we are concerned with somewhat larger units. Data are available for "Standard Metropolitan Statistical Areas" (SMSAs), defined as central cities of over 50,000 population, and the adjacent counties closely related to them.[17] But with the continued spread of residences and employments to adjacent rural areas and smaller towns the concept has now been introduced of larger "Economic Areas".[18] Thus the New York–New Jersey SMSA included only one New Jersey county and covered a 1975 population of 9.6 million (declining from 10 million in 1970); but it was flanked by the Newark SMSA (2 million population), New Brunswick SMSA (0.6 million), and Jersey City SMSA (0.6 million) to the west, and Nassau-Suffolk (2.6 million) and Poughkeepsie (0.2 million) to the north, all included in the newly defined New York Economic Area, extending northwards to include one county in Connecticut, with a population of 18 million (even this extended area however showing a population decline from 18.3 million in 1970).

Local demand, measured now not by employment but by incomes earned locally (including the self-employed as well as wage and salary earners) has been analyzed for a sample of some forty Economic Areas (including all the largest). Of the categories shown, the following are estimated to constitute local demand:

Contract construction
Wholesale and retail trade
Finance insurance and real estate
Transport communications and public utilities[19]
Services
Other industries[20]
Personal incomes from dwelling rent[21]
Government other than military.[22]

16. United States Department of Commerce, Bureau of Economic Analysis, *Local Area Personal Income 1970–75*, (1977).
17. For a more precise definition and discussion of criteria see United States Department of Commerce, *Metropolitan Area Definition*, Working Paper 28, (1969).
18. For a fuller discussion see *Survey of Current Business* (Nov. 1975).
19. Subject however to a maximum of five per cent of all local personal income. Any figure above this is regarded as an indication that the region is serving as a transport node, rendering considerable services to other regions.
20. This is always a small item.
21. *National Accounts* Table 2.1 shows this at 1.8 per cent of personal incomes, and this proportion is assumed for all economic areas. It is net of capital consumption, maintenance, indirect taxes, and interest, and includes income from owner-occupation.
22. Except for Washington, Federal Government civilian employment is assumed to be mostly for local needs. State capitals (except Boston) were excluded from the sample.

This leaves the following as "export earning" incomes:

Agriculture
Manufacture
Mining
Transport, etc in excess of five per cent of local personal income
Military
Dividends interest and rent
Transfer payments.

The two latter, now constituting on the average as much as twenty-eight per cent of personal income, are assumed (except for the small net income from residential rents) to represent income from outside the region, rather than income earned from supplying local needs, and thus to count as an "export".

As in Germany, the results (Table 58) show a considerable degree of uniformity, but with some unexplained variations. The proportion of incomes earned by supplying local services rises (though not substantially) with increasing size (measured by income) of the region. An attempt to relate this proportion to per head rather than aggregate income however gave a null result.

Table 58. U.S. Metropolitan Area Incomes.

Regional personal income, 1975, $ billion		Number of regions in sample	Percentage of person incomes of region ear by supplying local ne
Under 5		20	44.1
5-20		14	48.6
Pittsburgh	21.1		40.4
Detroit	35.5		41.5
San Francisco	39.0		52.8
Boston	39.3		49.4
Philadelphia	46.8		47.6
Chicago	57.6		48.4
Los Angeles	71.4		51.4
New York	128.2		52.1

Conflicting with the slight upward trend of local sales with size are the predominantly manufacturing cities of Detroit and Pittsburgh. These are not explained by lower per head incomes — in fact Detroit's per head income is well above the national average.

Within the grouped smaller regions, the higher figures seem to be found in Texas and other recently developed areas, and the lower in the older-established industrial areas in the Middle West (such as Detroit). For some reason, at given income levels, local service industries seem slower to develop in such cities.

The figures of course do not fully mean what they seem, for many reasons. In the first place, in the very large regions, as has already been pointed out, an increasing proportion of manufacture will also be for the local market. But conversely, an increasing proportion of their services, particularly finance and wholesale trade, may be serving national or international rather than local markets. San Francisco's high figure fairly clearly represents its activities in these fields.

These two sources of error pull in opposite directions. On balance, the former factor may be of greater strength, meaning that, in the larger cities the proportion of incomes generated by local sales may be a little higher than the above figures indicate.

This may be of importance when we come to calculate regional multipliers. So far we have dealt only with quantities of goods and services *presumed* to be exported or imported interregionally. It is a different matter to obtain actual measurements of such trade.

There are exceptional cases such as the American states of Hawaii and Alaska, or the Australian states of Tasmania and West Australia, which can be served only by sea traffic (or in West Australia's case also by a single line of railway) on which traffic can be recorded. In Hawaii's case imports are equal to over half the regional product. But these are unrepresentative regions.

Estimates of regional imports and exports are sometimes made by direct sampling of goods traffic crossing the regional border (imports and exports of services having to be made by other methods); or alternatively, by a method about as difficult, by detailed enquiries of a sample of traders in the region on the origins of their purchases and the destinations of their sales. A third method, less reliable, is to estimate the regional demand for each product and to subtract the region's output to estimate imports (or output less local demand for exports).

In very small economies interregional or international imports must form a high proportion of total resources, usually not paid for by capital inflow. An unusual inquiry into the economy of a village in Ghana in the 1930s gave the following figures (Table 59) for the average family of 5.9 persons.[23]

23. Beckett, London School of Economics Monographs on Social Anthropology, No. 10.

Table 59. Ghana Village Accounts.

	£		£
Cash income	21.4	Cash expenditure on local goods and services other than home produced food	4.15
Value of home produced food[a]	9.3	Home produced food	9.3
		Savings	1.9
		Imports	15.35
	30.7		30.7

a. The economic equivalent of this was 565 kg. of maize, the principal local grain.

Imports thus constituted half of resources. The cash income was mainly earned from exports of cocoa.

For India also, with a substantial amount of local handicraft output in place of interregional imports of manufacture, and much locally consumed agricultural production, the proportion of local sales to incomes has been estimated at 0.6.[24]

An early attempt to measure interregional imports was made in Denmark.[25] The family of an average manual worker employed in the oilseed crushing mills in Aarhus, with an annual income of three to four thousand kroner (£3 per week at the current rate of exchange, about the earnings of a semi-skilled worker in Britain at that time) was estimated to spend forty-five per cent of it locally, including eight per cent paid in local taxation, and fourteen per cent in rent. In computing the effects on the local economy of an expansion in employment in this large undertaking, Barfod introduced the further qualification that an estimated ten per cent of all salary payments, and twenty-five per cent of all wage payments, would go to workers whose homes and spending were elsewhere.

A pioneer study was made in the 1940s by Penelope Hartland of Brown University on direct measurement of the imports and exports of the New England region by sampling traffic across the regional border (at that time rail traffic was relatively more important).[26] The region appeared to have a very large negative

24. G. S. and A. P. Kulkarni, Gokhale Institute, Poona, private communication.
25. B. Barfod, *Local Economic Effects of a Large-Scale Industrial Undertaking* (London: Humfrey Milford, 1938).
26. Penelope Hartland, *Balance of Inter-Regional Payments of New England* (Boston: Federal Reserve Bank of Boston).

balance of commodity trade. Against this must be set however: (i) net export of services, particularly financial and educational; (ii) net receipts of dividends and interest by a comparatively wealthy population; (iii) possible liquidation of capital assets by retired people and others.

A precise allocation of sales and purchases was made in the regional accounts for 1954 of Kalamazoo County, Michigan, an industrialized area with larger paper and chemical works (analyzed separately in the accounts), with a population of some one hundred and forty thousand.[27] Of the manufacturing output of $440 million, $404 million was exported outside the region; of the non-government service output of $213 million only $37 million was exported. Personal incomes of $274 million included $46 million from outside the region (social services and some investment income). The manufacturing gross output of $440 million and non-manufacturing (including construction) output of $213 million included respectively, as much as $238 million and $50 million imported components. Savings (including business undistributed profits) created $32 million local investment plus $9 million net investment outside the region.

The acuteness of regional problems in Italy prompted a detailed study of the regional product and import and export trade of Sicily (being an island, records of goods transport to and from the mainland were available).[28] The regional accounts are shown (Table 60) (an input-output table was also presented).

Table 60. Sicily 1958 (billions of lire).

Gross product			
Agriculture, forestry, fishing	298	Private consumption	817
Manufacture	233	Government consumption	110
Services: Private	260	Gross investment	99
Public administration	130	Exports	279
Gross product at factor cost 1	823		
Do at market price (add indirect taxes less subsidies)	918		
Imports of goods and of non-governmental services	467		
Resources at market price	1,385		1,385

1. After debiting duplications of services rendered to business of 50 by public enterprises, 30 by financial institutions, and a small amount by extra-regional services.

27. W. Hochwald, "Dependent of Local Economics upon Foreign Trade: a Local Impact Study" *Papers of the Regional Science Association* 4 (1958), p. 259.
28. O.E.C.D. Report of the Regional Economic Planning Conference, Bellagio (1960) p. 337.

Services being taken into account, Sicily had a large negative trade balance, which must have represented public and private capital inflow. Imports constituted one-third of available resources.

The whole of southern Italy at that time had a gross product of 3,265 billion lire plus an import surplus (including imports from the rest of Italy) of 903 billion, giving 4,168 billion disposable resources, of which 846 billion (a much higher proportion than in Sicily) were devoted to gross investment.[29]

An official estimate of regional accounts was prepared for the Netherlands in 1960, and the results are shown in Diagram 12.[30] The relationship is remarkably linear, with a marginal propensity to import of about 0.3 as provincial income increases. There are no systematic differences between imports and exports.

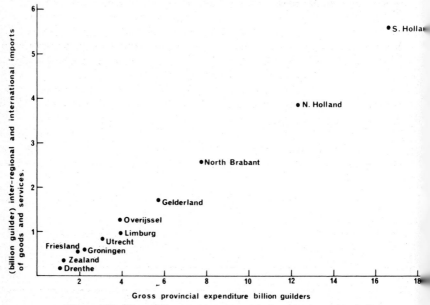

Diagram 12. (Note difference between vertical and horizontal scales).

For comparison with other countries, in 1970 2.67 guilders were equal to $US1 in purchasing power, indicating that 1.77 guilders in 1960 were equivalent to $US1 in 1970.[31]

29. Di Simone, *Mondo Economico* (1960).
30. *Regional Accounts of the Netherlands,* Netherlands Central Bureau of Statistics, Statistical Studies No. 20, (1970).
31. I. B. Kravis, A. Heston, R. Summers and Others, *International Comparisons of Real Product and Purchasing Power* (Baltimore: Johns Hopkins University Press, 1978).

For Britain there is some evidence, based on the official National Freight Surveys, of the interregional movement of goods measured by tonnage.[32] Estimates of interregional trade in services must be highly approximate; and "whereas the manufacturing industries are dispersing the service trades are becoming more localised".[33] There are however some alternative data of regional consumption of services.

An heroic effort has been made to use this information converting goods tonnages to approximate money values, and estimating approximately for trade in services.[34]

The results are plotted against total regional expenditure on the Diagram 13. They are very different from those of the Netherlands. The British figures show a much higher degree of interregional dependence, with a marginal propensity to import as high as 0.6. It will be seen however that as we approach the largest region in the southeast the slope falls to 0.3. As we saw with New York, in the southeast region, constituting a quarter of the whole country's demand, a higher proportion of manufacturing industry than usual may be found to be working for local demand.

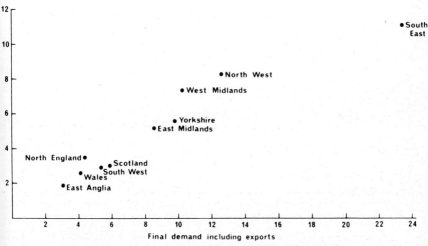

Diagram 13. Regions of Great Britain 1964–1967 (£ Billion).

32. For a detailed analysis see M. Chisholm and P. O'Sullivan, *Freight Flows and Spatial Aspects of the British Economy* (Cambridge: Cambridge University Press, 1973).

33. M. Chisholm and J. Oeppen, *The Changing Pattern of Employment: Regional Specialization and Industrial Localization* (London: Croomhelm, 1973), p. 108.

34. D. B. Steele, "Numbers Game (or Return of Regional Multipliers)" *Regional Studies* 6 (June 1972). A preliminary estimate, with calculation of multipliers, was published in *Oxford Economic Papers* (July 1969).

It has been suggested that Steele's trade figures have been over-estimated.[35] Even so the difference between the British and Netherlands results remains striking.

Differences between regional imports and exports were limited, except for the north (on the whole a depressed region) where imports (commodities plus services) were forty-six per cent above exports, matched by Yorkshire and the East Midlands, where exports exceeded imports by twenty-six and fifteen per cent respectively.

It must be borne in mind (and this makes the contrast with other countries more striking) that we are dealing here with comparatively large regions. Converting currencies on their purchasing power, the largest Netherlands region (South Holland) in 1960 would appear on this diagram as only £2.28 billion total demand and £0.77 billion imports; and Hawaii (in 1964) at £0.68 billion demand, £0.3 billion imports.

Many detailed studies of regional and local accounts are now available, too numerous to review. The investigators usually proceed to estimate "multipliers" and in some cases prepare an input-output table.

Once we have a good (in some cases not so good) set of regional accounts, we can then embark on the interesting task of estimating the regional multiplier. This describes the estimated ultimate effects of one additional unit of output or employment in a region. This method of analysis was borrowed, after some lapse of time, from the multiplier analysis of economic fluctuations. This latter was discovered by Kahn[36] (Giblin in Melbourne University had earlier obtained an approximately similar result, but had not formulated it precisely; and some independent work on the same lines appears to have been undertaken under Schacht in Germany). If one additional man is put on to earn wages, and he then spends his wages . . . and so on, until there appears, at first sight, to be no limit to the consequences which may flow from any increase in income. But we know that this is not the case, for several reasons. In some cases, additional labour and other productive resources are not available, so that the additional wages have to remain unspent, or be dissipated in paying higher prices for an unchanged quantity of goods.

But even if there are abundant unused productive resources — Kahn formulated his theorem against the background of the extremely severe unemployment prevailing in 1931 — there are still substantial limits to the process. As each man receives his wages, there are "leaks"

35. I. R. Gordon, "Return of Regional Multipliers — Comment" *Regional Studies* 7 (Sept. 1973), p. 259.
36. R. F. Kahn, "The Relation of Home Investment to Unemployment" *Economic Journal* 41 (June 1931).

before the next round of employment is created. Some of the increased wages may be saved; some will have to be paid in taxation, not immediately recompensed by central government spending; and a substantial proportion will be spent upon imports, international imports if we are applying the multiplier analysis to the national economy, international plus interregional imports for regional analysis. In such regional analysis, these "leaks" might amount to as much as two-thirds of any additional income. The first newly created income unit will thus generate only 0.33 further units of local income as it is spent, which, in their turn, will generate a further 0.11, and so on. We can save ourselves the arithmetic of working out the total by using the well-known formula for summing geometrical progressions of values less than 1. If the fraction spent locally is r, then the total additional amount earned, including the initial unit, will be $1/(1-r)$; in this case, the reciprocal of two-thirds, or 1.5.

By such a calculation, Barfod's figures for a Danish region in the 1930s would give a multiplier of 1.8, and the Kulkarnis' estimate for India as much as 2.5.

A pioneering study by time series of the regional multiplier in Britain was made by the American economist M. C. Daly, who compared Census employment data (unemployed being included in the tabulations according to their usual employments) by regions in 1921 and 1931.[37] He distinguished what he called "unimpeded" (in effect "export" industries) from "localized". Export industries included mining and defence, but only the central office staff of other government departments, the rest of their staff being regarded as localized. Localized industries include public works, building, building materials, distributive trades, and drink — "some firms with national sales have not affected the generally localized character of the industry" (there is no doubt that beer is a bulky commodity to transport). Daly makes the important point that construction industries are dependent on the rate of increase, rather than the absolute level, of employment in the export (and induced localized) industries. Agriculture was omitted, owing to the difficulty of judging the relative importance of milk and other locally-sold products — but this should not greatly affect the results. "I was ultra-conservative" Daly adds, "in adding to the list of localised industries, and if the allocations were imperfect, any improvements will increase the size of the multiplier".

For the whole country localized industries constituted 53.1 per cent of all employment in 1921 and 54.3 per cent in 1931 (if agricul-

37. M. C. Daly, "An Approximation to a Geographical Multiplier" *Economic Journal* 50 (June–Sept. 1940).

ture had been included these figures would have been 49.5 per cent and 51.2 per cent respectively). On the definition excluding agriculture the 1931 percentages ranged from 41.5 per cent in the East Midlands to 65.1 per cent in Greater London (the latter figure however may include some exported services).

Daly attempted to deduce a multiplier by comparing the percentage increases or decreases in the two types of industry in each region. But on re-examining his data, it appears that absolute changes give a more significant result (see Diagram 14). Three regions, for some reason, showed an exceptional growth of localized employment. But apart from these, we get a good approximation to a linear relationship with a slope of 1.15, that is, a multiplier of 2.15, including the initial change in "export" employment.

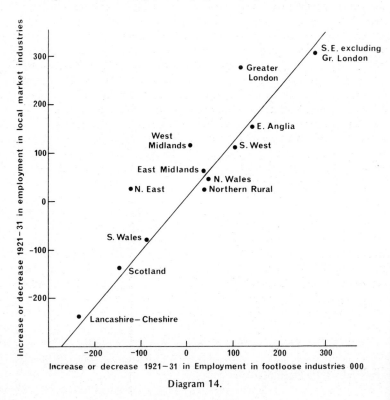

Diagram 14.

It is useful to have these results relating to a period now many years past in order to show us how great the change has been.

Multipliers now are far lower, and this probably applies to national multipliers too.

An analysis by the present writer of changes in employment, in the principal towns and industrial regions in Britain between 1931 and the 1960s (not published), using a more detailed classification than Daly's, showed a multiplier of only 1.4, similar to that obtained in Gordon's amendment of Steele's results for the 1960s.

In judging the reasons for this change we must remember that the theory of both national and regional multipliers was formulated in the 1930s, by economists who took for granted the existence of large reserves of unused labour and enterprise, waiting only for an increase in demand. (In addition, there probably was "disguised unemployment" in retailing and other local industries — but the absorption of such disguised unemployment kept the multiplier lower than it would otherwise have been.) There was little if any such usable surplus of unoccupied labour and enterprise in the 1960s — so local service industries had to compete with other industries for labour. The large volume of domestic service of the 1930s has almost completely disappeared, and some other local services (for instance, laundries) have declined in volume, or become relatively more expensive, as also for instance have restaurants and taverns. It is true that as real incomes rise the demand for services is expected to rise, all other things being equal — but there are significant price elasticities too. And most of these services are labour-intensive.

Much of what used to be spent locally on such objects is now spent on cars, household appliances, and the like, which are much more likely to be imported into the region.

But the biggest change has been in taxation. In the 1930s most wage-earners paid no direct taxation. Now high marginal rates of taxation take off a large part of any increase in income before it can be spent on local products (though we must not neglect the important qualification made apropos Scotland that insofar as increased demand leads to population inflow into the region, rather than raising the incomes of those already there, the relevant "leak" of spending power will then be at the average rather than the marginal rate of taxation, and the multiplier will be *pro tanto* higher).[38]

In his 1972 paper, Steele estimated regional multipliers within the range 1.16–1.31: Gordon suggested raising the figure to about 1.4. In another calculation,[39] taking Prest's figure of 0.185 as the general average of marginal tax rates, to which must be added 0.05–.10

---

38. M. A. Grieg, "Regional Multiplier Effects in the UK: A Comment *Oxford Economic Papers* 23 (1971), p. 280.
39. G. C. Archibald, "Regional Multiplier Effects in the UK" *Oxford Economic Papers* 19 (1967), pp. 30–32.

national insurance contributions, we are left with a reduced disposable personal income, changes in which are estimated (on 1952–63 data) to contain a local employment component of only 0.26. On these estimates the regional multiplier comes down to 1.25.

In a remoter region however the local component of expenditure may be higher, and may be more labour-intensive. So far we have failed to distinguish between induced changes in incomes and in employment. Assuming a marginal tax rate (including national insurance contributions) of 0.18 the establishment of a pulp and paper mill at Fort William in Scotland was estimated to give a regional income multiplier of 1.44–1.54, but an employment multiplier as high as 1.90–2.66.[40]

A large number of studies have been made in the United States, including some showing interesting results for much smaller towns than quoted above. The following summary, Table 61, is from C. L. Leven.[41]

Table 61. U.S. Local Expenditure

	Population '000	Proportion of income spent on local goods and services
Winnetka, Illinois	15	.11
Elgin-Dundee, Illinois	60	.38
Evanston, Illinois	80	.15
Decatur, Illinois	110	.48
Waterloo, Iowa	110	.48
Sioux City, Iowa	110	.45
Madison, Wisconsin	170	.53
Fort Wayne, Indiana	205	.48
Flint, Michigan	310	.33
Indianapolis, Indiana	620	.48
Milwaukee, Wisconsin Metropolitan Area	1,180	.45
New York Economic Area	16,000	.76

40. M. A. Grieg, "The Regional Income and Employment Multiplier Effects of a Pulp Mill and Paper Mill" *Scottish Journal of Political Economy* 18 (1971), p. 39.
41. C. L. Leven, *Design of Regional Accounts* (Baltimore: Johns Hopkins University Press).

The results in Table 61 are after allowing for savings not invested locally, estimated uniformly at six per cent of income. Local taxation is included but not national taxation.

Flint has already been mentioned for its exceptionally high proportion of manufacture in employment and personal incomes. Its low demand for local services cannot be explained in terms of per head income, which is above the national average.

Evanston and Winnetka, with their exceptionally low figures, are wealthy residential towns on the shores of Lake Michigan at the northern end of the Chicago economic area, probably mostly of two-car (or more) families. Their needs for services are clearly met mostly from outside the area, even probably for retailing — if only for the reason that "zoning" regulations in such wealthy areas tend to impede the establishment of all but the most urgently needed local services.

The very high figure for New York must include an estimate of the high proportion of manufacturing output consumed locally in such a large unit. It suggests a multiplier of 4. But this can work downwards as well as upwards. Converting 1970 data to 1975 prices by the GNP deflator of 1.375, local service sales at 1975 prices fell from $81.8 to $66.7 billion between 1970 and 1975, while "export" sales (other than transfer incomes) fell from $48.0 to $43.9 billion. There was however a rise in transfer incomes from $11.6 to $17.6 billion. It does indeed appear that the multiplier is high, working now on a declining economy.

The extraordinarily low level of local employment found in Evanston and Winnetka, and similar suburbs in the United States, contrasts with the planned new towns of Vällingby and Farsta adjacent to Stockholm, where forty per cent of the labour force are able to obtain local employment. Development of local service industries was encouraged, among other reasons, with a view to reducing the volume of traffic, an acute problem in Stockholm.

Many authorities are concerned now at the multiplier effect of tourist expenditure. This has been the subject of detailed study in Hawaii (Table 62), where tourism is of great importance to the regional economy.[42] It is to be expected, of course, that the distance from mainland America will raise the degree of self-sufficiency somewhat above that of comparable tourist centres elsewhere.

As a generator of local income tourist expenditure fell short of the other leading export industries, sugar, pineapple, and the military, whose total expenditures generated sixty-seven, fifty-three, and seventy-nine per cent local incomes respectively.

42. First National Bank of Hawaii, *The Impact of Exports on Income in Hawaii.*

Table 62. Expenditure and local income generation per $100 tourist gross expenditure.

	Expenditure	Local income generated
Hotels	29.1	18.0
Apartments	7.4	4.5
Restaurants	16.6	9.8
Tour agents & transportation	9.3	5.9
Retail stores (analysed separately)	37.6	16.6
	100	54.8

The proportion of tourist expenditure generating local incomes (Table 63) was not greatly different from that of the consumption expenditure of an average local family of four.

Table 63. Local incomes as a percentage of consumption expenditure.

	Family expenditure	Local income generated
Food	32.1	16.3
Housing	9.3	5.6
Fuel, light, refrigeration	3.0	1.0
Household operation	4.0	2.2
Furnishing and equipment	6.3	2.9
Clothing	7.6	3.8
Automobile	16.8	6.7
Other transport	1.8	1.1
Medical	4.3	2.3
Personal care	2.6	1.4
Recreation & education	7.8	4.3
Drink & tobacco	2.0	0.7
Other	2.4	1.3
	100	49.6

Walworth County, Wisconsin has been the subject of studies of local income generation ever since 1915. In 1963 it was estimated to have a regional output of $237 million, of which forty-four per cent represented exports of commodities, and ten per cent of tourism.[43] The authors distinguished (Table 64) the multiplier effects on sales, employment, and income, making further distinction between

43. R. J. Kalter and W. B. Lord, "Measurement of the Impact of Recreation Investments on a Local Economy" *American Journal of Agricultural Economics* 50, no. 2 (1968), p. 254.

Table 64. Multiplier Effects, Walworth Country.

	Sales	Employment	Income
Commodity exports	1.62	1.57	1.49
do including induced investment	1.87	1.78	1.77
Recreation exports	1.62	1.58	1.52
do including induced investment	1.87	1.70	1.80
Government	1.75	1.54	1.57
Investment	1.81	1.57	1.62

the immediate multiplier effect and the (larger) long-run effect when induced investment was also taken into account.

In a comparative review of tourism multipliers (Table 65) Walworth stands out high (though it is not clear whether the others also included induced investment).[44]

Table 65. Tourist Multipliers.

Pennsylvania, Sullivan County	1.56 - 1.62
England, Devon & Cornwall	1.29
Scotland, St. Andrews	1.34
Wales, Anglesea	1.25

In comparing these with Hawaii we must bear in mind that tourists travelling shorter distances will on the average have lower incomes, and are more likely to be camping or caravanning.

Account should be taken of Australian studies of regional incomes,[45] multipliers and input-output tables for two primary producing areas, the Powell–Mandeville study for an inland rural region producing wheat, sheep, and beef, centred on the town of Dubbo, of some seventeen thousand population, and the Jensen study for central Queensland, with mining as well as agricultural and pastoral output, containing the two seaport towns of Rockhampton and Gladstone (population forty-five and twelve thousand respectively at the time of the survey). Powell and Mandeville estimated farm purchases of variable inputs by use of a "representative farm" linear

44. B. H. Archer and C. B. Owen, "Towards a Tourist Regional Multiplier" *Regional Studies* Dec. 1971.
45. R. C. Jensen, Economic Record (Sept. 1976), and R. A. Powell and T. D. Mandeville, Economic Record (Aug. 1978).

programming model, that is, assuming that farmers always make optimal decisions, which may not be too far from the truth. Household expenditure was assumed to be analyzable in terms of the national input-output tables. Non-farm producers and traders were subjected to a questionnaire on the extent to which their sales and purchases were intra- or extra-regional, which of course elicited a far from complete response. Official statistics were available for agricultural, pastoral, mining, and manufacturing output, and trade turnover. For so many entries however the mere fact of the absence of many kinds of manufacturing production in the region could be taken as an indication that all requirements of the goods in question were imported. Farm households, which have been shown (in Australia at any rate) to have comparatively stable consumption in face of violent income fluctuations, are analyzed separately from non-farm. The regional output was $207 million with imports of $78 million and exports $92 million (difference explainable by taxes, interest, dividends, and also capital accumulation outside the region).

The central Queensland study likewise used the questionnaire method, which obtained a response (weighted by sectoral outputs) averaging forty-nine per cent. In this larger region with an output of $959 million, imports were only $155 million and exports $116 million, the difference perhaps representing capital inflow. But the ratio of imports to product was unexpectedly low — perhaps accounted for by distance and the transport costs incurred in purchasing from other regions.

In both studies some high multipliers — output, income and employment — were calculated; but these results were vitiated by failure to take marginal rates of income tax into account.

A much-needed warning has been published against too simple a treatment of the employment multiplier, at any rate in rural areas.[46] Davidson's analysis covered four zones in New South Wales, the low rainfall sparsely-settled pastoral zone, the intermediate-rainfall zone in which farmers combined sheep and wheat-growing, the high-rainfall zone producing lamb and high-quality wool, and the colder northern tablelands practising mixed farming.[47] Within each zone, non-farm population showed a close statistical relation to gross farm *income* (with a time lag); but the relationship between non-farm and farm *populations*, or employments, turned out to be negative. The explanation appears to be that farm labour is being displaced, not

46. B. R. Davidson, *Review of Marketing and Agricultural Economics,* New South Wales State Department of Agriculture, Dec. 1976.
47. From this zone were omitted areas of "export" production other than farming, that is, hydro-electric sites, and Armidale, an education centre.

only by equipment, fertilizers, and the like, but also by a rapidly increasing amount of farm contract services, supplied from the country towns. This consideration of course applies particularly in the wheat-sheep zone, where one unit of non-farm population is found for every $9,800 of gross farm revenue (at prices at the beginning of the 1970s), as against one per $19,800 in the Northern Tablelands. These relationships are rapidly developing, in all zones (Table 66).

Table 66. Rural Populations and Employment.

	EMPLOYMENT RATIOS			POPULATION RATIOS		
	Commerce & services/ primary & manufacture			Non-farm/farm		
	1961	1966	1971	1961	1966	1971
Pastoral	0.7	0.6	1.0	3.1	3.0	3.7
Wheat-sheep	1.2	1.4	1.7	2.4	2.6	2.9
High rainfall	1.4	1.7	2.0	3.5	3.8	4.5
Tablelands		Not available		2.4	2.5	2.9

Results of a similar nature (Table 67) were obtained in Scotland.[48] Regional employments were classified into "basic" and "service" (construction being omitted, on the grounds that it is sometimes a local service and sometimes part of an "export" project).

Table 67. Local Employment, Scotland.

	Urban[1]	Rural adjacent to urban	Rural
Service/basic employment 1966	1.25	.67	.97
Percentage changes 1951-61			
Basic employment	−11	−7	−17
Service employment	+13	+18	+10
Percentage changes 1961-66			
Basic employment	− 6	+ 1	− 1
Service employment	+ 2	+ 6	+ 1

1. Towns of 50,000 or more population.

48. J. R. Wagstaff, "Employment Multipliers in Rural Scotland" *Scottish Journal of Political Economy* 20 (1973), p. 245.

Again, service employment can rise while "basic" employment is falling. It is clear that regional employment multipliers must be treated with considerable caution.

Various adverse factors, their consequences aggravated by the regional multiplier, may leave some regions in a state of permanent depression. There may be considerations of economic externalities justifying action by public authorities to help such regions, whatever may have been the causes which brought them to their present state.

First there is the simple case of inequality, as with equality between persons. Full equality, or anything approaching it, is neither practicable or desirable. But public authority should act to mitigate extreme inequalities between persons, if only on the grounds of preserving political stability. By similar reasoning they should act to mitigate extreme inequalities between regions.

The basic theory of all economic adjustments through the market is that factors bearing on the movement of any variable act progressively to bring it into equilibrium. This theory however does not hold in the (fairly rare) cases in which some self-sustaining force comes to bear upon a variable, accelerating its movements away from equilibrium. An extreme example is the price of food during a famine, which goes up faster when people begin to buy and hoard what food is available. Distressed regions provide a milder but still real example. Usually they are already low in skill and enterprise. Continued movement of industry and population away from them will deplete these resources still further, and may move them into a downward spiral.

Even in the absence of such forces, regional adjustment may be extremely slow.

"Full employment" is subject to various definitions; but those controlling the economy of any country will naturally wish to make the best use of its labour resources, without provoking harmful situations of labour shortage. Where there are large inequalities between regions, national demand may rise to a point where it leads to labour shortages and delayed deliveries in the more prosperous regions, with all their harmful effects on costs, export sales, etc., while there are still large but immobile reserves of labour in the less prosperous regions. This may be the strongest consideration in favour of the policy of reducing regional inequalities.

Inequalities between regions and cities have often arisen for irrational reasons, or have been generated from non-economic causes, and need not therefore be respected by policy makers. An example has been the freight charges on Australian railways, which are state-owned but which, in response to capital city political pressures, framed their policy to encourage manufacture in the capital cities and to discourage it in the provincial towns (by low freight rates on raw materials and high rates on manufactured goods coming to the capital city).

Modern business, in every country, is increasingly dependent on contacts with politicians and bureaucrats, seeking favourable decisions on a large number of matters which they control, which factor leads to abnormal industrial development in capital cities.

But this had been true in the past too. The deteriorated economic condition of southern Italy, once one of the most economically advanced regions of Europe, has largely developed during the past hundred years, and as a product of politics. Before the unification of Italy in 1861 the south had as high a proportion of its labour force occupied in manufacture or handicrafts as did the north. But "Monetary and financial centres have to follow the political head-quarters . . . the very day the defeated king fled from Naples, the Rothschild of Naples left the town".[49] Thenceforward southern Italy found itself starved for capital, paying too high a share of the taxes, and receiving too low a share of government expenditure, injured economically both by the free trade policy at first pursued, and, after 1880, by the protectionist policy which favoured the production of wheat, as against the vine and olives for which southern Italy had greater natural advantage.

Much regional development too is simply a matter of chance. There might have been many other places where motor car manufacture could have developed; but the origin of two of its principal centres appears to have been due simply to the fact that Ford was born in Detroit, and Lord Nuffield in Oxford. The location of a principal centre of the United States confectionery trade at Hershey in Pennsylvania also appears to be due to an accident of birth.

" . . . Within broad limits the attractive power to-day of a centre for commercial and industrial expansion has a main origin in the historical accident that something was once started there and not in a number of other places where it could equally well or better have been started, and that the start met with success. Thereafter the ever increasing internal and external economies — in the widest sense of the word including also, for instance, a working population trained in various directions, lively communications, the feeling of growth and elbow room and the spirit of new enterprise, etc — fortified and sustained their continuous growth at the expense of other localities and regions where instead relative stagnation or regression became the fastened pattern."[50]

49. Economic Commission for Europe, *Economic Survey of Europe 1953.*
50. G. Myrdal, *Development and Underdevelopment,* Fifth Anniversary Commemoration Lecture, delivered in Cairo, 1950.

Hirschmann suggests that the reasons for the tendency of already rapidly growing regions to attract more industries "must be sought in the realm of social psychology . . . a climate particularly favourable to further growth of activity came into existence" as a result of "a psychology developed *ex post* to sanctify and consolidate whatever accumulation of economic power and wealth has already been achieved".[51]

"There is increasingly strong evidence that some large threshold size must be reached for an urban centre to free itself from the uncertainties of a narrow export basis for growth — in effect by achieving the necessary internal scale for self-sustaining growth. In North America a variety of studies point to a size not less than 250,000. In India a study reveals cost curves that declined steeply to the 130–200,000 size class, and remained level thereafter."[52]

Hoover also puts the threshold at a quarter million population. After this, he considers an industrial city can ensure its own continued growth through industrial diversification, political power, large fixed investments, a rich local market, and a steady supply of industrial leadership.[53]

R. P. Shaw, summarizing the evidence from a number of countries, including India and Russia, concludes that "there is an emerging consensus that an urban place of no less than 200,000 population will be required . . . to draw migrants or to retain relocated populations . . . and it must be built, or upgraded, rapidly".[54]

Public opinion polls are doubtless fallible, but a Gallup poll in the United States of America indicated that the present pattern does not do well in satisfying people's needs.[55] Of those now living in cities of half-million population or more, nearly fifty per cent say that they would prefer to live elsewhere; while of those living in other areas few express any interest in moving to big cities.

The British Government, faced for many years with the problem of what used to be called the "depressed areas", now more tactfully described as the "special areas", first sought to attract industry to them by giving tax concessions in the form of higher depreciation rates on fixed capital. This was about the most clumsy way possible of spending the available funds. It attracted to the special areas a

51. A. O. Hirschmann, *The Strategy of Economic Development* (New Haven: Yale University Press 1958), pp. 184–85.
52. B. J. L. Berry, *South and South East Asia Urban Studies Annuals* 1 (1970) (Sage Publications, Beverley Hills, California).
53. E. M. Hoover, *An Introduction to Regional Economics* (New York: Knopf, 1971), p. 156.
54. R. P. Shaw, "On Modifying Metropolitan Migration" *Economic Development and Cultural Change* 26, no. 4 (July 1978), pp. 690–91.
55. *Philadelphia Bulletin* (and other Journals), 23 March 1966.

limited number of highly capital-intensive industries, giving little employment. A more rational procedure would be to subsidize payrolls, or at any rate give relief from some of the heavy taxes or social security charges which they bear. This policy was adopted, to a limited extent, by the Wilson Government in Britain (1964–70), but was rescinded by its successor and not reintroduced. The Australian state of Victoria makes a small concession on payroll tax to industries away from the main metropolitan centre – an acute problem of boundary demarcation arose immediately after the introduction of this measure.

The economic incidence of payroll tax remission or subsidy has however not been properly analyzed. In the long run it may depend on the elasticity of labour supply. In the short run, this appears to be positive and high, especially in the case of female employment; this being so, the employer should gain from the subsidy and seek to expand employment. But in the long run there are indications that the supply elasticity of labour may be low, or even negative. If this is so, eventually payroll tax subsidies might serve to raise wages, discourage employers, and actually reduce employment.

A better device, which has enjoyed some success in the special areas in Britain, and is now being tried widely in developing countries, from the extremely successful Jurong Estate in Singapore, to courageous efforts by the impoverished Indian state of West Bengal, is the establishment by public authorities of "trading estates", leasing buildings and other facilities to incoming industrialists, and securing for them some of the economies of aggregation, which would not have developed by unaided market action.

Interest in regional multipliers mainly arises, understandably, from attempts to improve employment and incomes in poorer regions. It only occasionally happens (though it should more often) that multiplier analysis should be used to make a case *against* further development in regions already suffering from congestion, labour shortages, and the like. A university, for example, employing a number of high-income earners, with consequent fairly high demands for local services, may be expected to have a higher multiplier than usual, and thus be more than usually beneficial in a poorer region, but likewise more harmful in a region already congested.

Eversley and Blackman made a skilful estimate of such a multiplier by examining the occupational structure of Oxford and Cambridge cities, in comparison with other towns of similar size, as shown in the Census of 1911, at which time the Universities were almost those two cities' only "export service".[56] They estimated the multiplier

56. D. E. C. Eversley and J. M. Blackman, "Student Numbers and Total Town Populations" *Universities Quarterly* 15, no. 1 (Dec. 1960).

approximately at 1.5 additional employment for 1 additional student. In the 1960s Dr Eversley was teaching in the University of Birmingham, a city at that time suffering considerably from congestion and labour shortages. But the university authorities were not at all pleased when he pointed out the extent of the "university multiplier", and the case which it made against extending the university in Birmingham at that time.

More refined analyses of regional multipliers will make separate calculations for the effects of output, income, and unemployment; and in some cases will go further to estimate the amount of new fixed capital construction necessary to supply the estimated increase in local demand.

A still further stage is the preparation of regional input-output tables, analyzing the demands which each industry or service makes upon the output of others (changeable though these may be). The preparation of national input-output tables is a task of extreme difficulty and expense, requiring for its completion many years beyond the date to which it refers; and the results may be subject to considerable qualification if we attempt to make use of them, because of changes in technical methods, economies of scale arising from increased production, and changes in industry's demands for different inputs as their relative prices change. The compiler of a regional input-output table may, it is true, have fewer industries with which to deal, and may be able to fill many of his boxes with interregional imports because he know that there is no local production. But he faces greater difficulties in ascertaining the extent to which businesses sell their outputs or purchase their inputs within the region. Such difficulties indeed may also confront the compiler of any regional accounts, even in the simplest form, and even without attempting anything like an input-output table. There is a limit to the patience of busy traders being asked to classify their sales and purchases by regions.

The alternative method is the physical recording of goods (only by sample of course) crossing the regional border; but there have been few applications of this method (discussed above). It presents great difficulties; and it still leaves the compiler the problem of measuring interregional imports and exports of services.

13

Interregional Migration

A fundamental analysis of interregional migration was made by Ravenstein.[1] Its extent was found to be inversely related, in a determinate manner, to: (i) the distance between origin and destination, and (ii) the size of the settlement of origin. Large growing cities thus obtained most of their migrants from adjacent regions, which were then partly replenished from more distant regions – population building up, at all stages, in the larger towns.

A further important step, not denying but refining Ravenstein's principles, was taken by Stouffer, who introduced the principle of "intervening opportunities" (which has also proved useful in analyzing intra-urban traffic).[2] The extent of migration to a given destination depends, not crudely upon population and distance, but the number of "intervening opportunities" (usually measured by employments, sometimes by employment in specific trades, or by other activities), taking into account not only opportunities at the destination, but also the intervening opportunities *en route* to it. The principle is simple: the logarithm of the numbers travelling *to or beyond* a given distance is a linear function (decreasing) of the cumulated number of opportunities up to that distance.

The transition of the composition of the labour force, as the economy advances, from predominantly agricultural to manufacture and services, for which a few illustrative figures were given in an earlier chapter, is a well-understood phenomenon. It is of course basic to our analysis of location. As non-agricultural employment grows, some former agricultural workers will find employment in various-sized rural settlements, as we saw in Chapter 6, but most will go to increase employment, and population, in larger towns.

The key figure to observe is not the rate at which agricultural employment (measured either relatively or absolutely) is falling,

1. Ravenstein, *Journal of the Royal Statistical Society* (1885 to 1889).
2. S. A. Stouffer, "Intervening Opportunities: a Theory Relating Mobility and Distance" *American Sociological Review* 5 (Dec. 1940).

but the rate at which non-agricultural employment, measured in absolute numbers, is increasing. If, as is sometimes the case, this rate is no higher than the rate of increase of population, then the relative composition of the labour force will remain unchanged.

Until the 1950s it appeared that the maximum rate at which non-farm employment could grow was four per cent annually — not much in advance of the rate of population growth in some countries. This figure was based on observations of periods of its rapid growth in economies so diverse as Soviet Russia, Canada, and Japan. It was in fact a basic figure in a report on the economy prepared by the present writer for the Government of Pakistan in 1952.

Nineteenth and early twentieth century experiences (Table 68) of countries in the active phase of industrialization were summarized by Dovring.[3]

Table 68. Rates of Growth of Non-farm Employment (Percent per annum).

U.S.A.	1850-1880	4.2	U.S.S.R.	1913-1956	2.2
	1880-1910	3.6			
			Great Britain	1801-1831	2.1
Spain	1900-30	2.7			
			Belgium	1846-1880	2.1
Netherlands	1899-1930	2.6			
			Norway	1865-1890	1.9
Japan	1890-1915	2.6		1890-1920	1.7
	1915-1940	1.8			
			Italy	1911-1931	1.3
Finland	1910-1940	2.4		1931-1951	1.6
Switzerland	1888-1910	2.2	Portugal	1900-1930	1.3
Denmark	1855-1880	1.3	France	1861-1891	0.7
	1880-1911	2.2			
Sweden	1880-1910	2.2			
	1910-1940	1.3			

But subsequent experience has been very different. With better transport and communications, and education, the rates of increase of non-agricultural employment, and hence of urban employment and population, have been greatly accelerated. The available information for developing countries is given below (Table 69).[4]

3. FAO Monthly Bulletin of Statistics (Rome) (Aug—Sept. 1959). Some of the data refer to non-farm population.
4. Data from the *International Labour Office Yearbook of Labour Statistics.* Very small countries have been omitted.

Table 69. Rates of Increase of Non-agricultural Employment % per year (most recent figures).

Syria	1970-1976	8.2	Mexico	1970-1977	4.6
Dominican Republic	1960-1970	8.1	Peru	1961-1970	4.6
South Korea	1970-1978	7.0	Nicaragua	1963-1971	4.3
Thailand	1970-1976	6.4	Brazil	1960-1970	4.2
Libya	1964-1973	6.2	Ecuador	1962-1974	4.2
El Salvador	1971-1975	6.2	Paraguay	1962-1972	3.6
Costa Rica	1963-1973	6.1	Indonesia	1961-1971	3.6
Tunis	1966-1975	6.0	Honduras	1961-1974	3.6
Colombia	1964-1970	5.9	Morocco	1960-1971	3.1
Algeria	1954-1961	5.4	Bolivia	1950-1976	3.0
Fiji	1966-1976	5.4	Egypt	1961-1966	2.8
Panama	1960-1970	5.2	Jamaica	1960-1977	2.6
Phillippines	1970-1976	5.0	India	1961-1971	0.0
Sri Lanka	1963-1971	4.9			

In Latin America, taken as a whole, non-farm employment is estimated to have risen 3.6 per cent per annum for 1950–1960, 3.1 per cent per annum for 1960–65, with overt and disguised unemployment meanwhile rising from five to eight per cent of non-farm employment.[5]

In these movements we have the cause of the recent rapid growth of cities, and of migration from rural areas in the developing countries.

It is frequently said that this urban growth is unbalanced, in that it is proceeding in advance of industrial employment, causing many of the city dwellers to fall into unemployment, open or disguised, with an inordinate expansion of service employments. This, and some related ideas, have been shown to be incorrect.[6] Over the period 1950–1970, in most cases, the industrial proportion (the author does not define "industry", but apparently it includes construction and transport as well as manufacture) of the labour force and the urban proportion of the population rose together, preserving approximately a 1:2 ratio (in the most advanced economies the figures are of the order of forty and eighty per cent respectively). Latin America did however depart from this rule. The orders of magnitude of the proportion in 1970 are shown in Table 70.

5. S. Barraclough, FAO Monthly Bulletin (July–Aug. 1969).
6. S. Preston, "Urban Growth in Developing Countries – Demographic Reappraisal" *Population and Development Review* 5, no. 2 (June 1979), pp. 197–208.

Table 70. Latin America.

	% of labour force industrial	% population urban
Temperate zone	30	75
Tropical zone	20	55

Examination of all the available data of the rates of out-migration of agricultural labour force in the last intercensal period gave an average for the advanced countries of 18.5 per thousand per year, for the developing countries only 13.7 — and this rate is lowest in the least developed countries. We are dealing with pull, not with push.

The case for pull rather than push is also made by evidence from nineteenth century Russia.[7] The rate of migration to Moscow and St Petersburg was found *not* to be related to population pressure in the province of origin, but to be related to the extent of the province's "cultural modernization".

Likewise emigration from Ireland in the famine of the 1840s was led by the wealthier peasantry.[8]

Extreme poverty in Java did little to help the schemes promoted by both Dutch and Indonesian administrators for migration to the sparsely-populated outer islands.[9] Gross migration from Java totalled only 406,000 for the 1950–1967 period, and it is conjectured that "there was in fact net migration into Java".

However extreme circumstances "push". In Egypt the relatively high rate of urbanization (observed by Napoleon's statisticians in 1798) was due to the rural depopulation that had resulted from centuries of insecurity.[10] However, because of preceding rural underpopulation, and with irrigation improvements, urban growth rates remained below rural until about 1907.

Another factor which is sometimes forgotten is that a large proportion of the observed growth of cities in the developing countries comes from their own natural increase. The average for all developing countries was found to be sixty-one per cent (India sixty-eight per cent, Indonesia sixty-four per cent, Brazil fifty-five per cent). This is principally the consequence of recent great reductions in mortality.

7. B. A. Anderson in R. D. Leed ed., *Population Patterns of the Past* (1977).
8. M. Chisholm, *Geography and Economics* (London: Bell, 1966), p. 134.
9. G. McNicoll, *Bulletin of Indonesian Economic Studies* (March 1969), p. 78.
10. Hamdan, "Studies in Egyptian Urbanism" quoted in *Geographical Review* (Jan. 1961), p. 137.

This was certainly not the case in the past. In the early stages of economic growth urban mortality was so much above rural that substantial migration was required merely to keep the cities in existence, quite apart from providing for their growth. Infant mortality in eighteenth century Stockholm was 387 per thousand, probably the highest rate ever recorded.[11] Graunt's life table for seventeenth century London left only four hundred survivors to age sixteen per thousand births, which would not have sufficed to maintain the population, even with maximum rates of reproductivity.[12] The eminent astronomer Halley (after whom the great comet was named) was also a pioneer demographer. His survival rate to sixteen, based on data from Breslau, stood at five hundred per thousand births, which might just have sufficed to maintain the population. An estimate for (white) U.S. population in 1830 gave the ratio of age-specific mortalities between large towns and rural at 1.4 for the age group fifteen— nineteen, for all other age groups 2 or more.[13] Even in 1940 the aggregate standardized ratio (for whites) still stood at 1.23 for males and 1.12 for females.[14] A Norwegian study showed for 1949—52 ratios of 1.20 for males and 1.01 for females, the ratios having gradually declined from 1.36 to 1.1 respectively in 1899—1902.[15]

Actual estimates of migration have been made for the city of Norwich, which was growing fairly steadily through the eighteenth century, but required net inward migration of 8 per thousand per year in the first half and 5 per thousand per year in the second half of the century.[16]

Still more striking (Table 71) are the figures from Stockholm.[17]

Our ancestors were faced with an extremely bad (though improving) level of medical practice; and an extraordinary lack of hygiene. This

le 71. Demographic Balance Stockholm.

	1721-60	1761-1810	1811-60	1861-1910	1911-40	1940-60	1961-66
ral increase per 000 per year	− 10.9	−12.8	− 9.3	+ 5.8	+ 1.7	+ 7.0	+ 2.2
n migration '000 per year	+21.1	+11.7	+19.6	+16.3	+13.6	+ 7.5	− 8.2
age population '000	51.5	74.4	82.6	211.4	449.8	745.9	795.8

11. R. Artle, *American Economic Review* (May 1971), p. 355.
12. I. S. Sutherland, "John Graunt: A Tercentenary Tribute" Journal of the Royal Statistical Society 126 (1963).
13. Jaffe and Lourie, *Human Biology* (Sept. 1942).
14. *Metropolitan Life Insurance Bulletin* (Feb. 1948).
15. *Statistisk Sentralbyra* (Oslo), Okonomiske Studient No. 10.
16. Edwards, *Yorkshire Bulletin of Economics* (Nov. 1969).
17. *Statistisk Arsbok for Stockholms Stad 1967*, p. 53.

latter did far less harm to the rural than to the urban population. Manchester ("what Manchester thinks today England thinks tomorrow") set a particularly bad example. "Filled though that city is with radicals and philosophers, they cannot drain it" said Drummond, a hostile critic in Parliament. Professor Kitson Clark, the eminent Cambridge historian, has set out to excuse the municipal administrators of those days, on the grounds that the technology of water supply and drainage was not yet understood. He should have consulted some of his colleagues who teach ancient history — the main drainage of Rome was constructed in dim times of antiquity.

It is sad to see municipal administrators in developing countries similarly neglecting their duties now.

Our most complete knowledge of the extent of interregional migration (cumulated over the years) comes from those census authorities who have recorded and classified birth places. Alternatively we can estimate it within given periods by comparing total change in the population of a region with the recorded births and deaths of that region. This method depends on accurate birth and death registrations, which are only available in the advanced countries, since various dates in the nineteenth century (though back to the eighteen century in Sweden). It is migration to urban areas which is our principal concern — migrations between rural areas are of minor significance.

To offset the high urban mortalities of the past, high in-migration was needed, with rates diminishing as the nineteenth century advanced; while increasing rates of industrialization again required in-migration; and we have to observe the resultant of these conflicting factors.

In France, where family size fell long before the rest of Western Europe, natural increase in urban areas became trivial after 1876, and negative by 1906—10. Almost the entire growth of urban areas was provided by migration, including increasing migration from abroad after 1906, while rural France was rapidly depopulating. The supply of migrants, measured by the proportion of each generation which at the age of forty-five years was residing away from the Department in which they were born, rose gradually from twenty per cent of the generation born 1816—20 (the first generation of the Railway Age) to thirty-seven per cent of the generation born 1922—26.[18] The process was however interrupted as a consequence of the fearful loss of life in the 1914—18 war, which left more incentive for country men to remain at home, where farms etc. were now more easily obtainable.

An exceptionally rich nineteenth century study shows that in 1890

18. Y. Tugault, "Geographical Mobility in France over One Century — Study of Various Generations" *Population* 25, no. 5 (Sept. 1970).

or thereabout some fifty to sixty per cent of the inhabitants of the larger German cities were born outside the city.[19]

A study by decades, going back to the beginning of the nineteenth century (dependent however on uncertain birth and death figures) for Manchester showed the proportion of net increase due to migration rising from thirty per cent in 1801—10 to sixty-two per cent in 1821—30 (a decade of very high Irish migration), falling to twenty per cent after 1850.[20] For Liverpool (nearer to Ireland!) the proportion rose from forty-six per cent in 1801—10 to sixty-nine per cent in 1841—50, but fell to net out-migration by the 1880s.

For the whole period 1841—1911 net migration constituted only twenty-five per cent of the population growth of London and large industrial towns, and was of minor importance elsewhere (except for certain "residential" towns, and naval and military bases).[21]

For really high figures of migration we turn to the Japanese Census of 1930 (Table 72) at the culmination of a period of active migration, and also when mortality was above present rates.[22] The country was divided into regions according to the proportion of occupied males in agriculture, as an indication of the degree of industrialization.

Table 72. Japan: Percentages born outside prefecture of residence (ages 20 - 70).

% male labour force occupied in agriculture	Below 20	20-39	40-49	50-59	60-69	70 and over
Migrants: Male	63.6	33.2	34.7	10.1	9.2	7.7
Female	62.7	31.1	28.3	10.2	9.1	7.2

In Brazil the 1940—50 population gain of the seven largest cities consisted of net migration to the extent of over seventy per cent.[23]

The distribution by age of interregional migrants shows a falling proportion for the older men and women. But we cannot tell from this how much represents an actual return to their former homes, or merely different circumstances when they were of the usual migrating age. The reversal with age of interregional migration is a subject of each on which little is known. A unique study in France recorded the males of each generation and the proportions engaged in agriculture at succeeding Censuses (Table 73) which showed a rise after the age of forty-five to forty-nine (being engaged in

19. Meuriot, *Des Grandes Agglomerations Urbaines*
20. Cannan, *Economic Journal* (1894).
21. Cairncross *Manchester School* January 1949, p. 85.
22. S. Kuznets et. al., *Economic Growth, Brazil, India, Japan* (Durham, N.C.: Information given is for males and females in each quinquennial age group; likewise for out-migration.
23. E. T. de Barros, World Population Conference (1954).

Table 73. France: Percentages of males in each generation engaged in agriculture.

Date of Birth	1856-1860	1861-1865	1866-1870	1871-1875	1876-1880	1881-1885	1886-1890	1891-1895	1896-1900	1901-1905	1906-1910
Age 15-19								34.7		36.3	30.9
20-24						26.0	23.6		24.2	26.3	24.5
25-29					34.2	31.0		26.5	26.5	25.8	26.6
30-34				33.9	31.9		26.3	23.7	24.4	26.0	
35-39			35.1	33.4		27.7	25.0	23.0	24.8		24.8
40-44		37.1	35.7		31.7	27.5	25.0	23.7		26.2	
45-49	38.8	38.2		35.7	31.9	27.8	25.9		24.8		
50-54	40.4		39.4	36.1	32.5	29.1		25.2			
55-59		42.4	39.8	36.6	33.6		27.8				
60-64	44.6	42.0	39.5	37.0		32.0					
65-69	42.3	40.0	38.0		34.6						

(The oblique vacant spaces are due to the absences of the usual quinquennial Census in 1916 and in 1941).

agriculture does not always mean a return to their former homes, but usually so).[24]

The uniformity of the rise above age forty-five to forty-nine is striking, likewise the fall before it. It follows that in a developing economy agriculture has to employ an excess of the young and of the old.

The Japanese figures above show rates of female migration below male, though not markedly so. In some Asian cities there is a marked male surplus. But in other countries, about the 1930s, appeared the curious phenomenon − now again disappearing − of an excess of females in the large cities, mostly of the marriageable age. Tugualt's figures (Table 74) for France, quoted above, show female migration exceeding male for the first time in the generation born 1891−95.[25]

Table 74. France: Migration By Sexes.

Generation of Birth	1891-95	1896-1900	1901-05	1906-10	1911-15	1916-20	1921-25
Percentage residing outside Department of birth (at age 45)							
Males	34.6	33.6	32.8	33.7	37.8	37.5	36.0
Females	35.0	35.6	35.8	36.1	38.4	39.8	38.0

The excess female migration was at its highest in the 1906−10 generation, and is still with us (this accumulation of unmarried women in the cities may be a partial explanation of why the 1906−10 cohort showed exceptionally low reproductivity).

An explanation which immediately comes to mind is that the 1896−1905 cohort suffered the greatest loss of potential husbands through the 1914−18 war, and so had to come to the cities in search of employment. But then why did the discrepancy continue for succeeding cohorts? And why was it found in Sweden? Measures of the rate of migration outflow to the towns from rural Sweden showed female migration from 1901 to 1935 at more than double the male rate at younger ages but at higher ages usually below male rates.[26]

Similar data for urban female surplus in this period are found elsewhere.

24. *Statistique Générale de la France* (July−Sept. 1948 Supplement).
25. Y. Tugault, "Geographical Mobility in France over One Century − Study of Various Generations", *Population* 25, no. 5 (Sept. 1970).
26. Quensel *Ekonomisk Tidskrift* (Sept. 1940).

In Australian capital cities, on the other hand, the female surplus at ages fifteen to twenty-nine which had been marked in the 1930s, has now disappeared — mainly because of substantial and predominantly male migration from Europe.

In Brazil the Census of 1970 (Table 75) shows a large female surplus in the cities, even down to the ten to fourteen age group.

Table 75. Females per '000 Males, Brazil 1970.

Age	10-14	15-19	20-24	25-29	30-39	40-49	50-59
Urban and suburban	1031	1155	1138	1120	1087	1045	1085
Rural	953	966	991	949	944	889	847

Even in Djakarta, once predominantly male, change is appearing (Table 76).

Table 76. Females per '000 Males, Djakarta.

	10-14	15-19	20-24	25-29	30-34
Census 1930	923	960	959	948	932
Census 1961	997	1012	1004	1038	863

For the three leading metropolitan areas in the United States (Table 77) the 1970 Census shows the female surplus at its maximum at the ages twenty to twenty-four, and exceptionally high in New York, where the female surplus at these ages had risen from 1100 in 1940.

Table 77. USA Females Per 1,000 Males.

Age	15-19	20-24	25-29	30-34	35-3
New York Metropolitan Area	1014	1229	1133	1108	109
Chicago Metropolitan Area	968	1193	1056	1044	103
Los Angeles — Long Beach Metropolitan Area	1010	1123	1003	981	99

In England and Wales the 1973 estimates for population aged fifteen to forty-four give a national figure of 974 females per 1000 males, with the ratio rising only slightly to 1005 for Inner London — and this is found to be entirely accounted for by the concentration of women in the three "fashionable" boroughs of Westminster, Camden, and Kensington-Chelsea. There had been a much larger female surplus in London in 1939.

It might be supposed that rates of interregional migration would bear some relation to the expected increment of income, capitalized over future working life. A study[27] in the United States (Table 78) of out-migration from the south, capitalizing income differences at six per cent discount rate, showed some remarkable differences by race and education.

Table 78. Effect on Net Migration Rate $(\times 10^5)$ of $1,000 Increase in Present Value of Expected Income Gain.

(Man aged 27)		White	Black
Years of schooling	8	145	0
" " "	12	299	3
" " "	16	306	62

For older men, of course, the response is very much less, and appears to be actually negative for blacks. The consequence of increased education, Bowles considers, quite apart from its effect on expected earnings, which has already been taken into account, is to increase initiative and willingness to take risks — and education therefore should be given additional economic credit for this reason. Regarding blacks — their expected earnings, and discriminatory elements therein, having already been taken into account — Bowles considers that the factors at work are less willingness to take risks and also a higher subjective rate of discounting the future. But generally speaking, with increased education we should expect increased inter-regional migration.

In every country, and for centuries of time, the net movement of interregional migration has been towards capital cities and other heavily industrialized areas. About 1970 there came a sudden reversal of this trend, well documented (see Table 79), apparently in almost all industrial countries.[28] We have as yet no explanation for this. In Chapter 9 we did see that "economic potential" began to lose its attractiveness in areas where it was highest, a number of different factors probably being at work. It may also be that, since about 1970, there has been, all over the developed world, a greatly heightened consciousness of the environment, pollution, congestion, lack of access to open space, and similar considerations. Perhaps, in fact, people

27. S. Bowles, "Migration as Investment — Empirical Tests of Human Investment Approach to Geographical Mobility" *Review of Economics and Statistics* 52, no. 4 (Nov. 1970).
28. D. R. Vining and T. Kontuly, "Population Dispersal for Major Metropolitan Regions: an International Comparison" *International Regional Science Review* 3, no. 1 (Fall 1978).

Table 79. Metropolitan Areas Migration.

Country	Central Region	% of population in central region	Annual average net internal migration to central region per '000 of its 1960 population			
		1960	1955-9	1960-4	1965-9	1970-4
France	Paris	18.1	5.1[a]		1.4[b]	−2.4[c]
Italy	North West	25.9	8.2	13.5	6.2	5.5
Hungary	Central Industrial	26.0	9.0	9.7	5.7	4.3
W. Germany	North Rhein-Westfalen	29.5	3.4	−1.5	−2.0	−1.2
Sweden	Greater Stockholm	33.6	3.6	4.8	3.2	−0.9
Japan	Tokyo-Osaka-Nagoya area	36.6	9.2	15.9	14.5	7.2
Norway	South-East	48.6	2.7	3.0	2.7	1.1
Finland	Helsinki region	56.4	5.0	6.2	6.0	6.9

a. 1954-63   b. 1962-68   c. 1968-75.

are belatedly and slowly becoming aware of the considerations regarding the optimum size of city set out in Chapter 8.

In Australia net migration has been directly measured since 1970. For the period 1970–78 the Sydney district shows an average annual net out-migration of 2 per thousand, Melbourne a net in-migration of 0.8 per thousand. Perth, Brisbane, and Adelaide (with populations in the 0.75–1 million range) continue to show substantial net in-migration figures. Approximate estimates for the period 1961–66 already show internal migration for Sydney and Melbourne negative, but this was masked by high overseas immigration.

In the United States of America the population of the whole New York Economic Area (not merely the New York Metropolitan Area) is now declining, and of the Chicago Economic Area is stationary.

The British figures (Table 80) form a striking addition to the Vining–Kontuly table. The principle field of attraction in the past, the South-Eastern region, fell from net in-migration of 2.7 per thousand per year in the 1950s to 0.4 in the 1960s, and to an outflow of 2 in 1975–76.[29] For Greater London[30] itself the net rate of out-migration was as high as 10 per thousand, while the remainder of the southeast region showed a positive figure of 4.0. The other main zone of industrial attraction in the past, the West Midlands, centred on Birmingham, showed a sharp reversal; so did, conversely, the declines in Wales and Scotland. Strong attraction is now exercised by East Anglia and the south west. We may recall the discussion of economic potential in Chapter 9, and its increase consequent on Britain joining the European Economic Community — these two latter are regions standing to gain.

"Economists say that people leave poor regions; it is demographers who insist that regions are poor because people leave".[31] This prophetic aphorism foretold the time when statesmen would come to realize that depopulation was not economically advantageous, as it is so commonly supposed to be, but the reverse. For forty years the regional development policy of succeeding British Governments had been to attract (or compel) industry away from London and Birmingham; in 1976 the Labour Government quite suddenly put the whole

---

29. *Regional Statistics, 1977*; earlier data summarized by D. Eversley, "Population Changes and Regional Policies Since the War" *Regional Studies* 5, no. 4 (Dec. 1971), p. 215. The figures include international migration, which has been at net rates (usually outwards) well below one per thousand population.
30. Area within approximate twenty-four kilometres of the centre, originally demarcated by Sir Robert Peel for police administration.
31. C. P. Kindelberger, *Economic Growth in France and Britain 1851–1950* (Cambridge, Mass.: Harvard University Press, 1964), p. 238.

Table 80. Net regional migration per '000 population per year.

	1951-69 average	1974-75
West Midlands	1.2	− 3.9
East Midlands	1.6	1.1
Scotland	− 6.2	− 0.9
Wales	− 1.1	2.1
East Anglia	5.6	12.1
South West	4.1	8.3

policy into reverse, and announced that its principal object now was to attract industry back to these declining cities (together with one or two others, particularly Liverpool).

With equal suddenness, the Conservative Opposition also reversed policy, in the same direction, on the same day.

14

Urban Densities

The ancient city of Uruk,[1] about 3000BC, covered more than 450 hectares[2] with an average residential density of about 100 persons/ hectare. Another study made Ur (not to be confused with Uruk) a city covering 1000 hectares with a density of perhaps 500 persons/ hectare.[3] This was the city, one of the wonders of the world at that time, which the patriarch Abraham was willing to leave for the austere life of a desert nomad. In ancient Greece densities ranged from 86 persons/hectare in Corinth and 200 in Athens to an estimated maximum of 315 in Selinus.[4] In the large city (920 hectares) of Alexandria under the Roman Empire density was some 420 persons/ hectare, but in the seaside-residential city of Pompeii 230.[5] In Rome itself the density may have been as high as 700. In the fifth century AD the new imperial city of Byzantium occupied 4500 hectares, with a more tolerable density of about 220 persons/hectare.[6] By the ninth century however, repeatedly threatened by besiegers, the area had shrunk to 2160 hectares, and by the time of its final capture in 1453 its population had shrunk to about one-tenth of its ancient level.[7]

Great cities were built in ancient China.[8] The Chou metropolis Hsia-tu covered 4800 hectares. A density estimate for the ninth to the third centuries BC (130 persons/hectare) can be made for the smaller city Ch'i-Ch'eng, covering 1600 hectares. The Tang metropolis

1. Adams, *Scientific American* (Sept. 1960), p. 166.
2. Hectare = 10,000 square metres = 1/100 square kilometre = 1/259 square mile = 2.47 acres.
3. Sir Leonard Woolley, *Ur of the Chaldees: a Record of Seven Years of Excavation* (Harmondsworth: Penguin, 1938).
4. Doxiadis Institute, Athens, private communication.
5. Duncan Jones, *The Economy of the Roman Empire: Quantitative Studies* (Cambridge: Cambridge University Press, 1974).
6. S. Runciman, *Byzantine Civilization*.
7. Professor Cavanna, private communication.
8. Eberhard, *Economic Development and Cultural Change* (1955–56).

of Ch'ang-An, designed in 742AD, of 7950 hectares, housed some two million inhabitants at an average density of some 250 persons/ hectare.[9] A house, believed representative, occupied 185 square metres — it must have housed a large family and servants.[10] Pien-Ch'ou, originally built AD781 on an area of 750 hectares was rebuilt in 955 on an area of 4300 hectares, to house about a million inhabitants, again at an average density of 230 persons/hectare. But those cities were altogether exceptions. The usual Chinese town covered only 6 hectares. An average density of 230 persons/hectare also prevailed in eighteenth century Edo (Tokyo), housing a population of 1.3 million.[11] But this average was a composite of 150 persons/hectare in the *samurai* and priestly quarters, and as much as 660 persons/ hectare for the 600,000 working and trading population. So dense a population, in wooden buildings, posed a high fire risk, and for this and other reasons further migration to the city was forbidden. Nevertheless there were devastating fires, covering most of the city, in 1659, 1771 and 1806.

Densities have been estimated for as many as ninety-two mediaeval European cities (Table 81).[12] The measurements were made at various dates between 1348 and 1550, namely, after the first (and in most cases after the subsequent) attacks of the Great Plague — earlier densities were probably higher.

Table 81. Mediaeval Densities.

Persons/hectare	Under 80	81-125	126-175	Over 175	All densities
Number of cities	27	44	13	8	92

The median was about 100, which appeared to be unrelated to the city size, which ranged from under 50 to over 200 hectares. These densities are not very different from those of a present-day African village (in Ghana) estimated at 112 persons/hectare.[13] Family "compounds" averaging 165 square metres and 8 occupants, covered only twenty-five per cent of the ground, the remainder being open space and public buildings.

9. Goodrich, *A Short History of the Chinese People.*
10. J. Tyrwhitt, "The City of Ch'ang-an" *Town Planning Review* 39, no. 15 (April 1968).
11. Tonuma, *Area Development in Japan,* No. 6 (Japan Centre for Area Development Research 1972).
12. J. C. Russell, "Late Ancient and Mediaeval Population" *Transactions of the American Philosophical Society* (1958).
13. Beckett, *Akosoaso* London School of Economics, Anthropological Monograph, and private communication.

Mediaeval densities were small in comparison with those of ancient cities, including those of China. It must be remembered that mediaeval cities were walled, while ancient Rome (until Aurelian's reign in the late third century AD) and Alexandria were unwalled — but showed higher densities.

In mediaeval Oxford the average tenement was 357 square metres.[14] If we assume an average family of five this indicates a direct density of 140 persons/hectare — lower if we take road and public building space into account. Paris in 1329 (before the Great Plague) (Table 82) was estimated to have a much higher density.[15] However in 1861 the four central *arrondissements* (I–IV) had a density of 690, which still stood at 672 in 1901, and 390 in 1936.

Table 82. Persons/hectare in Paris.

1329	1590	1637	1789	1861
550	350	375	164	214

Some other eighteenth century estimates included Leyden 400, Liege 335, Amsterdam 330, Rome 300, Brussels 200, Bologna 175, The Hague 170, Lyons 165, Ghent 100, Bordeaux 90. The smaller towns sometimes but by no means always showed lower density. Sheffield had a density of 1000 persons/hectare in 1800, 560 in 1850, rising again to 740 in 1901.[16]

A general review of average urban standards in Europe gave 125 persons/hectare up to 1850, 100 in 1900, and 67 in 1950.[17] We demand more space as our economies advance. Thijsse,[18] of the School of Social Science at The Hague, whose ideas about the best pattern of settlements for the modern world were discussed in Chapter 8, aims at fifty persons/hectare (one hundred persons/hectare in the residential area covering half the area of the city, with the remaining half being used for industrial, commercial, and recreational purposes). If however people are to live in detached houses (a comparative rarity in the Netherlands), density will have to fall to twenty, or ten, if people are to have substantial gardens.

These averages however have concealed some areas of very much

14. Pantin in Trevor-Roper ed., *Essays in British History* (1964).
15. Demangeon, *Paris La Ville et sa Banlieu*, Landry, *Traite de Demographie* and (for the eighteenth century) De Dainville, *Population* (July–Sept. 1958); and Census figures.
16. Sheffield City Council, *Sheffield Replanned* (1945).
17. E. Brutzkus, "Prerequisites for Preservation of Historic Urban Quarters" *Ekistics* 31, no. 182 (Jan. 1971).
18. Private communication.

higher densities, such as prevail still in many large cities in poorer countries. A density map for London in 1695, centring on the ancient Roman landmark of the London Stone, from which road mileages were measured, shows an interesting contrast (Table 83) with the densities shown by the first Census in 1801.[19] By 1801 commercial developments were already displacing residences at the city centre, and the zone of maximum density was displaced slightly outwards. One sub-registration district showed a figure of 630, rising to a maximum of 771 by 1851, and the Spitalfields district still showed 788 in 1901.

Table 83. Historic London Densities.

Distance from centre km	Below 0.4	0.4-0.8	0.8-1.2
Persons/hectare 1695	538	474	454
1801	432	427	568

As late as 1931, densities of 586 persons/hectare were found in London in the Parish of St George in the East, Stepney, and 560 in the Netherfield district of Liverpool. Below these figures were found 361 in the Westgate Ward of Newcastle and 328 in the Medlock Ward of Manchester; the rest of urban England was by then below 250.

The densities of the most populous districts in New York (Table 84) were at their highest about 1900.[20]

Table 84. New York Densities.

	1850	1900	1940	1957	1968
Persons/hectare in highest density districts of Manhattan	635	1540	1000	855	660

In the most densely populated part of Brooklyn a maximum density of 565 was attained in 1930.

Such densities may be supported (with difficulty) by communities which possess the wealth and technique to construct very high buildings. Considerably lower gross densities may nevertheless impose greater hardship on communities which do not possess the means to build beyond two or three storeys. In Singapore 300,000 of the population live at an average density of 750 persons/hectare, and 2500

19. Judges, *Economic History Review* (Oct. 1935).
20. E. M. Hoover, *An Introduction to Regional Economics* (New York: Knopf, 1971), pp. 343–44.

persons/hectare in the worst districts.[21] A density as high as 3000 persons/hectare has been recorded for some parts of Hong Kong, under exceptional circumstances, with a great flow of immigrants entering a city narrowly constricted between mountains and sea.[22] Still in 1961 the Wanchai area had a density of 2100 persons/ hectare, and three contiguous wards covering 250 hectares averaged 1500.[23] Hollingsworth raised the question of whether, in the light of these figures, some mediaeval urban populations might have been underestimated. He also made the shrewd point that the fact that so much of the transport has to be by porterage (Chinese porters use yokes — whose high costs are reviewed in Chapter 1) creates a strong economic incentive to high densities. Buildings of seven to eleven storeys, of which there are some in Hong Kong, make possible local densities as high as 5000 — but Atkinson estimated 750 persons/ hectare as the maximum possible density before sanitary conditions deteriorated, even under Hong Kong's strict and hygienic regime.[24] He classified customary urban densities, based on single storey houses, at 250–500 in black Africa and 500–750 in north Africa. However the *medinas*[25] of Casablanca are inhabited at 1,300– 1,700 densities, and some 200,000 people,[26] or thirteen per cent of the city's population, are living in unsewered *bidonvilles* (shanty towns) at a density of about 1,000 persons/hectare. In the older part of Karachi density was estimated at 1,500, and in the *bustee* (hut) zone of Calcutta at 2,720. The maximum Indian density recorded was 3,750 in the Bhuleshwar area of Bombay.[27]

Apart from these exceptional cases, the results which we obtain (Table 85) will depend on how narrowly we define our areas — the

Table 85. Indian Central Area Densities Persons/Hectare.

	1881	1901	1921	1931	1941	1951	1961
Calcutta[1]	285	465	510			840	
Poona[2]	393			455	576	875	1013

1. Berry & Others, *Geographical Review*, July 1963, quoting Kar.
2. Gokhale Institute, *Social Survey of Poona*.

21. *Town and Country Planning* (Nov. 1955).
22. R. M. Hughes, "Hong Kong: an Urban Study" *Geographical Journal* 117, no. 1 (March 1951).
23. Hollingsworth, *Historical Demography*, p. 281.
24. Atkinson, *Town Planning Review* (July 1960).
25. Economic Commission for Africa, *L'Habitat en Afrique*, (1963).
26. A. Wells, "Low-Cost Housing Casablanca" *Ekistics* 29, no. 171 (Feb. 1970).
27. J. E. Brush, *Geography in a Crowding World*.

high figures for Poona given below are for the small area within one third of a kilometre of the city centre – but the trends are clearly upwards.

Surabaya, the second city of Indonesia, shows substantially lower densities of 1.9 million people in the "old city" at 265 persons/hectare, and 0.9 million in the "new city" at 40 persons/hectare.[28]

With a few exceptions, densities are high near the centre of a metropolitan area, and fall off with increasing distance from the centre. The present writer appears to have been the discoverer of the principle that density falls off in accordance with a negative expotential function of distance from the centre.[29] (An early study by Bleicher in Frankfurt showed that densities fell off with distance from the centre, but fitted no exponential or other function to the data).[30] This result was strictly empirical; theoretical justifications for it have however been developed by Muth[31] and E. S. Mills,[32] who has developed Muth's formula with an assumed price elasticity of demand for housing of -1.

Where y is gross residential population density measured in persons/hectare, and x is the distance from the centre of the city in kilometres, then (except in the central business zone):

$$y = Ae^{-bx}$$

It will be seen that A is the density at the centre of the city, where x is zero; or rather a hypothetical density, which would be found if the observed densities were extrapolated inwards towards the centre of the city. In fact the centre of the city is mainly occupied by business and public buildings.

The coefficient b, on the other hand, which may vary very greatly between cities, is best considered as a measure of the spread or "sprawl" of a city (an unpleasant word much used by town planners to describe a phenomenon which they greatly dislike). With a high value of b the city is compact, that is, density falls off rapidly to rural levels at quite a short distance from the centre. With a low value of b density falls off gradually and the city spreads out over a considerable distance before rural density is reached.

28. P. R. Fouracre and D. A. C. Maunder, *Transport and Road Research Laboratory Supplementary Report 370.*
29. C. Clark, "Urban Population Densities" *Journal of the Royal Statistical Society* 144 (Series A) (1951) Part IV.
30. Bleicher, *Statistische Beschreibung der Stadt Frankfurt am Main und ihrer Bevolkerung* (Frankfurt am Main, 1892).
31. R. F. Muth, *Cities and Housing: a Spatial Pattern of Urban Residential Land Use* (Chicago: Chicago University Press, 1969).
32. E. S. Mills, *Studies in the Structure of the Urban Economy* (Baltimore: for Resources for the Future by Johns Hopkins University Press, 1972), p. 111.

The coefficient *b* must be determined in the first instance by transport factors. Without a cheap and adequate system of transport people are very unlikely to build their city in a dispersed manner. But other factors may be important also, such as social customs. Some people · prefer to live in comparatively densely aggregated cities and (particularly in the Latin countries) resent it if their homes are so far from their work places that they are unable to go home for their midday meal.

It was found that the fit of the equation could be improved by taking densities per hectare of land zoned for residence, rather than gross area.[33]

Integrating, we obtain a simple relationship showing that the total population of the city should be:

$$2 \pi A b^{-2}$$

This, however, overstates the true population fo the metropolitan centre because it extrapolates up to the hypothetical density *A* in the centre of the city, and does not allow for the comparative absence of population from the central business zone.

This issue was faced by Newling,[34] who amended the equation to

$$y = Ae^{bx+cx^2}$$

where *c* is always negative and *b* positive where there is a density "crater" around the city centre, otherwise negative.

In this equation *A* now represents the actual, comparatively low density at the centre. Density rises to a maximum in a rim around the central crater, and then falls off in a function increasingly dominated by the cx^2 term. The distance from the centre of the crest of the rim can be determined by differentiation as $b/2c$, with density $Ae^{b^2/4c}$.

The formation of such a "rim" is well illustrated by the data for Stockholm.[35] In the nineteenth century (when there were comparatively few commercial buildings, and traders lived on their own premises) an almost perfect linear relation (in logarithms) prevailed, with very high densities (nearly five hundred persons/hectare gross area available for building) at the centre. With the depopulation of the old city centre to make room for public and commercial buildings (1950 central density down to about one hundred persons/hectare) a new focus of maximum density (some three hundred person/hectare) has appeared about 1.5 kilometres away from the old centre.

33. Chicago Area Transportation Survey Research News 1958, pp. 3–10.
34. Newling, *Geographical Review* (1960), pp. 242–252.
35. Kant, *Lund Studies in Geography* Series B No. 24, p. 349.

In Bombay the area of maximum density is now 1.6 kilometres from the city centre.[36] In the United States the "rim" phenomenon is accentuated by the formation of black "ghettos", of high residential density, in the older suburbs close to the city centre. Attempts have been made to explain ghettos simply in terms of low negro incomes; but other factors besides economics are at work. Assuming the same relationship between residential location and income as is found for low-income whites, Kain obtained theoretical distributions of negro residences in Detroit and Chicago which differed widely from the actual.[37]

Straszheim came to the same conclusion.[38] Concentration in the ghettos reduces employment opportunities, because of travel expense and lack of public transport, with the increasing movement of employment, particularly in manufacturing, to the outer suburbs (see Chapter 15). Regression analysis of negro employment by districts in the two cities shows strong negative terms for distance from the ghettos. On the other hand proximity to the ghetto probably raises negro prospects of employment in the higher paid occupations.[39] Negro business and professional men may enjoy local oligopoly.

Table 86. Paris Densities — Saunders's Equation.

	A (persons/hectare)	b (Per km)	k
1936	282	.397	2.14
1954	277	.369	2.00
1962	254	.320	1.87
1968	228	.284	1.82

An alternative formula[40] for the density-distance relationships explaining the central "crater", and also allowing for some differences in the shape of the curve, is

$$y = A \ (1+kbx)e^{-bx}$$

Reverting for the present to the simpler equation, the integral

36. J. E. Brush, "Spatial Patterns of Population in Indian Cities" *Geographical Review* 58 (July 1968).
37. J. F. Kain, "The Development of Urban Transportation Models" Rand Paper p. 3059 (1965) and *Regional Science Association* 14 (1965), pp. 147–174.
38. M. R. Strazheim, *Quarterly Journal of Economics* (Feb. 1974), p. 40.
39. P. Offner and D. H. Saks, "Note on Kain's J. Housing Segregation, Negro Employment and Metropolitan Decentralization" *Quarterly Journal of Economics* (Feb. 1971).
40. E. Saunders, *Regional Studies* (March 1975), p. 67.

for total population $2 \pi A b^{-2}$ is also defective because it assumes that the city is able to spread uniformly in every direction, whereas in fact most growing cities find expansion prevented in some directions by sea, lakes, rivers, swamps, or mountains. Where the sea or other such obstacle subtends a comparatively uniform angle to the centre of the city, a proportionate allowance can be made.

If a given total population is to be housed in a city, this can either be done by raising A, with b given, or lowering b, with A given, and the latter effect is squared. In most modern cities a heavily falling value of b has made it possible to house a much larger population, with an actual fall in central densities. Where the city is on the edge of a sea or a lake, on the other hand, higher densities are required to house a given total population (b being given) than in an inland city — sea-ports have always been notorious for a comparatively high degree of overcrowding.

The distribution of people between high and low density residences is influenced by their incomes, present and expected work places, the number and age of their children, and also by many elements of personal choice, their comparative taste for open life or for city amenities, and the strength of their comparative dislikes for travel on the one hand and for the dirt, noise, and crime of the city on the other.

On the set of historical relationships (Diagram 15 — semi-log scale) for London A is measured (or rather estimated) from the point where the curve cuts the vertical axis, and b by its slope. Between 1801 and 1841 population greatly increased. No mechanical transport was available, the b coefficient (slope of the curves) remained high — the curves for the two dates are almost parallel — and population growth could only be accommodated by packing people in more tightly all round, as is the situation in some Asian cities now.

By 1871, with the use of steam transport, this situation was clearly changing. The slope of the curve had altered; the relative rate of growth of the outer districts was much higher than that of the inner, while in the innermost ring there had been an actual fall in the population since 1841, much of the space having been taken for commercial buildings, railways, and so on.

From that time onward the tendency has continued. Between 1871 and 1921 all districts within a radius of 3 kilometres of the centre of the city actually lost population, while those outside this radius gained. Between 1921 and 1951 all districts within a radius of 11 kilometres of the centre lost population. The slopes of the line have fallen from 0.78 in 1801 to 0.09 in 1961 — more recent information is considered below — while central densities are now far lower than previously.

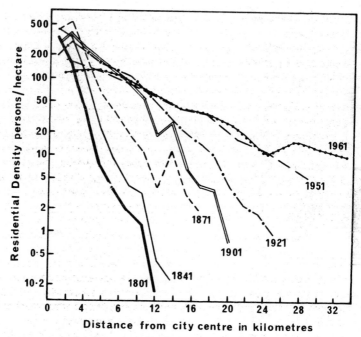

Diagram 15. Residential Population Densities — London.

After assembling data on the A and b coefficients for a number of cities and times, two important generalizations have been made. Data collected for a large number of cities in the United States of America for four Census periods showed that, while b coefficients in general are rapidly declining (cities becoming more spread out) they are also related to the "age" of the city ("age" being defined as the time elapsed since the city passed 50,000 population).[41] The b coefficient shows an all-round fall at each Census; but the data also show a slope with the age of the city (subject to a few exceptions, such as cities developed early in the nineteenth century still showing a high b coefficient in 1900). In other words, the spreading out of a city is a slow process, and newly formed cities are found to be still comparatively compact. Given the age of a city, the b coefficient falls with rising city size. The age of cities is of course strongly inter-correlated with their size. What we are observing is a combined effect of age and size.

An interesting exception is provided by San Francisco — the same

41. B. Edmonston, *Population Distribution in American Cities* (1975).

will be observed in the distribution of employments dealt with in the next chapter – a city built on a narrow peninsula only some ten kilometres wide. It is true that there are bridge connections to the north and east, but they call for long and costly journeys. The *b* coefficient (measured per kilometre) changes abruptly from 0.18 for the first 15 kilometres to 0.07 after that distance. The same is to be expected in any city on such a peninsula site, Seattle for instance.

Muth gives the density gradient an income elasticity of -.63 (not very well determined) – a prospective rise of per head real income in a decade of thirty per cent should reduce *b* coefficients by some twenty per cent. But he also found that the apparent relationship between income and distance from the centre was fully explained (in Chicago at any rate) by the age of the buildings – with this factor eliminated the relationship disappears.[42]

So much for the fall in the *b* coefficient; it has also been observed that the *A* coefficient (extrapolated maximum density) has been falling too, at any rate since some time in the nineteenth century. Rene Bussière has made the striking discovery that when we plot the historical series for *A* and *b* we find, on the data for Paris and London, close linear relations between them since the middle of the nineteenth century, with the slope, in both cases, changing about 1901, as is seen in the Diagrams 16, 17, and 18 (densities in persons/

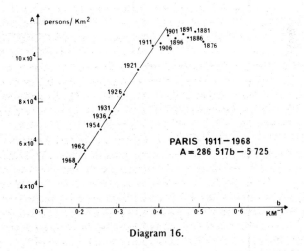

Diagram 16.

42. R. F. Muth, *Cities and Housing: a Spatial Pattern of Urban Residential Land Use* (Chicago: Chicago University Press, 1969), pp. 311 and 318.

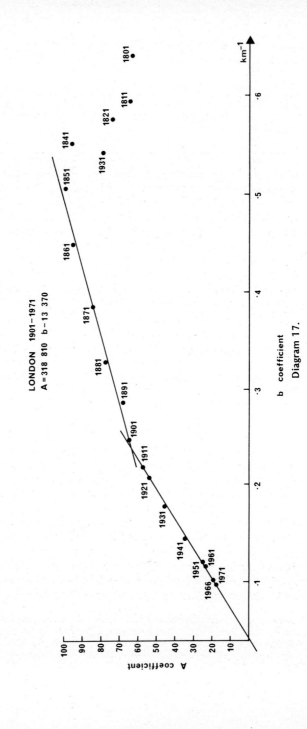

LONDON 1901–1971
A=318 810 b–13 370

A coefficient

b coefficient

km⁻¹

Diagram 17.

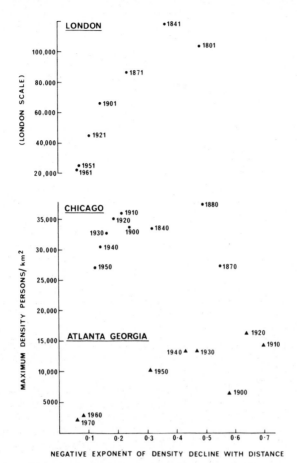

Diagram 18. Relations between A and b Coefficients.

square kilometre — divide by 100 to obtain persons/hectare.[43]) Bussière considers that such linear relationships apply generally in European cities. Similar diagrams were prepared for two United States cities for which Edmonston gave historical data. For Atlanta the relationship is at first horizontal, then linearly declining, but with the levels of density much lower, and the change in slope not

43. R. Bussière, *Modele urbain de localisation residentielle* (Centre de Recherche d'urbanisme, 74 Rue de la Federation, 75015 Paris). Recently published data by De Borgen, *Annals of Regional Science* (Nov. 1979), also show a clear linearity for Brussels (since 1900) and Antwerp and Ghent (since 1910).

appearing until 1940. For Chicago, at an intermediate level of density, the change in slope appeared about 1910, but the subsequent relation has been curved — the *b* coefficient falling less rapidly than was to be expected from the fall in the *A* coefficient. The reason for this is obscure. A value of *b* below 0.1 is not the prerogative of very large cities — witness Atlanta.

For Sydney in 1973—74 a fairly detailed distribution (Table 87) is available for residential population (some data are also included in the table for employment and land values, which will be used in Chapters 15 and 17). The data are classified by municipalities, which are mostly small areas, though some of the information for outer zones is recorded under shires, which contain extensive areas of uninhabited or very lightly inhabited land. In these cases therefore the measurement of area was confined to the built-up land as shown on the Census map.

Table 87. Sydney Densities[1].

Range of distances from centre	Mean distance	Built-up area	Residential population	Manufacturing employment	Retail employment	Assessed land value $'000
km	km	'000 ha		Per hectare		
Sydney Municipality	1.5	1.34	40.3	32.7	17.5	1,191
Other						
0-5	4.0	4.19	42.5	12.1	1.96	405
5-7.5	6.3	7.63	42.8	5.86	1.69	246
7.5-10	9.0	4.94	31.6	5.61	.97	193
10-15	12.5	24.5	25.5	2.19	.80	136
15-20	16.5	41.4	17.9	2.66	.64	97.8
20-30	25.9	36.0	12.4	1.16	.40	63.3
Over 30	34.8	27.8	11.8	.71	.31	65.1

1. Australian Bureau of Statistics, New South Wales Branch, Local Statistics, 1976.

The residential densities show the usual central "crater" followed by exponential decline. Measuring distance in kilometres and density in persons/hectare the equation

$$y = 73.5e^{-.086x}$$

fits satisfactorily up to about twenty kilometres beyond which point densities tend to flatten out to a uniform low distribution.

Table 88 gives the figures for London and certain other European cities arranged in historical sequence (persons/hectare, and rate of decline per kilometre of natural logarithm of density).

Some cities however clearly do not fit into a negative exponential pattern. A density map of the Spanish city of Pamplona shows isolated blocks of very high density, with layers of low density or unbuilt land in between. On enquiring the cause of this, the writer was informed that it was solely a matter of decision by the municipal authority.

Perhaps similar ideas of town-planning prevail in Latin American cities, about whose density patterns little appears to have been recorded.

Some further values are given (Table 89) for Australia and New Zealand. They are not brought up to date for a reason which will be explained below, namely indications of a change in the exponential pattern.

Information is available for the three leading Japanese metropolitan areas (Table 90).[44]

An interesting series is available (Table 91) for Kingston, Jamaica, showing a remarkable decline in the b coefficient (bus travel in the 1960s was available at only one penny per mile).[45]

In a large city, where the great majority of inhabitants have to walk to work, high densities and concentration near the city centre — that is, high values of both A and b — are unavoidable. The present writer has made a number of visits to the unhappy city of Calcutta, world famous for its squalor and overcrowding. But it has undoubtedly improved in a number of ways since he first saw it in 1947. The civic authorities, in spite of manifest incompetence and corruption, have moved many of the squalid huts which used to occupy all available vacant space near the city centre, and rehoused their inhabitants in somewhat better dwellings in the suburbs. But the inhabitants did not appreciate this. The best opportunities for casual employment, they pointed out, were near the city centre. Dwellings in suburban areas, necessitating long journeys on foot, imposed great hardships on them.

In the ancient world Minerva, the Goddess of Wisdom, was usually shown accompanied by her symbol, the owl. There is much truth in the trenchant proverb — "The owl of Minerva flies in the evening". As with the running of stage coaches and sailing ships, so often we come to attain a good understanding of a problem or a technique only in the last few years before it becomes obsolete. The same must sadly be said, after less than three decades, of the negative exponential method of analyzing urban residential densities. While for a time it may still be useful in some cities in developing countries, and in small towns, we find that in large cities in advanced countries the b

---

44. Kono, International Union for the Scientific Study of Population, Sydney Conference 1967 and the 1950 Census figures.
45. B. Newling, private communication.

Table 88. Historic Density Functions.

		A	b			A	
London	1801	1040	.78	Berlin	1885	1120	
	1841	1080	.58	Frankfurt	1890	550	1
	1871	865	.38	Vienna	1890	660	
	1901	586	.23	Berlin	1900	1580	
	1911	530	.21	Madrid	1920	1420	
	1921	499	.20	Birmingham	1921	401	
	1931	430	.174	Liverpool	1921	1275	
	1939	331	.142	Frankfurt	1933	340	
	1951	246	.120	Budapest	1935	1080	
	1961	227	.116	Zurich	1936	328	
	1966	184	.099	Dublin	1936	270	
	1971	173	.097	Birmingham	1938	201	
				Oslo	1938	308	
				Manchester	1939	143	
				Copenhagen	1940	231	
				Stockholm	1940	425	
				Aarhus	1950	279	
				Leeds	1951	116	

Table 89. Australian and New Zealand Densities.

		A	B
Brisbane	1901	66	0.58
	1933	96	0.47
	1947	143	0.45
Christchurch	1911	154	1.00
	1936	154	0.84
	1951	212	0.83
Dunedin	1911	43	0.42
	1936	35	0.22
	1951	31	0.12
Melbourne	1933	250	0.35
	1954	137	0.22
Sydney	1911	100	0.30
	1947	135	0.19
	1954	93	0.16
Wellington	1911	108	0.75
	1936	96	0.53
	1951	73	0.48

Table 90. Japanese Metropolitan Densities.

	TOKYO				OSAKA				NAGOYA			
	1950	1955	1960	1965	1950	1955	1960	1965	1950	1955	1960	1965
A coefficient (persons/hectare)	156	302	371	316	85	224	288	275	77	88	111	119
b coefficient	.21	.13	.12	.10	.20	.17	.18	.15	.44	.16	.16	.15
Limiting density (persons/hectare)	8	10	10	15	5	12	15	18	5	6	7	9

Table 91. Kingston Density Functions.

	$\underline{A}$	$\underline{b}$
1891	190	1.01
1911	264	.90
1943	143	.55
1960	158	.33

coefficient is tending towards zero, indicating an almost uniform density pattern, around a small uninhabited central business zone. The problem then becomes the ascertaining of this uniform density (which may indeed change with time) towards which the city is tending; there is a simple technique for this.

The question first came up regarding Amsterdam. At the 1957 Conference of the International Statistical Institute the present writer read a paper on the negative exponential function. In the discussion, the Director of Municipal Statistics for Amsterdam stated that he had tried it and that it did not work; "niet op te gaan". Over a radius of 6 kilometres, Amsterdam had an almost uniform residential density averaging some three hundred persons/hectare, with no sign of decline with distance. He was asked whether this indicated that Amsterdam was subject to strict town planning regulations, to which he agreed. Asked further how long such regulations had been in force, he replied "About three hundred years". These changes take time.

The method of analysis now proposed is simple. The wards, or other units into which the metropolitan area is divided, are classified according to their density at the beginning of the period under observation. Their rates of gain or loss of population in the subsequent decade, or other period, are plotted against these initial densities. It soon becomes clear that there is a long-run "preferred" density, below it attractive and above it repulsive to population.

One of the first metropolitan areas in which this method was tried was Pittsburgh.

It is immediately apparent that a density of some ten thousand persons/square mile (forty persons/hectare) of land not occupied by heavy industry, railways, parks, and the like, is "preferred", in the sense that wards with lower densities are gaining and with higher densities losing population. It must be noted that this is a net density after the exclusion of land occupied by heavy industry, railways, parks, — gross density will be lower.

For Chicago the data (Table 92), are more abundant, as the Plan Commission records data separately for each square mile, and a contingency table can be prepared. "Preferred" density here seems to be higher — something between forty and sixty persons/hectare.

able 92. Numbers[a] of Blocks in Chicago at Various Densities.

Density 00/sq. m.	Density Change 1950–60 (%)					
	Increase			Decrease		
	Over 50	10–50	0–10	0–10	10–50	Over 50
30–70		3	2	12	9	
20–30		2	4	26	8	
10–20	7	20	9	25	16	
5–10	14	14	3	4	5	1
Under 5	5	7	1	4	7	

Omitting blocks with population below 1,000. From Dickinson, *City and Region*, pp. 38, 140; Original sources from Chicago Plan Commission.

An interesting method of analysis which gives us an historical perspective shows the earlier built-up zones of Los Angeles with densities trending downwards, and the more recently built-up trending upwards, to a preferred density somewhere between eight to ten thousand square mile, thirty to forty persons/hectare.[46]

An interesting example for a lower-income city is provided by Kingston, Jamaica (Table 91). Up to 1911 approximately parallel lines indicate all-round increases in density rising to 264 persons/hectare. But since then central densities have been falling, and in 1960 the equilibrium point at which density is neither rising nor falling appears to be at about 115 persons/hectare.

The evidence from London ("Greater London", the area within approximately a twenty-four kilometre radius from the centre) shows however how rapidly "preferred" density can change (Diagram 19). In the 1960s likewise in the 1950s, it was somewhere about forty persons/hectare — by the 1970s it was twenty or less.

This however must be considered in the light of the fact that the Greater London area was one of rapidly declining population (7.99 million in 1961, 7.44 in 1971, 7.03 in 1976). Similar diagrams plotted for some smaller British metropolitan areas, over the period 1951–76,

46. Duncan, Sabagh, and Van Arsdol, *American Journal of Sociology* (Jan. 1962).

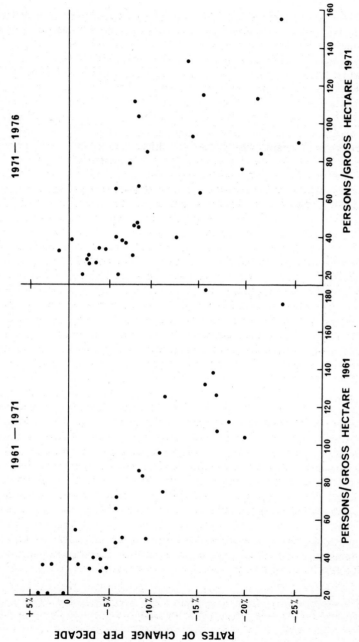

Diagram 19. Population Changes Greater London Boroughs.

also showed preferred densities in the neighbourhood of twenty persons/hectare for West Midlands and South East Lancashire (with comparatively stable populations) but also for Merseyside (Liverpool area), with declining population. The Avon (Bristol-Bath) area however, with increasing population, showed a figure of about thirty.

But Australian and New Zealand cities, with stable or increasing populations, can also show declining preferred densities. In Melbourne in 1961–66 the number of districts showing population gains began to exceed the number showing losses at a density of some thirty-five persons/hectare. The higher densities were found, of course, nearer the city centre. Up to a radius of some ten kilometres the old exponential formula worked fairly well – it may be significant that this was also the zone served by tramways. Further out (greater dependency on car transport?) the density-distance relationship showed a strong tendency to flatten. Even in the 1930s there were already slight signs of such a break in the curve.

The corresponding figure for Sydney was nearly fifty – the difference can probably be explained by greater transport difficulties in Sydney, due to the city's extraordinary topography, broken up by long arms of the harbour. Transport difficulties make people more willing, other things being equal, to put up with higher density dwellings.

By 1966–71 the Melbourne turning point had fallen to about thirty. Brisbane, with a population of some 0.75 million, had a preferred density of about twenty-five in 1961–66: by 1971–76 this had fallen to fifteen or less. In Canberra, a planned city where people have their density preference chosen for them, an average of some twenty-five has also prevailed. In Perth, also with a population of some 0.75 million, rapidly growing, and with very low densities, no district exceeding twenty-five persons/hectare, all districts but one were gaining population in 1961–66, whereas in 1971–77 all districts with densities above fifteen were losing population.

In Adelaide, on the other hand, with a population of nearly a million, the preferred point has remained at twenty-five between the periods 1966–70 and 1971–76.

A study by the present writer of 1966–71 population changes in New Zealand indicates preferred densities of about forty for Auckland (population 650,000) and twenty for Christchurch (population 276,000).[47]

Cities are forming at these low densities because low density is what people want, when they can afford it – nothing could be clearer than this. Low density, of course, is the measurable part of the complex

47. C. Clark, New Zealand Town Planning Quarterly (June 1974).

of attributes which go with it, mentioned above — comparative freedom from noise, pollution, and so on. But we have to analyze the demand for residential land as such, apart from the houses which stand on it. This difficult task was undertaken by Winsten and Savigear.[48] Using three-dimensional models, they first pointed out that we must separately analyze persons/room and rooms/hectare. The former is largely influenced by the number of children in the family (children are generally supposed to require less space than adults). Families with children tend to live in the outer suburbs, which factor raises the persons/room ratio there. This ratio is lowered with income (measured by the only substitute information available locally, namely "social class index", or the proportion of men in higher-paid occupations). The inner areas, on the other hand, have comparatively few children, but high room occupancy — a response to high rents. This high room occupancy is considered to be the principal repulsive factor driving people away from inner areas.

With these persons/room considerations set aside, we can now turn our attention to analyzing rooms/hectare. The situation in London in 1951 (it may have changed considerably since) is shown in Diagram 20 (note that the density is calculated per acre, and not of gross area,

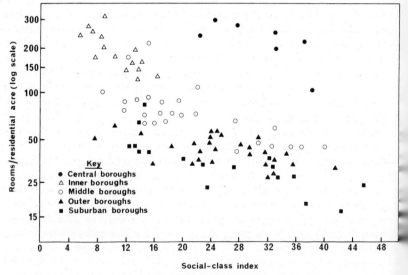

Diagram 20. Social-class index.

48.   Winsten and Savigear, *Journal of the Royal Statistical Society* (1966) Part 2.

but of land designated residential). The boroughs (units for which information is available) are classified into five groups by increasing distance from the centre. The first observation is that the innermost boroughs are mainly occupied by higher-income residents, probably with few or no children, living at high densities, because they are willing to "trade space for time", in the authors' felicitous phrase — put up with high density in exchange for reduced time of travel to work.

This phenomenon of high-income families living near the city centre is more marked in Continental Europe. In the United States of America it has been observed in Tucson, and a few other cities, but certainly not generally.

But these are the exceptions. For everyone else, the curve is declining, that is, higher income means lower density, subject to the qualification that, at a given income level, lower densities are enjoyed by those who live further out — usually at the expense of higher travel time and cost. But the principal thing to notice is the shape of the curve. It is much steeper in the range 0–16 than it is at the higher income levels. It is the poor who have the highest income elasticity of demand for more space.

With such clear indications that people prefer low-density living, and indeed that the strongest demand for it comes from the poor, who are now living at high densities, it is surprising how much effort and influence are being devoted to attempts to restore high-density living near the city centre. The movement outwards of residential population has been accompanied by similar movements (Chapter 15) of business and employment, and by falling land values (Chapter 17). There are thus obvious financial interests in any attempts to restore city centre residential densities, which may be able to obtain (in the accustomed manner) political action such as underground railways and construction of public housing in high apartment blocks near the city centre. But besides these direct financial interests we have to face the considerable influence, social, intellectual, and political, of what have been felicitously described as the "idealists of the city".[49] These include a body of architectural opinion, generally of Le Corbusier's school of thought, politicians of big city power, evangelistic bureaucrats of an essential conservatism rooted in the forms and aesthetic of the past; and also the "ideologists of the proletariat", for whom urban masses, poverty stricken and over-crowded, must be the source of truth.

The natural tendencies for inner city population, employment, and land values to decline should be reversed, they contend. The

---

49. Maurice Ash in a letter to *The Times* (London), 18 December 1976.

inner city is becoming dead, with few residents, and only a daytime population of workers, and that diminishing. What is wanted, they say, is an inner city alive at night, full of theatres and restaurants; they tend however to take *fin-de-siècle* Paris and Vienna as their models, rather than the more drab example of nineteenth century London.

This is indeed to prefer the tastes of the few to the needs of the many.

In Britain these ideas were reinforced by a concept so ludicrous that it can hardly be described – but it actually happened. An influential body of opinion urged that the urban multitudes should be required to live in high apartment blocks instead of low density suburbs for the purpose of "saving" agricultural land. This movement was particularly strong under Mr Harold MacMillan's rule as Minister of Housing in the early 1950s.

Quite apart from the inherent undesirability of tower blocks, now generally recognized if only from the point of view of the health of inmates, calculations based on their additional construction and main- tenance costs per unit of dwelling space lead to the conclusion that it is worthwhile housing people in tower blocks rather than in low-rise rise buildings, with a view to saving agricultural land, if we set a value of about £250,000 on each hectare so saved.[50]

The justification of town planning, for the obtaining of certain "public goods", was set out in Chapter 8. But a clear perversion of this principle is found in proposals for "urban renewal". While it has influential advocates elsewhere this concept has mainly been applied in the United States, where it has been the subject of vast expenditure, mainly from Federal funds, state and municipal authorities having been more cautious – though the University of Chicago, most unwisely, put in a contribution for "renewal" of its own neighbourhood.

It is true that in the United States the problem is complicated by the existence, in every large city, of a "ghetto" in which the black population is confined, illegally but effectively, by tacit understandings among real estate dealers not to sell houses in white districts to black families. Because of their comparative poverty, coupled with this constraint, the black families are to be found in the older, cheaper, and more run-down parts of the inner suburbs. Without any thought for the welfare of the inhabitants. black or white, massive schemes of redevelopment were prepared for bulldozing and rebuilding large areas, to be mainly filled with apartment blocks, at much higher rent than those which they replaced.

50. P. A. Stone, "The Economics of Housing and Urban Development" *Journal of the Royal Statistical Society* 122 (Series A) (1959). Part IV.

An aggregation (Table 93) of 297 urban renewal projects in the United States showed the extent of the reduction of residential land.[51]

Table 93. "Urban Renewal" Percentages of Land Use.

	Residential	Commercial	Industrial	Streets	Public and open space
Before "renewal"	45.8	11.7	6.1	31.7	2.0
After "renewal"	34.5	16.4	14.6	27.8	6.7

The commercial and industrial objectives appear untenably high. The counter-slogan "Urban renewal means negro removal" was all too well justified. In addition, as Professor J. Q. Wilson of Harvard pointed out, these schemes cut right across the normal development of political and social life in the inner city areas. For this criticism, President Johnson condemned the Professor as a "public enemy".

It is easy to discern the alliance of political forces which produced these anti-social results. In the first place, there were the politicians and bureaucrats making jobs for themselves, advocates of the "federal bulldozer" for its own sake. Associated with them were the property owners in the inner suburbs who saw their property values declining, and who expected that compensation could be assessed (as it was) to pay them more than current market values for their properties. Municipal politicians were worried about declining revenues from municipal taxation and the high costs of providing services for a poor population, and were looking forward to something less costly and better tax-paying in its place. Finally, there were the banks, insurance companies, and the like looking forward to what they expected to be large, secure, and remunerative property investments.

The principal effects of urban renewal in the United States have been to displace the poor, and compel them to find more expensive housing, and to provide a subsidy from public funds for the owners of the inner city land. There are no reasons why this should be done.

On the other hand we must not move totally to the opposite position, of leaving the problem of "blighted areas" (places where population, business, and property values are heavily falling) entirely to the free market.

There may sometimes arise significant adverse externalities, that is, some disadvantages against which the parties concerned cannot act by ordinary market means. If a house is unpainted and in bad repair,

51. Kain, *European Regional Science Association,* Ghent Conference, quoting from a paper by E. F. R. Hearle and J. H. Niedercorn, *The Impact of Urban Renewal on Land Use,* then in course of publication by the Rand Corporation.

it is up to the owner to have it repaired, or to sell it to someone who will. But if all the neighbouring properties are neglected, a point may be reached where the whole character of the district changes, and the individual proprietor, however carefully he repairs his house, may still find it difficult to sell. At a later stage banks, insurance companies, and building societies may draw a "red line" around the district, refusing to make loans on any property in the district, which they now regard as bad security. The result will inevitably be a further spiralling downward movement in property values, and in the state of repair. To those proprietors who are willing to maintain their properties this is an adverse externality which they cannot meet without help from public authority, which should be given to them, not in the form of any grandiose project of "urban renewal", but a more modest procedure of assisted loans for reconditioning.

In a number of European countries, but in New York alone among American cities, the failure of owners in "blighted districts" to maintain their properties is largely a consequence of rent control. "Next after bombing, rent control is the surest way of destroying a city", said the sage Swedish economist Assar Lindbeck. Rents received sometimes may not even meet maintenance costs. In New York, apartments are now being abandoned at the rate of nearly a thousand a week.

The problem is made worse in Britain by the existence of a very large amount of public ("council") housing, where occupants enjoy considerable subsidies, and who cannot be ejected except in the most extreme circumstances.

"Public housing" in the United States is run however on the opposite principle — those whose family circumstances improve are required to leave. This has the effect of concentrating in public housing what are euphemistically described as "families with problems". In some cases public hosuing has acquired such a bad reputation that tenants are now unwilling to occupy it. Even at zero rentals, it has had to be demolished.

Rent control and British "council" tenancies are not part of our present subject matter. But we must take into account some of their consequences. In the older, inner suburbs, where the most marked population decline has taken place, and where also many of the older dwellings have been demolished, a larger proportion of the population will be living in council houses or flats, or in rent-controlled private dwellings. These are the people, it need not be added, who have most to lose by leaving their present residences. Moving to the area of another municipal authority, they would find themselves very low down in the waiting list for council dwellings. This has a considerable effect on the economics of the area. Dwellers in council dwellings and rent-regulated private dwellings include (though they certainly do not consist of them exclusively) many of the aged, the infirm, the chronically unemployed, and the lowest paid. These not only raise the costs of local government in their own area; but also, in view of most of the employment opportunities now being in the outer suburbs, the amount of unemployment increases. This has particularly serious effects among juveniles, who now constitute a substantial proportion of the unemployment totals.

15

Urban Land Use

As a warning to any geographical zealots who may try to apply Von Thümen's principle to urban land use, Hoover calculated that on this principle a university with a 120 hectares land requirement would have to occupy a ring-shaped campus twenty-five metres wide and fifty kilometres in extent. Such a lay-out, he adds, would preclude both a sizeable stadium, and getting to classes on time.[1]

We have hitherto been thinking of urban densities in terms of persons/hectare, in a range bounded by extremes of three thousand to fifteen. To make a closer analysis of urban land use we must invert these figures, and think in terms of square metres/person (hectare = ten thousand square metres), within a range whose extremes lie approximately between three and seven hundred.

It must be remembered that in the United States we are dealing now, not with metropolitan areas as previously defined, but (with one exception) with central cities as defined for administrative purposes — for it is only from surveys by city planning authorities that we can obtain detailed records of land use. Measurements refer to space actually utilized, excluding vacant land, but including land specifically set aside for recreation.

Great variability is found (Table 94) in United States cities, from under one hundred to over six hundred square metres/person. This is not found, as might have been expected, to be significantly related to size of city, but rather to its age; it is the more recently developed cities which have been able to allow more abundant space for all activities. The data for United States cities in 1960 were therefore classified "old" or "new" according to whether the city's factor of population increase between 1910 and 1960 had been greater or less than two.

The first striking feature is the amount of space required for roads. It is clear that much road design is an investment for future urban growth. Small and growing towns make lavish provision,

1. Hoover, *Introduction to Regional Economics* (New York: Knopf, 1971), p. 110.

Table 94. Land Use in Cities.

	All uses m²/person	Residences	of which multiple family	Roads	Railways	Industry	of which light industry	Commerce	Public buildings	Parks and recreation
Small towns[a] under 4,000 population	766	27.4		57.1[c]		9.4[b]		3.7		13.9[d]
Small towns[a] 4-20,000 population	690	42.0		34.0[c]		9.8[b]		2.7		9.6[d]
U.S. cities about 1950:[e]										
Satellite cities:										
Population under 5,000	1,091	27.5	1.1	32.6	4.5	6.6		3.1	3.0	22.9
5 - 10,000	870	37.4	1.8	33.1	3.8	2.4		1.5	7.0	14.5
10 - 25,000	536	51.1	3.4	24.6	3.0	1.5		2.1	4.7	12.7
Over 25,000	234	40.2	9.4	26.9	5.6	13.7		3.0	3.4	6.8
Central cities:										
Population under 50,000	404	39.4	5.4	28.2	5.0	5.7	2.7	3.2	5.2	13.1
50 - 100,000	324	37.3	6.5	35.2	6.2	4.9	2.1	2.8	6.5	10.8
100 - 250,000	325	41.5	5.8	27.4	5.2	5.8	2.5	2.8	5.8	11.1
Over 250,000	204	40.2	11.8	24.5	4.4	8.8	3.9	3.9	8.3	9.3
U.S. cities about 1960[f]										
Los Angeles	330	52.6		20.8		9.6[h]		6.1		10.8[d]
Other "new" cities[g]	325	43.5		26.8		6.8[h]		4.8		18.1[d]
New York	93	26.6		34.4		9.9[h]		2.3		26.8[d]
Other "old" cities	219	37.9		23.4		14.1[h]		4.4		20.2[d]
Chicago	147	35.1		26.8		15.3[h]		7.0		15.9[d]
Chicago historic data[i] 1940	125	31.0		32.4	10.0	9.0		6.7[j]	3.2	7.7
1923	128	34.0		32.4		18.1[h]		6.9	3.5	4.9
1890	177	22.9		43.0	9.4	12.7		3.5	2.7	5.6
1870	172	27.5		37.3	10.8	10.5		4.1	1.1	8.7
Chicago zone data 1956 (central business district)				36.0	2.1			57.4[l]		

Table 94. (cont.)

		Percentage Distribution of Urban Land Use								
	All uses m²/person	Residences	of which multiple family	Roads	Railways	Industry	of which light industry	Commerce	Public buildings	Parks and recreation
Miles from central business district										
0 - 2		10.1		32.4		27.0[h]		18.7[j]	4.7	6.9
2 - 4		25.1		29.0		22.4[h]		11.6[j]	4.8	7.1
4 - 6		33.3		28.4		18.8[h]		9.5[j]	4.0	6.1
6 - 8		38.4		29.0		13.0[h]		7.3[j]	3.5	8.6
8 - 10		42.3		28.8		10.9[h]		5.7[j]	3.3	8.5
10 - 12		41.6		29.1		17.6[h]		4.1[j]	1.8	5.5
Over 12		35.5		24.1		25.4[h]		3.6[j]	2.3	9.1
Whole metropolitan area		32.1		25.4	9.3[k]	6.3	5.7	3.7	3.9	18.9
Calculated marginal[f] requirements for city growth	368	64.9		6.5				10.3		10.8[d]

a. Data from Queensland, averages of six and five towns respectively
b. Mainly public utilities
c. Including railways
d. Including public buildings
e. Bartholomew, Land Uses in American Cities (1955)
f. J.H. Niedercorn and E.F.R. Hearle, Recent Land Use Trends in 48 Large American Cities (Rand Corporation Memorandum RM3664, 1963)
g. Population growth 1910-60 over twofold
h. Including railways
i. Subsequent data on Chicago from reports of Chicago Plan Commission
j. Including parking grounds
k. Including communication and public utilities
l. Including parking grounds amounting to 8.9 per cent of the whole area

gradually falling with size of town — marginal requirements for roads taking only 6.5 per cent of the land — with the figure at a minimum of about 20 per cent. Los Angeles, contrary to expectation, shows a low figure. The Chicago figures show the high proportion in the city's early years and the fall as we proceed outwards from the centre.

Commerce, of all kinds, apart from its expected concentration near the city centre, requires only a small proportion of urban land. The figure for New York is surprisingly low. There is nothing unusual in the column for public buildings — apart from the rise in their demand for land since 1870. Park and recreation land varies very much with municipal policies — New York has a good record here. Railways occupied much land in nineteenth century cities — Chicago's ten per cent figure however was probably a maximum. The demands of industry were not great. They show a tendency to be high in the outer suburbs, which tendency, as we shall see below, has been accentuated since the times to which this table refers.

It is the residue of land after meeting these demands which is available as residential land (including private gardens, but not including roads and so on in residential areas). It is seen to be somewhat higher in the new and growing cities, and taking sixty-five per cent of land at the margin, but its absolute amount shows a maximum at about fifty per cent.

So it must be borne in mind that when we speak of densities measured gross of fifteen persons/hectare we are considering densities on actual residential land, excluding roads, of at least thirty, and perhaps forty or more persons/hectare.

Information on land use is available for the world's largest metropolitan area, Tokyo (Table 95).[2] Only four land use classifications are given, and these are *gross* of road space; so all values must be divided by a factor of about 1.4 for comparison with figures given in the previous table.

Table 95. Tokyo Percentage Distribution of Land Use.

Mean distance of zone from central business district km.	Residential	Commercial	Industrial	Other (mainly recreation and farm)
1.4	16.9	70.9	11.3	0.9
3.8	63.0	28.5	5.7	2.8
6.2	46.2	11.5	38.3	4.0
8.5	74.0	10.4	6.4	9.2
11.2	62.4	3.1	5.2	29.3
12.8	56.4	3.4	5.9	34.3

2. Source described later in this Chapter.

There is no unexpected feature, except perhaps the high concentration of industrial land at about six kilometres distance from the business centre.

Actual park space in Tokyo,[3] as distinct from horticultural land and other private open space, amounts to only 1.2 square metres/person, as against 19 in New York, 23 in London, and 27 in Frankfurt.[3] What parks Tokyo has are of great beauty — and a small charge is made for admission. The proposed new capital city for Japan is to have 143 square metres/person space in all, of which 15 per cent or 22 square metres/person will be open space, comparable to the open space per person in London or Paris, 18 per cent roads, 38.7 per cent residential, only 2.6 per cent for central government buildings, and as much as 7.9 per cent for schools.[4]

The planned new town of Peston in the United States of America provided 370 square metres/person of developed area, of which twenty-two per cent was to be parks and play-grounds; the British new towns only 220 square metres/person on the average, with twenty-six per cent open space, with the exception of Cumbernauld in Scotland, with a higher density of 143 square metres/person (the object being for everyone to be within walking distance of the centre), but with thirty-three per cent open space.[5]

The above measurements all refer to site area occupied; an alternative measure is floor-space occupied. Where the demand for space is highest the construction of multi-storey buildings (at substantially higher cost than lower buildings per square metre floor space both to build and to maintain) makes it possible to obtain more floor space for each square metre of site; but there is a limit to this process. Not only must height limitations be borne in mind but also the non-usable portions of buildings (elevator space, etc.). The Empire State Building in New York, at the time of its construction in 1931 the tallest building in the world, reached a ratio of over 20:1 rentable floor area/site area;[6] the city authorities now impose a limit of 15:1. Even such a ratio is rare. A survey by the metropolitan planning authorities in Sydney in 1968–69 (a metropolitan area of some 2.75 million population) showed at the business centre (see Diagram 21) the floor space/gross area ratio no more than 3:1 or 4:1 at the maximum, and that only for the first half-kilometre from the centre. This high usage is almost entirely accounted for by office space — office work can be carried on in high buildings with less inconvenience

---

3. *The Developing Economies* (Dec. 1972), p. 519.
4. *Nihon Keizai Shimbun* (Tokyo), 18 February 1975 (English Edition).
5. Best, *Town and Country Planning* (Feb. 1964) and P. A. Stone, *Estates Gazette* (1962).
6. *Construction Review* (May 1968).

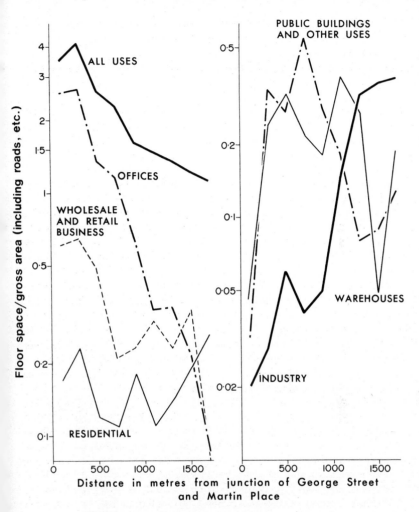

Diagram 21. Central Sydney Floor Space Use 1968–69.

than activities calling for the movement of goods. Other demands are less concentrated on central sites; demands for space by industry do not become significant until 1 kilometre distance is reached; and these now show a tendency to be displaced further outwards. Residences begin to represent a significant proportion of all floor space at 1.5 kilometres distance.

Sydney is more favoured with parks and gardens; but in the case of cities which are unwilling or cannot afford to set aside land for public open space we may note Newling's interesting observation in Kingston, Jamaica, that no greenery appears until the floor space/ site area ratio has fallen below 0.6:1.[7]

A survey extending over a wider area is available for Chicago (Table 96).[8] The centre is largely occupied by commerce and related service industries. There is some concentration of retailing and whole-saling. The distribution beyond 10 km tends to stabilize. The figures refer to the 1950s, and both manufacture and retailing have further dispersed since then.

Floor space data are also available for Glasgow.[9] The ratio to *net* site area (excluding road space) in the city centre is 5, falling abruptly after approximately 2.5 kilometres to 0.35, then 0.25 at 5.5 kilometres, and 0.15 at 9 kilometres.

Detailed information on floor-space utilization in the various zones of a metropolitan area is very limited in amount. More abundant, though still limited, is information on the distribution of employment. In the discussion at the 1957 meeting of the International Statistical Institute (see Chapter 14) in which the Director of Municipal Statistics for Amsterdam showed that the distribution of residential densities in his city was almost uniform, he went on to analyze the distribution of employments, which was found to follow fairly closely a negative exponential (semi-log) distribution.

Measuring density in employments/hectare and distance from the centre in kilometres the fitted expression is

$$y = 450e^{-0.74x}$$

This exponential distribution for Amsterdam (with a very high central density, comparable with that found in London) appears however to be an exceptional form. In all other metropolitan areas for which a detailed distribution diagram of employment has been obtained the better-fitting function is found to be not exponential (semi-log) but a power function (log-log). (A more refined treatment indicates that a gamma function might fit best.)[10] Using a power function for London in 1971 employment density per gross hectare was found to vary (approximately) inversely with the 1.34th power of distance from the centre.

7. Private communication.
8. *Chicago Area Transportation Survey,* Vol. 1, p. 109.
9. R. N. Davidson, "Pattern of Employment Densities in Glasgow" *Urban Studies* 7, no. 1 (1970), p. 69.
10. M. Mogridge, Papers from the Urban Economics Conference, July 1973. Centre for Environmental Studies, London.

Table 96. Utilization of Floor Space in Chicago.

Distance from business centre km	Ratio floor space/ gross area	Percentages Occupation of Floor Space						
		Commerce and service industries	Public buildings	Wholesaling	Retailing	Public utilities transport communication	Manufacture	Residences
0 - 1.1	2.4	47.5	9.6	11.5	14.8	4.3	4.9	7.4
1.1 - 4.0	1.15	8.3	10.4	11.9	6.6	12.5	21.6	28.7
4.0 - 6.4	0.9	4.1	7.1	3.0	7.3	6.6	20.0	51.8
6.4 - 10.5	0.41	4.2	6.5	1.4	5.1	4.3	15.6	62.9
10.5 - 16.1	0.23	4.3	6.2	1.2	5.5	2.0	8.5	72.4
16.1 - 20.9	0.08	2.6	7.0	1.2	5.0	2.1	10.4	71.7
20.9 - 30.6	0.015	3.7	7.4	1.2	5.2	1.3	12.1	69.2
30.6 - 43.4	0.002	5.2	8.4	1.6	8.1	2.6	10.7	63.3

Diagram 22 gives the London data.[11] Between 1951 and 1971 employment in the centre remained about constant, rose strongly in the two-four kilometres radius (this zone is now known to traffic engineers as "The Gluepot"), then fell up to the ten kilometre radius,

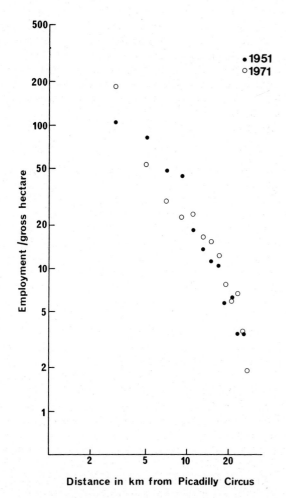

Diagram 22. Greater London Employment Densities.

11. 1971 data from large sample results provided by Greater London Council, 1951; less precisely from Census data for boroughs and urban districts grouped into two kilometre rings (to compare with 1971).

above which it rose. The approximate linearity on the log-log diagram ceased abruptly, in both years, at eighteen kilometres. The fitted negative slopes have declined (that is, employment becoming more dispersed) from 1.48 in 1951 to 1.34 in 1971.

Another sample showed that in the short period 1966–71 employment within the ten kilometre radius fell nearly ten per cent from 2.39 to 2.17 million. In Greater London outside the ten kilometre radius employment remained approximately constant at 1.9 million. The region as a whole was depopulating, with the principal incidence of depopulation on the inner zones.

For five other British metropolitan areas as well as Great London Evans records areas and employments (Table 97) in aggregated zones.[12] From the area of each aggregation can be computed its average external radius.

Table 97. Distribution of Employments.

	Greater London	West Midlands	S.E. Lancashire	Merseyside	Tyneside	Clydeside
Imputed external radii of succeeding zone aggregations km.	2.94	1.10	0.94	1.10	1.12	0.7
	9.83	8.12	5.92	5.97	3.78	7.0
	24.5	14.8	17.8	11.1	8.7	16.3
Employments/hectare						
First zone	522	320	602	415	199	70
Ring between first and second aggregations	42.5	26.2	23.7	22.4	24.4	23.4
Ring between second and third aggregations	12.1	11.6	9.1	7.4	10.8	4.2

If on a log-log diagram we plot the above employment densities against the mid-point of the radii (e.g. 42.5 against the mid-point of 2.94 and 9.83) – which of course biases the result – we nevertheless obtain a consistent picture of parallel lines, all with a slope of about -1.45. At any given distance from the metropolitan centre the London employment density is approximately ten times that of Tyneside – but the slopes are much the same.

Stockholm has a wide dispersal of employment, with a gradient of only 1.25.[13]

Oslo, with 300,000 labour force in the metropolitan area, has its highest density at 400 employments/hectare.[14] It is considered

12. Evans, *Economics of Residential Location*, p. 28.
13. Kant, *Lund Studies in Geography* Series 8, No. 24, p. 355.
14. T. H. Rasmussen, "The Development of a Planned Plurinuclear City Region: Greater Oslo" *Regional Science Association* 14 (1965), pp. 105–16.

desirable to keep average density within 1.1 kilometre radius down to 250 (that is, one-third of the metropolitan labour force in the central four square kilometres) so that rush-hour traffic does not become too congested, and also because it is desirable to limit the area of the central business district — "too great a size seriously restricts personal contact". The rest of the labour force should be employed in outlying employment areas each less than two square kilometres in extent, and provided with adequate parking space. Smaller cities certainly do face lesser problems.

A number of metropolitan employment density gradients are shown on Diagram 23 (log-log scales). London's five hundred employment/ hectare in the central business district looks small in comparison with Tokyo's two thousand. In spite of great differences in density levels, the curves show similar gradients, though Adelaide shows a higher slope, and Amsterdam, as noted previously, is exceptional.

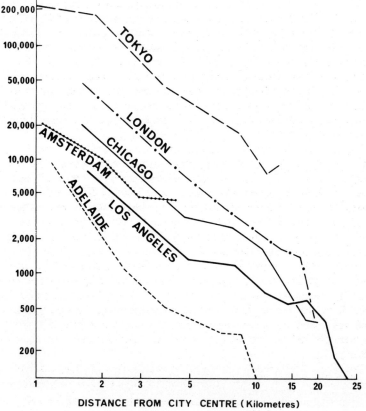

DISTANCE FROM CITY CENTRE (Kilometres)
Diagram 23. Employment/Km^2.

We now examine the distribution of employments of different kinds. The floor-space data for Sydney showed the nature of the demand, principally for office space, within 1.5 kilometres of the centre. London data from the 1962 Traffic Survey (drawn on semi-log scale) shoed that while at the business centre non-manual employment density was nearly twice manual employment density, yet over most of the metropolitan area manual and non-manual employment showed a remarkable similarity in distribution.

The first factor influencing the location of employment within a metropolitan area is, of course, the need for space per unit of value added. Only where this is low can businesses afford to locate in the high-rented central area. So we find office work at one end of the location scale, scrap metal yards, car wreckers, and so on, at the other.

But there is more to it than this. Central locations are required by certain industries, independently of their space requirement per unit of value added, though of course they will do their best to keep it down. Such industries are (i) those providing personal or business services to those working or residing in the neighbourhood — restaurants, hairdressers, post offices, secretarial bureaus, and the like, and (ii) those exceptionally dependent on "external economies", that is, on specialized firms who can provide them with adequate and, above all rapid supplies of required components and services. Examples of such industries are publishing (newspapers, periodicals, and books) and fashion (not staple) clothing, with its many demands for specialized subcontract work.

There is an interesting illustration of this latter principle. The clothing trade grew up in old-established centralized and concentrated locations, particularly East London and the garment district of New York — traditional inertia, thought some town-planners, and this pattern need not necessarily be repeated elsewhere. During recent decades Los Angeles has become a new fashion-clothing production centre. Contrary to some expectations, here also, the clothing trade occupies a concentrated centralized area.

Some detail is available (Diagram 24) for Los Angeles.[15] The concentration of restaurants and other service industries is noticeable. Aircraft, one of Los Angeles's principal industries, is mainly located away from the metropolitan centre. This is not only because of the need for extensive space for storing and testing aircraft, but also because the aircraft firms find these suburbs a better source of skilled labour.

Detailed information (Table 98) is available on the land use and employment for the Tokyo metropolitan area, probably the world's

15. Unpublished information kindly made available by the California State Labour Department, 1963.

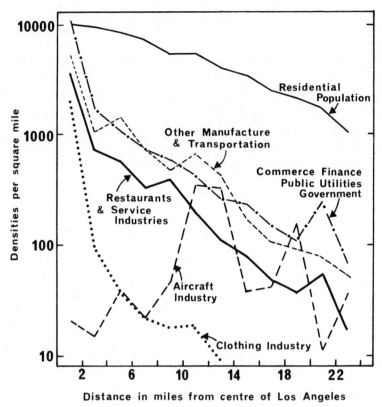

Diagram 24. Los Angeles — Residential and Employment Densities.

largest, with a labour force of over seven million.[16] The metropolitan area (*to*) includes, towards the inland, some semi-rural (*shi*), and rural (*gun*) areas, and some outlying islands. Employment and land use data are available for these areas; but to tabulate them would be misleading, because at distance from the central business district comparable with theirs are other muncipal areas along the coast. Table 98 therefore is prepared only from data of the twenty-three wards (*ku*) of the main city.

If the data are plotted log-log a change in slope (accelerated decline in density) is observed after 10 kilometres for all employments except manufacture, where the decline continues at an approximately unchanged rate. If however we treat this "bulge" at the 8.5 kilometres

16. *Tokyo Metropolitan Area Municipal Statistics*, 1978.

Table 98. Tokyo Employment.

Average distance of zone from business centre km	Number of wards (*ku*)	Area hectares	Employments/Hectare							
			Construction	Manufacture[a]	Wholesale retail trade	Finance insurance & real estate	Transport & communication	Services	Govt.[b]	TOTAL[c]
1.4	2	715	124	397	653	210	172	263	117	1,947
3.8	4	2,970	364	105	138	222	370	811	165	437
6.2	5	4,521	217	900	606	100	203	321	51	239
8.5	4	4,221	154	597	400	66	137	280	47	237
11.2	5	14,057	67	272	161	27	49	121	18	722
12.8	3	9,042	70	323	159	28	59	110	21	779

a. Including public utilities
b. Including local government
c. Including some minor employments not specified

point as abnormal and measure gradients over the whole length of the lines we obtain the (negative) gradients shown in Table 99.

Table 99. Tokyo Employment Gradients.

Finance	2.02
Government	1.91
Wholesale and retail trade	1.73
Transport and communication	1.61
Services	1.46
Manufacture	1.21
All employments	1.52

The all-employment slope is not very different from that found elsewhere. As expected, finance shows the highest slope. Government employment, even in a national capital, could be more dispersed, as the experience of other countries shows. Japan does not yet have so much dispersal of retailing to suburban shopping centres, though no doubt this will come. Services follow the general employment pattern. Manufacture has a remarkably wide dispersal — rebuilding after wartime damage may have been a factor.

The 1971 figures for London (Diagram 25) show a considerable change since 1962, with a lower slope of -1.34, a low slope for factory and a high slope for office employment, with shop employment now about the same slope as the all-employment figure. Up to 10 kilometres from the centre factory employment has a slope as low as 0.6, but beyond that point the decline accelerates. Transport employment is even more dispersed, and education also shows a slope below one. Warehousing and health services both show a slope of about 1.2, government employment 1.5.

An analysis of the factors influencing changes of location within the Greater London area between 1951 and 1961 showed that the principle motive forces were growth of output, and capitalization, that is, labour-intensive industries found movement more difficult — less so however for industries with a high female proportion in their labour force.[17] The expanding industries of vehicles and mechanical and electrical engineering showed the highest mobility — not so chemicals however, where choice of sites may be limited.

17. Tulpule, *Regional Studies* (April 1969), p. 37.

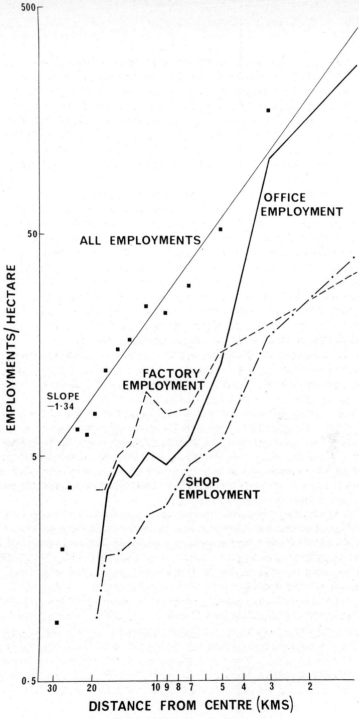

Diagram 25. Greater London 1971.

Chicago[18] shows a gradient 1.54 for commerce out to a distance of twenty kilometres; for manufacture 0.9, falling off abruptly after about fifteen kilometres. The smaller city of Milwaukee[19] shows a gradient for manufacture as low as 0.74, falling off suddenly at ten kilometres distance.

Data for Philadelphia in 1943 show a slope of about 1.2 for manufacture to a distance of eight kilometres from the city centre, after which density falls off rapidly.[20] Within one mile from the city centre the density of manufacturing employment was 28.6 per hectare of all land.

Sydney (data given in table in Chapter 14) shows a slope of -0.96 for manufacture, that is, density almost exactly in inverse proportion to distance from the city centre; and a similar slope for retailing, apart from the high concentration near the city centre.

In the smaller manufacturing city of Brisbane (population 0.75 million, manufacturing employment sixty thousand) density was only 5.1 manufacturing workers within three kilometres of the city centre, falling off with a slope of 1.28.

Melbourne, with its peculiar asymmetric development eastwards and southwards to the hills and the bay shore, to the comparative neglect of the flat country to the north and west, also shows (1966 census) an average slope of -1.4. The northern and western suburbs show much lower employment densities, both manual and non-manual, than do their counterparts at the same distance from the centre. In this case male and female employments have been tabulated separately, female employment being of much greater relative importance in the non-manual sector. In neither sector however was the male—female ratio found to change significantly with distance from the centre.

All the studies quoted above have been based on laborious detailed examination of small-area statistics within metropolitan areas. An alternative method,[21] which provides much more abundant information, but of much lower quality, covers eighteen cities, at four different dates, measuring employment densities for manufacture, wholesale, retailing and services, by a crude method which measures

18. Chicago Area Transportation Study, Vol. I, pp. 20–24 and Vol. II, pp. 22–34.
19. City of Milwaukee, *Industrial Location in Milwaukee County.*
20. O. D. Duncan, Cold Spring Harbour Symposia on Quantitative Biology 1957.
21. E. S. Mills, *Studies in the Structure of the Urban Economy* (Baltimore: Johns Hopkins University Press, 1972).

only for "central cities" and "outer rings" (as defined by the Census Bureau). Mills did not use the log-log but the semi-log (Ae^{-bx}) formulation; however this will suffice to give us some idea of the comparative orders of magnitude of the gradients. The average values of the b coefficient are shown in Table 100 (Mills's results for residential densities have already been quoted in Chapter 14). It is certainly good to have values extending over such a time-range, and to observe the persistent fall of the coefficient, that is, wider dispersal of activities.

Table 100.

Employment Gradients in the United States

	Values for 6 metropolitan areas				Values for 18 metropolitan areas			
	1920	1929	1939	1948	1948	1954	1958	1963
Manufacture	.95	.82	.77	.76	.68	.55	.48	.42
Wholesaling		1.43	1.24	1.01	1.00	.86	.70	.56
Retailing		1.02	.90	.76	.88	.75	.59	.44
Services			1.12	.88	.97	.81	.66	.53

N.B. Gradients per mile not per kilometre.

Boston had an exceptionally low gradient for manufacture. Fitted in more detail than Mills's data, it was found to be 0.23 in 1958, falling to 0.17 in 1967.[22]

It is a mistake however to regard this dispersal as a function of time alone. Couch subjected Mills's data to multiple regression with population and industrial employment in the metropolitan area, as well as time, as explanatory variables.[23] For wholesaling, retailing, and services the regression coefficients showed the gradients making a positive response to total population, but a negative response (decline) to industrial employment and to time. The gradients for manufacture,

22. E. A. Hanushek and B. N. Song, "Dynamics of Post-War Industrial Location" *Review of Economics and Statistics* 60, no. 4 (Nov. 1978), p. 515.
23. J. D. Couch, "Employment Density Functions – Theory for E. S. Mills's Conundra" *Journal of Regional Science* 18, no. 2 (Aug. 1978), p. 294.

on the other hand, showed the exact opposite, falling with the population of the metropolitan area, rising with industrial employment and with time. (Mills also had suggested that if population and income were to be kept constant the gradient for manufacture might rise with time). Couch's explanation of these phenomena is interesting and plausible — namely that manufacture has an elastic demand for land but an inelastic demand for labour (rising population *per se* therefore disperses it more widely); while wholesaling, retailing, and services are in the converse position.

For more detailed observations of the distribution of employments within the metropolitan area, we usually have to rely on information from traffic surveys. The details given in the 1962 London Traffic Survey only distinguished manual and non-manual employments. But more detail is available (Table 101) for 1971–72, and also (Table 102) for the more dispersed West Midlands urban area near Birmingham — in this case in the form of employment/square kilometre.

A more refined approach to density measurement is to consider the numbers employed in manufacture, commerce, and so on, not per hectare of gross area, but manufacturing employees per hectare used in manufacturing, similarly for commerce . . . Just as pressure on available space — expressing itself in land prices — drives manufacture to dispersal, but permits more concentration of office employments, where space requirements per worker are less, so within the land devoted to manufacturing, or retailing, we should expect to find, for example, the producers and retailers of jewellery showing a more dense concentration in central sites than, say, the producers and retailers of furniture. Within the land devoted to manufacture in Chicago is found a higher density gradient of 1.23, with a very high density of some 1000 workers/hectare in the inner-most manufacturing zone up to two kilometres from the business centre.[24] Commercial employment density in this zone is lower, at 940, and falls off very steeply until it stabilizes at about 100 workers/hectare to a distance of ten kilometres from the business centre.

Employment is widely dispersed (slope -1.23 on the log-log diagram). The feature of difference is that manufacture, which constitutes nearly sixty per cent of all employment, is dispersed in almost precisely the same manner as other employments.

In Glasgow retailing shows a density of nearly 2,000 employments/

---

24. See Footnote 18.

Table 101. Percentage Composition of Employments — London.

Distance from centre (kms)	Office	Factory	Shop	Health service	Transport	Education	Public	Construction & public utility	Warehousing
0 – 2	68.2	7.4	8.8	2.5	0.9	1.9	4.4	3.4	2.5
2 – 4	60.9	10.8	9.6	3.2	3.6	2.6	2.8	3.3	3.1
4 – 6	24.4	27.7	11.1	5.8	7.6	6.3	4.1	6.2	6.8
6 – 8	20.0	27.6	15.3	5.8	7.4	8.1	5.9	4.2	5.7
8–10	20.6	34.2	13.5	5.9	6.5	6.2	3.1	8.7	4.3
10–12	21.2	40.5	11.3	3.8	7.5	5.0	2.5	4.5	3.6
12–14	24.0	34.0	12.4	3.6	5.5	6.1	4.4	6.2	3.8
14–16	29.6	32.5	11.7	4.9	5.6	6.3	2.4	4.2	2.7
16–18	28.3	28.5	14.4	3.9	5.3	8.2	3.7	5.2	2.7
18–20	18.0	45.2	11.5	2.8	4.1	8.0	2.4	3.6	4.2
20–22	20.6	36.1	8.7	2.8	17.4	4.8	1.9	4.1	3.6
22–24	18.3	35.2	12.2	5.5	6.0	6.5	5.6	6.6	4.0

Past the 6 kilometre radius, a considerable uniformity of composition of employment is found

Table 102. West Midlands Employment and Residences Per Square Kilometre[a] 1964.

Boundaries of rings from centre[b], kilometres	0–6	6–8	8–10	10–12	12–14	14–16	16–18
Areas of rings in square kilometres:							
Theoretical	113.1	88.0	113.1	138.2	163.4	188.6	213.6
Actually measured	117.3	65.8	107.8	164.5	163.0	222.6	142.3
Employment per square kilometre:							
Manufacture not motor cars	2,010	711	1,180	522	455	181	53
Motor car manufacture	116	269	115	112	194	12	37
Construction	161	88	107	53	73	27	25
Public Utilities	74	30	32	9	13	7	25
Transport and Communication	290	108	96	41	52	27	11
Retailing.	268	201	193	67	60	34	29
Wholesale and other trading. . . .	183	40	36	11	25	11	3
Professions and administration	645	283	468	91	183	215	34
All employment	3,749	1,731	2,227	907	1,054	515	216
Residences	5,078	4,877	3,898	1,592	2,460	1,259	957

(a) Per square kilometre of whole measured ring area

(b) Centre of gravity of employment of whole area, found to be approximately on the mid-point of the boundary between Districts 7 and 41, that is, 4.4 kilometres in an approximately north-westerly direction from Birmingham business centre (District 1)

hectare[25] (comparable with Tokyo!) of retailing land up to 2.5 kilometres from the business centre, then falling precipitously to 125. The plans for a new town in England provided for employments/ hectare at the densities shown in Table 103.[26]

Table 103. Employments/Hectare.

Commerce and offices	1,180	Public buildings	50
Retailing	425	Wholesale and storage	30
Manufacture	120	Education	15

The amount of space used per employee is related to distance from the centre; but it is also strongly related to the date at which the plant was constructed. Hoover and Vernon showed that the amount of space (total area of building plot) per manufacturing worker in the New York metropolitan region averaged 97 square metres for plants built before 1922, 186 square metres for plants built 1922–45, and 425 square metres for plants built since 1945.[27] A manufacturer's location decision within a metropolitan area is influenced primarily by the bulk of the goods produced or handled. The change to road from rail transport has given many formerly centrally-located industries handling bulky goods a strong incentive to move to suburban locations. Modern factories, designed for electric power and forklift trucks, occupy large single-storey buildings, with plenty of space for vehicles to move and park in place of the old-fashioned compact multi-storey factory or warehouse, designed originally, in some cases, for transmission of power from steam engines. Another consideration not to be neglected is that an attractively landscaped suburban location facing a main road gives an industrialist good publicity. Another important factor has been the decline in residential densities in the inner city areas, which is itself a factor driving out many industrial employers who used to depend on the abundant supply of cheap labour, particularly female labour, which in the past was found in the inner cities. The outward movement of employments, in its turn, gives further incentive to the outward movement of residential population, and the process becomes self-reinforcing. And the aircraft manufacturers in Los Angeles, mentioned above, are not the only employers who have found that suburban

25. R. N. Davidson, "Pattern of Employment Densities in Glasgow" *Urban Studies* 7, no. 1 (1970), p. 69.
26. W. S. Arkins and Partners, Harlow Transportation Study 1969.
27. E. M. Hoover and R. Vernon, *Anatomy of a Metropolis: The Changing Distribution of People and Jobs Within the New York Metropolitan Region* (Cambridge, Mass.: Harvard University Press, 1959).

locations not only give them the space which they need, but also a better supply of skilled labour.

Whatever may be the position with manufactures, retail and service industries are certainly not distributed uniformly or at random over the metropolitan area, but in business and shopping centres of various sizes and functions. The customer gains greatly in minimizing the time and travel needed to visit the various shops and services. The trader finds advantage in aggregation, as we have seen, even in proximity to his competitors.

The distribution of such centres, and the functions which they perform, within a metropolitan area, bears a striking resemblance to the distribution of rural centres. This has already been noted in Chapter 6 (Berry's diagram for a ' semi-urban area adjacent to Chicago[28]) with a determinate near-linear relation between the number of functions performed and the logarithm of the number of traders.

One classification (though there are many alternative classifications) is shown in Table 104.[29]

Table 104. Classification of Shopping Centres.

	Approximate number of functions performed (Berry)	Minimum space requirement (hectares)	Gross floor area as proportion of total space	Population served '000
Neighbourhood centre	20 – 40	1.6	0.16	7–20
Community centre	40 – 60	4	0.23	20–100
Smaller regional centre	60 – 80 ⎱	16	0.23	100 or over
Major regional centre	80–100 ⎰			

As the floor space may include upper storeys and basements, the proportion of the site area occupied by buildings is less than the above column indicates, and the space available for car parking more. Car parking space requirements per vehicle average thirty-seven square metres (four hundred square feet).

There are a number of indications that a unit of one hundred thousand population within a metropolitan area can provide itself with nearly all its local retail and service requirements except the most specialized; it is not of course suggested that it would be a self-contained unit for employment, for which 0.25–0.5 million is probably needed (see previous chapters).

In a continuously built-up metropolitan area, with an average density (if we are looking into the future) of thirty persons/hectare,

28. B. J. Berry, *Metropolitan Planning Guidelines: Commercial Structure* (North East Illinois Planning Committee), p. 117.
29. Urban Land Institute, Washington, Technical Bulletin No. 30.

such regional shopping centres should be on the average some six kilometres apart.

If we had a free hand in designing a large new town the best pattern might be a "flower" with a small centre performing specialized functions, surrounded by "petals" each containing some one hundred thousand population, largely self-sufficing for commerce and services. Such a pattern would give maximum access to recreation land.

It is interesting to compare planned units for a much denser population (without cars) in Soviet Russia for "micro-regions" of thirty to fifty hectares and 5000–15000 population (implied gross densities 170–300 persons/hectare!).[30] Residential densities would be even higher, as roads and commercial and recreational land would have to be provided. However no dwelling would be more than three to five hundred metres from the shopping and service centre, which could be reached without crossing a main road.

If we express the shop floor areas in Table 104 per head of population they add up to a little over one square metre. It is interesting to see that a much lower-income population (in the plans for Gandhinagar, a new capital for Gujarat State) is expected to require 0.5 square metres/person shopping space, of which 0.2 square metres was to be in the town centre.[31]

The provision of local shopping and service centres is a different matter from the proposal, which might be of very great social value, for building houses, not along streets, but clustered around and facing an open space intended for children's play, and recreational functions, inaccessible to vehicular traffic, which would approach the houses from the outside.[32] Living in such a manner should greatly improve neighbourliness and remove feelings of isolation. But the numbers who could inhabit each cluster would be a few hundred at the most — not enough to support an economically competitive shopping centre.

30. Abrasimov, Secretary of the Union of Soviet Architects, reported in *Pravda* (Moskva), 6 June 1960.
31. Newcombe, *Journal of Town Planning Institute* (March 1968).
32. L. Wolfe, *The Reilly Plan* (after a plan prepared by Sir Charles Reilly for Birkenhead in 1947).

16

Urban Traffic and Transport

In the two previous chapters we have analyzed the distribution in urban areas on the one hand, of residences, and on the other hand, of employment in manufacture and in other forms of business, and the factors influencing such distributions. These locations of residences and business are of course the source from which urban transport and traffic arise.

This chapter cannot do more than give an outline of what has now become a vast and ever-expanding subject. Traffic engineering and management is now a business in which large numbers of experts are actively engaged, as well as being a field with its own large output of research, teaching, and scientific literature.

Some references were made in the previous chapter to goods traffic within urban areas, which is expected to be at its heaviest to and from factories and warehouses. In the past such businesses needed proximity to railway lines and waterfronts; but now that most goods traffic is by road they have been freed from this constraint, and there has been a sustained movement to more spacious suburban locations. While goods vehicles contribute to traffic difficulties, the most acute problems arise from the large and increasing volume of passenger vehicle traffic, to which this chapter will be devoted.

Widespread interest is now felt and strong feelings aroused on the question of urban passenger traffic, particularly the increasing use of private cars rather than public transport. Will the rising price of fuel reverse this trend? Can we or should we attempt to reverse the trend towards low residential densities, recognizing however that this could only be done by great efforts sustained over a long period of years?

It may be worth stating the principal conclusions before we examine the details. These are derived from the pioneering book on the subject, *The Urban Transportation Problem,* a combined study in economics and engineering.[1] This book was published in 1966, since which date

1. J. R. Meyer, J. F. Kain, and M. Wohl, *The Urban Transportation Problem* (Cambridge, Mass.: Harvard University Press, 1966).

rises in labour relative to other costs have told still further against labour-intensive rail and bus transport relative to private cars.

It is frequently said (with justification) that direct cost comparisons are invalid, on the grounds that a railway is supposed to meet all its costs, whereas bus and private car transport has all the costs of its road, and sometimes of its parking space, provided at public expense. One of the great merits of the Meyer, Kain, and Wohl study is that it takes all these public costs, including land required for roads and parking, fully into account. They added however that in the United States of America expenditure on urban roads, in comparison with rural, is not high, and does not appear to be subsidized, that is, is less than the sum of all taxes paid by road vehicles (true also in other countries).

Interest is reckoned at six per cent, and all capital investment depreciated according to its estimated average service life, ranging from fifty years for structures to twelve years for buses.

As is well known, the cardinal problem of public transport is that vehicles and staff have to be available to carry the heavy traffic in the short morning and evening rush-hour periods, but are largely unoccupied during the rest of the day. Under these conditions it is reasonable to charge all the overhead expenses to the rush hour traffic. The results are presented in a series of diagrams (see Diagram 26 for a representative example), on various assumptions about residential density along the transport corridor, and length of the downtown distribution system.[2]

The principal conclusions are outstanding, namely that is worth constructing a suburban railway (it is a different matter to use a railway already constructed in the past) only when the rush hour traffic on any given route reaches the very high figure of 40,000 passengers per hour. Such volume of traffic can only arise in a city which is not only very large, but also of high residential density, which is true only of very few cities in the world. (One of these cities, of course, is Tokyo, where some railway lines have been carrying 120,000 persons/hour, and believe that they could carry up to a theoretical maximum of 160,000 persons/hour.)[3] For traffic between 10,000 and 40,000 per hour the most economical form of transport is by bus, running on priority tracks or freeways for the main part of its route. This should be well within the capacity of a single lane, which has been estimated at

2. Over-all home-downtown passenger-trip costs for high residential density along corridor, hourly downtown passenger trip originations of ten per block at the home end, ten-mile line-haul facility, and two-mile downtown distribution system route length.
3. Kagayama, *Traffic Quarterly* (Oct. 1965).

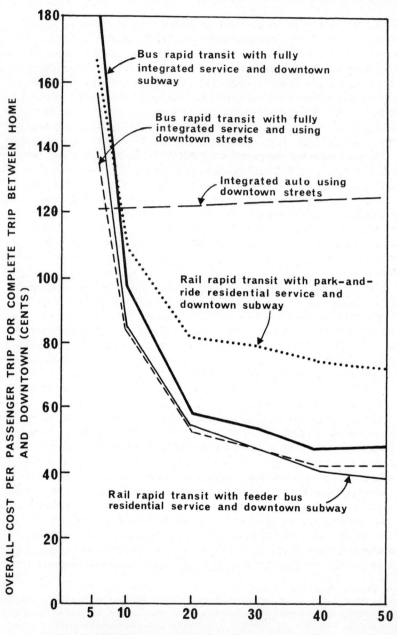

Diagram 26.

1,450 buses/hour at a speed of fifty-three kilometres/hour.[4] Such buses are to collect passengers in residential areas and then run express to the central business district in reserved lanes on freeways (the costs of which have been charged to them in this comparison). They would then have to use the central business districts streets for distribution. Running railways to the edge of the central business district, followed by transfer of the passengers to specialized vehicles, is rarely economic. Below ten thousand travellers per hour the private car is the most economical.

A more economical bus service is *not* to be expected in the larger cities. A survey of British municipal bus services led to the conclusion that the provision of bus services showed diseconomies of scale.[5]

The city of Nottingham has been conducting an extensive experiment on priority rights for buses, including a radio device which enables a bus driver approaching a traffic lamp to alter it in his favour. The results however have been disappointing. A government report states that the experiment gives "little reason to expect car drivers to transfer to bus".[6]

Experiments in the United States indicate that a technology is now available to allow control and selection of traffic entering freeways. This will mean that it will be possible for traffic at all times on the freeways to run uncongested. This will make it possible to give priority to buses, perhaps to commercial vehicles, or perhaps to fully occupied cars.

The monorail, which has captured so much public attention, ever since Edwardian times, proves to have very serious stability and switching problems and is also costly.

While the *Urban Transportation Problem* was published in 1966, its principal conclusions first appeared in the form of an expert report by the three authors, commissioned by President Kennedy. Kennedy however appears to have acted first and to have read the report afterwards; he went directly against its main conclusions and asked Congress to authorize $500 million (which would buy a great deal more then than it would now) for the construction of urban railways. The response was ambiguous. In Los Angeles, a city notorious for its low residential densities and dependence on private car transport, a survey showed that only 4.7 per cent of those questioned said that they would use a rapid transport system if constructed plus 2.6 per cent

4. Herman, Third Conference Australian Road Research Board, 1966.
5. J. S. Wabe and O. B. Coles, "Short and Long-Run Cost of Bus Transport in Urban Areas" *Journal of Transport Economics and Policy* 9, no. 2 (May 1975) p. 127.
6. Department of the Environment, *Transport and Road Research* (London: 1976), p. 8.

who said that they probably would.[7] On the other hand 86.8 per cent said that they believed Los Angeles needed a rapid transit system. People somehow think that it would be good for other people, but not for themselves. Repeatedly, the Los Angeles city authorities have been on the brink of deciding to construct a suburban railway system, then have wisely rejected the proposal. A professional estimate was that it would handle only 2 per cent of the traffic, at a cost of $800 million, whereas a $1,600 million investment in freeways was expected to handle twenty per cent of the traffic.[8]

The city which did accept President Kennedy's offer of a subsidy, by a narrow majority in a local referendum, was San Francisco. San Francisco does indeed have an unusual problem, owing to the long Bay crossing to the eastern suburbs. The present writer was in San Francisco shortly after the referendum; one honest citizen explained that he had voted for the proposal on the grounds that he thought that it would increase the value of his property. The Bay Area Rapid Transit venture has been an unmitigated financial disaster.[9] Interest and depreciation charges alone cost approximately $1 per journey, before making any provision for operating costs. These costs were at prices of the early 1970s, and would be a great deal higher now.

With the low residential densities prevailing in all modern cities, the use of a suburban railway system would require "park and ride" (or alternatively "kiss and ride", where the wife drives the husband to the railway and then returns home); both forms of transport involve substantial costs, but may obviate the purchase of a second car.

But all these relativities should be altered, many people say, by the great rise in the price of fuel. Investigations show that they are mistaken. What has risen so markedly has been the price of crude oil. But the price which the vehicle operator pays for his fuel is something very different. Some eighty to ninety per cent (until the recent rise in crude oil prices) of the price paid by the vehicle operator for fuel represented the costs of international and internal transport, refining, storage, and distribution – not to mention a very substantial bite of taxation. These elements in the cost of fuel may be expected, on the whole, to have risen in price no more than the general price level.

What we must examine therefore is the *crude oil* element in relation to total transport costs, beginning about 1970, then allowing for subsequent rises in crude oil prices. The initial figures (Table 105) for 1970 are extraordinarily low (even if we make a small addition for the crude oil component in refining and transport costs).

7. Meyer and others, *The Urban Transportation Problem* (Cambridge, Mass.: Harvard University Press, 1966, p. 105.
8. G. W. Hilton, *Traffic Quarterly* (July 1967).
9. J. F. Kain, private communication.

Table 105. Fuel and total costs in United States cents/vehicle kilometer, about 1970.

	Overall cost[a] per passenger trip cents	Do per passenger/ km	Do per vehicle/ km[c]	Energy requirements kilojoules/ vehicle km[d]	Equivalent in kg. crude oil	Value crude at 1970 prices[e]	Crude energy cost as % of all costs
Motorcycle				2,040	.046	.044	
Car	81[b]	4.5	7.1	4,360	.10	.096	1.4
Bus	34[b]	1.89	94.5	12,180	.27	.259	0.3
Suburban train[f]			47.4	220,000	5.0	4.8	1.0

a. Including full allowance for public costs incurred for roads, parking, and so on.

b. From diagram in Meyer, Kain, Wohl, p. 300. Refers to medium residential density along corridor, ten miles line haul, and two mile down town distribution system, with over 20,000 passenger volume per hour per corridor at maximum load points.

c. Calculated from average loading assumptions (1.6 and 50 respectively) stated in the text.

d. Brown & Lawlor, Consumption of Transport Energy in Australia 1975-6 Canberra: Bureau of Transport Economics.

e. 1970 prime crude f.o.b. Ras Tanura, Arabia $1.30/barrel, i.e. 0.96 cents kg (International Financial Statistics).

f. N. Clark, Bulletin No. 11, Transport Section Civil Engineering Department, University of Melbourne. p. 19 show direct operating costs in 1970-71 at $4.6/train mile or $6.8 including full allowance for interest and depreciation i.e. $4.23/train km. or $4.74 U.S. currency.

In allowing for the effects of the rise in the price of crude oil, we must take into account only the *real* rise in price, that is, the extent to which oil prices have risen more than the general price level which itself, in the leading industrial countries, has about doubled since 1970. The oil exporting countries claim that, apart from their large initial price rise in 1973, subsequent crude oil price rises have only about kept pace with the rise in the world prices of manufactured goods which they import. This no longer appears to be true.

But even if we allow that the price of crude oil has risen five or even ten fold, in real terms, that is, in excess of the rate of the general rise in prices, this will still only make a slight difference to the relative costs of different forms of urban transport.

The costs in the table relating to crude oil consumption are per vehicle/kilometre. If we want to know costs per passenger/ kilometre we must of course specify the average number of passengers per vehicle. Meyer *et al.* assume an average of 1.6 passengers per car, which may be high – 1.1 passengers per car for "park and ride" (by railway). The bus calculations are made on filling the average American-sized bus with fifty seats (in other countries buses are generally smaller). But this calculation is made for the cost per vehicle/kilometre in the rush hours only, when it is presumed to be filled. Taking the day as a whole, the average rate of occupancy must be far lower.

Some bus operators are only able to expect an average occupancy, taking the day as a whole, as low as twenty per cent.

The basic predicament of the public transport operator, something so obvious that people fail to see it, is that, however skilfully he organizes the movement of his vehicles, in the rush hour, when he needs them most, nearly half his vehicles must be travelling in the wrong direction.

The extent of train occupancy depends, of course, upon the size of the city. In other words, going back to our original comparison, if the rush hour traffic is as high as forty thousand travellers per hour, it is possible to carry them closely fitted into long trains, running at short intervals, at low cost; but this is not possible in smaller cities, with lower traffic volume.

Returning to the question of crude oil consumption (or its equivalent in coal for generating electric power for railways) we see that fuel use in private cars can be reduced to the same order of magnitude as the use in public transport, if more passengers are carried per car – and also, it might be added, if cars were smaller. Estimates of price elasticity of demand for fuel will be considered below. Even very substantial rises in the price of fuel are not however likely to have large immediate effects, but they may in the long run, by encouraging the use of smaller cars.

Consideration should be given (this principle has already been applied in Singapore) to giving parking and traffic priorities to smaller cars, and also to those carrying a full complement of passengers. This brings the authors of *The Urban Transportation Problem* to one of their most drastic proposals, namely the abolition of the system of taxi licensing. They see however little possibility of their proposal being adopted, principally, as they candidly admit, because of the degree of graft in municipal politics. (The City of Washington does however have almost free entry into the taxi business; likewise London, though confining operators to the use of a peculiar type of vehicle, with the imposition of an unnecessarily difficult geographical test.) At present, in most cities, cars can be shared, outside the family circle, only by a system of car-pooling, difficult to organize, and imposing complete rigidity of daily movement time-tables. To offer a lift, even to a friend, while asking him to pay something towards the cost of the journey, infringes insurance requirements. Taxi monopoly it certainly is — anyone retiring from the business can sell his licence for a very large sum. Present holders of licences would of course have to be compensated, but the monopoly should be abolished, and anyone (except perhaps those with known criminal records) should be allowed to carry passengers on any terms which he is able to negotiate. Also everything possible should be done to encourage multiple hiring. Anyone who defends the taxi monopoly, and restrictions on multiple hiring, while at the same time complaining about the use of fuel, is totally incoherent. The abolition of the taxi monopoly would cheapen travel, save fuel, reduce congestion; and would have one further great advantage, to which hardly any attention has been drawn, namely that it would provide employment opportunities for the unskilled.

City centre employment is now almost everywhere stationary or declining. In London, after a rise[10] in the numbers entering the Central London area 7.00–10 a.m. from 1,178,000 in 1953 to 1,394.000 in 1960 (mostly by public transport), in the short period 1966–71, employment[11] within two kilometres of Piccadilly Circus fell 7.6 per cent, as against the fall in the whole London region of 5.2 per cent. (The two to four kilometre distance zone, where congestion is also acute, showed a fall of only 3.0 per cent.) In Melbourne the fall was more dramatic.[12] Between 1961 and 1971 the number of work-

10. *The Paper Metropolis,* quoting a London Transport Executive.
11. Greater London Council, private communication.
12. K. O'Connor and C. A. Maher, Geography Department, Monash University, Australian and New Zealand Association for the Advancement of Science, 1977 Conference.

travellers to the Central Business District expressed as a proportion of all workers fell by proportions ranging from 13 to 32 per cent for the various suburban districts of residence — median fall 25 per cent, with the fall most marked for travellers from the outer suburbs. The Melbourne authorities, in spite of having their succeeding predictions of increased city centre employment repeatedly falsified, have been engaged in the enormously expensive undertaking of constructing an underground railway, in the expectation that the trend will be eventually reversed.

In many (not all) cities in the United States the fall in employment in the Central Business District began as early as the 1950s.

In Chicago the peak had been reached in 1948 — shortage of cars apparently had the effect of discouraging the suburbanization of employment.[13]

It would certainly be unwise to plan for the expansion of city centre employment, as do most projectors of urban railway systems.

In the previous chapter we saw something of the nature of the employments still carried on in the city centre. Increasingly, travel to the city centre is now required from the two opposite ends of the social spectrum. On the one hand professional men, financiers, government and business administrators, and the like; on the other hand, comparatively low-paid workers in the locally needed services — transport, restaurants, and the like. There may be a case for subsidizing the travel of the poorer group, but there is no case for subsidizing the transport of high-income workers. The average family income of workers using public transport in the United States in 1960 was found to be $6,466, as against the all-workers' average of $5,660.[14]

Public transport to city centres is now generally subsidized by national and local taxation, often heavily, and in any proposals for newly constructed public transport (like the Bay Area Rapid Transit in San Francisco, mentioned above), it is taken for granted that the main cost will be met from public funds. In Australian capital cities, taking into account all costs including interest and depreciation, fares paid on suburban railways cover less than half, in some cases less than a quarter of the costs.[15] For bus and tram services, though now requiring considerable subsidies, the case is not so extreme.

The Chicago Area Transportation Survey estimated that bus

13. *Chicago Area Transportation Survey* Vol. 2, p. 121.
14. M. Wohl, "Users of Urban Transportation Services and Their Income Circumstances" *Traffic Quarterly* 24, no. 1 (1970).
15. Nicholas Clark, Bulletin No. 11, Transport Section Civil Engineering Department, University of Melbourne, 1973; and other sources.

services were unremunerative for population densities below 9500 persons/square kilometre of residential land, that is, for 105 square metres/person or more of residential land. Turning back to the Table 105 in Chapter 15, and multiplying together the first two columns (total square metres/person x proportion of land residential) we find that it is generally only in the "old" cities that such densities prevail.

Insofar as subsidies are justified by the genuine economic externality of reducing congestion, while railways and subways deserve more subsidy (reckoned per passenger/kilometre carried during rush hours) than buses, subsidies at present orders of magnitude cannot be justified. Subsidies to bus services should also be available for private bus services at the same rate as for public.

If rail and subway services to the centres of large cities were charged at full cost, including interest and depreciation (less any subsidy genuinely calculated to represent their value in reducing congestion), two consequences would follow. The employers of the lower paid service workers in the city centre would have to raise their wages, in some cases reduce the service offered, or move to suburban locations (for example, some of the retail businesses still carried on in city centres). Meanwhile the higher-paid salaried and businessmen, who in most cases could not change their workplace, would have an incentive to move their residences closer to the centre (while at the same time having less incentive to reside close to railway or subway stations).

These movements would have their reflections in the price of urban land (to be dealt with in Chapter 17). They would reduce the demand for and the price of business land in the city centre; and of residential land in the outer suburbs, particularly land now high priced because of its proximity to railway stations. There would be countervailing movements raising the prices of business land in the suburbs and of residential land nearer the city centre; but these would probably be of a lesser order of magnitude. In net effect, the subsidies on rail and subway suburban transport are subsidies to the owners of certain types of land — for which there is no social justification.

The proposal to tax congestion as an adverse economic externality is not new — it was proposed by Pigou as long ago as 1920,[16] when road congestion was a rarity. Smeed showed that, if V is actual average speed and A speed on the uncongested road, then the costs imposed by congestion on other users are proportional to $(A-V)/V^2$.[17] The

16. A. C. Pigou, *The Economics of Welfare* (London: Macmillan, 1920).
17. R. J. Smeed, *Manchester Statistical Society Proceedings* (1961).

reduction in average speed by increasing numbers of vehicles, and other factors, is described by Wardrop.[18]

Let v = average speed miles/hour

w = roadway width in feet

q = average flow car equivalents/hour (bus = 3 equivalents, goods vehicles 1.5, motorcycle 1/3, light van 1)

f = controlled intersections/mile

λ = average proportion of effective green light time

Then $v^{-1} = (31 - 140/W - .0244\, q/w)^{-1} + f(1000 - 6.8\, q/\lambda w)^{-1}$.

The additive second term shows the effect on speed of number of intersections, whatever the traffic volume — hence the case for freeways.

A simpler formula (also favoured by Smeed[19]) can be used for most purposes, namely $q/w = 68 - 0.13v^2$; meaning that however low the average speed, traffic in vehicles/hour cannot exceed 68 x road width in feet; this is the capacity of the intersections.

For some purposes we need to relate average speed to distance from city centre — as we proceed outward numbers both of vehicles and of intersections decrease. Angel & Hyman[20] found in Manchester that at distance x from the city centre

Average speed miles/hour $= 18.5 - 12.5e^{-.56x}$

These formulae must not however be regarded as permanent, as road conditions improve. Inverting the formula to make speed (v) a function of volume in passenger-car equivalents/hour (q) the results for London were[21]

1952 $\quad v = 31.3 - q/89$

1964–6 $\quad v = 30.2 - q/116$

From these functions, and estimates of the loss inflicted on other vehicles by congestion delays, numerous calculations have been made of economically optimum rates of congestion tax. A study by Roth is quoted (Table 106) because he specifically takes into account the elasticity of demand for car travel; clearly, if the elasticity of price response is very low, a higher tax will be needed to discourage the congestion-creating vehicles.[22] The formula used is slightly different from that quoted above:

18. J. G. Wardrop, "Journey Speed and Flow in Central Urban Areas" *Traffic Engineering and Control* 9, no. 11 (1968), p. 528.
19. R. J. Smeed, "Traffic Studies and Urban Congestion" *Journal of Transport Economics and Policy* 2, no. 1 (Jan. 1968).
20. Angel and Hyman, Centre for Environmental Studies Working Paper CES WP 65.
21. Thompson, *Journal of Transport Economics and Policy* (Jan. 1968).
22. Roth, *International Statistical Institute Proceedings* (1963).

Table 106. Optimum Rate of Congestion Tax ("old pence"/mile).

Average speed miles/hour	Vehicles/hour	Assumed price elasticity		
		2.2-3.4	0.7-1.1	0.4-0.7
12	1,100	7.7	10.2	11.6
10	1,283	10.6	14.1	19.6
8	1,467	15.2	19.6	22.8

$$v \ (miles/hour) = 24 - .0109 \ (vehicle/hour)$$

Whereas total costs per vehicle (note that these are in the "old pence" of the 1960s of 240 to the £, not 100 to the £ as now) are estimated at 4.1 pence/mile plus 224 pence for each hour journey length.

Engineers have available a whole array of devices, once the political decision is made to impose a congestion tax, which will make it possible to tax travel or parking in congested areas, varying the rates between streets or between times of day if required, by impulses sent to a sealed meter in the car from cables in the road, or by other devices. Before such taxation can rationally be imposed however we have to have an estimate of the price elasticity of demand for car travel, on which subject unfortunately the information is still confused. We must look for long-run rather than short-run elasticity; in the short run people may make fewer or shorter shopping or social trips, but it is in the long run that they made decisions about living nearer their work, running a smaller car, and so on. We must also distinguish the price elasticity for car travel, all other things being equal, from the cross-elasticity of demand for public transport. If this rises, it will reduce private car transport, but in most modern cities the proportion of traffic carried by public transport is now so low that even a substantial change in it should only have a minor effect on demand for private transport.

We must also remember that people respond to duration as well as to price of journey. Insofar as congestion can be reduced, people will undertake more travel, thus partially offsetting – to an extent not yet investigated – the effect of the congestion tax.

We may first consider a thorough study which shows (Table 107) how many other factors have to be taken into account besides the money cost of the journey, and the fundamental distinction between work journeys and shopping journeys.[23]

23. T. A. Domencich, G. Kraft, and J. P. Valette, "Estimation of Urban Travel Behaviour: An Economic Demand Model" *Highway Research Record*, 238 (1968).

Table 107. Demand Elasticities.

	Work journeys	Shopping journeys
Money cost	− .07	−1.65
Distance	− .49	− .88
Time in car	− .82	−1.02
Journey time out of car . . . . . (walking from car park, etc.)	−1.44	−1.44
Cross elasticities:		
Public transport distance . .	+ .14	+ .09
Public transport access	+ .37	−

Separate analyses for work and shopping journeys, taking a number of factors into account, gave the above results.

The price elasticity is very low for work journeys, as might have been expected. Types of journeys not covered (social, recreational, and so on) may be expected to show an elasticity similar to shopping journeys, and we may construct a weighted average of the figures 0.07 and 1.65, remembering however that work journeys constitute well over half the mileage. Note also the high elasticities for time, in both cases, which may produce the offsetting effect on traffic volume mentioned above.

For price elasticities of demand for public transport we have results ranging from 1.3 to 0.2, and similar ranges for demand for private transport, and for the income elasticities (Table 108). The confusion is somewhat mitigated however when we remember that both price and income elasticities tend to fall, as has been observed for many commodities, with rising real income. This is apparent when we compare the results in the table for different countries, or the fall in the Norwegian elasticities between the 1930s and the 1950s.

One consequence of such a fall in elasticities with rising real income will make the checking of congestion by taxes of any kind progressively more difficult.

Kain's negative income elasticity of demand for public transport is an isolated figure, and may be due to local factors in Detroit. From observations of the stability of the ratios between travel time and earnings in Chicago, Muth concludes that the income elasticity of demand for marginal transport costs is about one.[24]

The difference of both income and price elasticities between large

24. R. F. Muth, *Cities and Housing: a Spatial Pattern of Urban Residential Land Use* (Chicago: Chicago University Press, 1969), p. 309.

Table 108. Price and Income Elasticities of Demand for Urban Personal Transport.

		Price Elasticities		Income Elasticities	
		Public Transport	Private Transport	Public Transport	Private Transport
SA	Baum[1]	.18			
	Curtin[2]	.21			
	Powell[3]	.3	2.1	.4	4.3
	Phlips[4]				
	Short Period	.17		.95	
	Long Period	.43		.95	
	Fuel Short Period		.11		5.8
	Fuel Long Period		.68		1.54
	Wheaton[5]			.25	
	Kain[6]			-.76	.21
	Lane[7]				
	Price elasticity		.73		
	Duration elasticity		.87		
	Chicago Area Transportation Study[8]				
	Price elasticity	.89			
	Duration elasticity	1.85			
	Warner[9]				
	Price elasticity	1.0	.2		
	Duration elasticity		.2		
AUSTRALIA	Powell[10]				2.5
UK	Thomson[11]		1.3		
	Department of the Environment[14]	.3			
GERMANY	Baum[1]	.32			
	Nord Rhein — Westfalen experiment[8]	low			
FRANCE	Bresard[8]	1.0			
NETHERLANDS	Amsterdam & The Hague[12] ..	.75		2.2	
	Amersfoort[12]	1.3		.8	
NORWAY	Amundsen,[13] 1930's	.7	2.4	2.7	4.0
	1950's	.9	1.9	1.8	2.7
	Fuel 1930's		2.2		6.4
	1950's		1.0		2.0

1. H.J. Baum, *Journal of Transport Economics and Policy*, January, 1973. Medians of twelve cities ranging from .08 to .30 in the United States and seven cities ranging from .27 to .41 in Germany in 1955-6.
2. Curtin, Highway Research Record, No. 213, 1968; work journeys.
3. *Southern Economic Journal*, October 1968.
4. University of Louvain, private communication.
5. American Economic ·Review (Sept. 1977), p. 624. White non-manual workers, San Francisco. Allowance made for time as well as money cost of journey.
6. Review of Economics & Statistics, Feb. 1964; Detroit data; related to family incomes.
7. Review of Economics & Statistics (August 1970), p. 321.
8. See Text.
9. *Stochastic Choice of Mode in Urban Travel*, Evanston 1962.
10. *Econmetrica* (July 1966).
11. Journal of the Royal Statistical Society (1967). Mean of results obtained by several different methods.
12. Netherlands Economic Institute Die Entwikkeling van het locaal personen vervoer in Amersfoort 1955 (Population of Amersfoort 63,000).
13. Artikler fra Statistisk Sentral byra No. 7 (1963).
14. *Transport and Road Research* (1977), p. 8, Department of the Environment, London. This estimate is for season ticket (commuting) travel: for midday reduced fare travel elasticity was estimated at 0.8. The same publication (1976, p. 2) estimates 0.3 elasticity for bus travel from an international study.

and small towns in the Netherlands is striking. These represent long-period elasticities largely representing, it may be, peoples' choice of residence in relation to their work places.

An interesting result in relation to the recent rise in the price of fuel was obtained in the United States of America.[25] This was derived from a study of bus travel in Tucson, eliminating the effects of length of route served, school holidays, and the "queueing period" for gasoline (Dec. 1973–March 1974). The elasticity of bus travel with respect to the price of gasoline was as high as 0.42. As gasoline constituted only about one third of the total expense of car travel, the elasticity of bus travel with respect to the full relative price of car travel will be much higher — though it is not permissible to multiply 0.42 directly by 3.

On the other hand, the ratio of public to private transport in such a city is probably very low, so that a five per cent or more rise in bus travel may mean a fall of only one per cent in private travel.

A very interesting analysis of numbers of journeys in relation to time required for journey (which may be assumed to be approximately proportional to expense) for Paris in 1947,[26] when few cars were available, relates of course to the cherished French custom of going home for midday *déjeuner,* requiring four daily journeys. At this time a little over one-third of all workers (average journey twenty minutes each way) went home at midday. Those who did not had an average journey of forty minutes each way; so (although a limited number spent much longer) the *average* daily travel time was eighty minutes, alike for four-journey and two-journey travellers. This suggests (although with qualifications) a price elasticity of about one. There is a curious similarity to the results of the British National Travel Survey, which will be given below. The suggestion that combined price elasticity for all types of journey is about one is also made by Wardrop.[27]

Travellers of course are not homogeneous in their response to price, and questionnaires show a distribution of replies. A questionnaire among car travellers to Central London in 1965 (average journey, eighteen kilometres) as to how many of them would change from car to public transport for their journey to work under various circumstances showed that fifty-one per cent would do so if public transport were free, and forty-four per cent at a fare of one shilling (.05£).

25. D. E. Agthe and R. B. Billings, "Impact of Gasoline Prices on Urban Bus Ridership" *Annals of Regional Science* 12, 1 (March 1978), pp. 90–96.
26. Bresard, *Population* (Paris) April–June 1948), p. 371.
27. Wardrop, *The Theory of Traffic Flow* (Amsterdam: Elsevier Publications, 1961).

Thirty-five to forty per cent said that public transport would have to become quicker, more frequent, or more comfortable.[28]

But a more recent study estimates that free public transport would reduce peak hour car use for travel to and from work (by those not needing their cars at work) by only twenty-two per cent.[29] One reason may be that "perceived cost" of car travel is only .02£/kilometre.

In Chicago, at zero fares only thirty-two per cent would travel by railway, and fifteen per cent at a twenty cent fare (at prices of the early 1960s).[30] For those without access to the railway, and whose alternative to car travel would be the subway-and-elevated system, or buses, the proportions attracted by zero fares were only eighteen and thirteen per cent respectively. The authors went on to ask how many would travel by public transport if they were *paid* a dollar for each journey which they took. Even on this hypothesis, twenty-six per cent would still refuse railway transport, twenty-nine per cent subway, and thirteen per cent bus transport.

The belief that price elasticity of demand for urban transport might be at or above one induced Chicago Transit Authority in 1953 to make the interesting experiment of halving fares in non-rush hours.[31] Traffic increase, however, was disappointing, and there was a net revenue loss of five per cent. Critics may persist that the reduction was not maintained for long enough to give time for a number of people to alter their place of residence to take advantage of the lower fares. On the fact of it, this indicates a price elasticity of about 0.9, even in the short period, for non-work journeys.

Some estimates have been made for Chicago of elasticity with respect to both price and time (quoted in Table 117).[32] The time required to travel by public transport between the central business district and various outlying areas, expressed as a multiple of the time required for automobile travel, may be as high as 3, or as low as 0.6. This ratio, raised to the power of -1.85 and multiplied by 41.1, gives the expected percentage of journeys made by public transport, with quite a good fit. An equally good fit, however, is obtained by raising relative price to the power of -0.89, and multiplying by 7.4.

These exponents of 0.89 and 1.85 should give price and time elasticities for all journeys, including work journeys.

28. Penelope Williams, "Low Fares and Urban Transport Problem" *Urban Studies* 6, no. 1 (1969), p. 84.
29. A. J. Daly and S. Zachary, *Transport and Road Research Laboratory Supplementary Report 338,* (1977).
30. Moses and Williamson *Journal of Political Economy* (June 1963).
31. Schroeder, Metropolitan Transport Research.
32. *Chicago Area Transportation Study,* quoted by Mortimer, *Highway Research Bulletin* 203 (1958).

In a more recent German experiment, on the other hand, in the highly industrial district of Nord Rhein-Westfalen public transport monthly tickets were cheapened by two-thirds (by means of a special subsidy) over a period of eight months for ten thousand employees travelling to work by car.[33] Only thirteen per cent of them changed to public transport, indicating a low elasticity for work journeys.

We should apply these estimates of price elasticity to the changes in the relative prices of public and private transport which have been taking place. (Table 109)[34] In the 1950s and 1960s there was a great relative cheapening of private transport. Since 1972 there has been a reversal of this trend, not only because of gasoline and oil prices, which represented twenty-six per cent of the total cost of private transport in 1972, and rose by eighty-two per cent between 1972 and 1978. In this period non-fuel costs of private transport rose by forty-eight per cent, but public transport charges (apparently through increasing subsidization) rose by only thirty per cent.

Table 109. U.S. Public and Private Transport prices 1935 base.

	1935	1947-9	1955	1972	1978
Private	100	155.5	182.1	273.1	426.3
Public	100	122.4	202.8	461.9	610.2
Public/private	1	.787	1.114	1.691	1.431

"Public Transport" refers to intra-city travel only: "private" includes all journeys — intra-city cannot be separated from long distance — but the cost trends should be similar. In spite of the reversal of price trends, the volume of intra-city public transport increased by only eight per cent between 1972 and 1978, while the volume of private transport (including long distance) rose by twenty-two per cent. Many cities were abandoning or contracting their public transport services.

In the United States of America combined expenditure on private car travel plus intra-urban public transport as a percentage of all private expenditure rose from 9.2 in 1929 to 12.7 in 1953–56, since when it has slightly declined. There were only minor changes in the relative price of travel, so we may conclude that its income elasticity of demand was a little below one.

33. Quoted in *The Future of the British Car Industry* (1975), London: Central Policy Review Staff, 1975, p. 32.
34. Calculated from *United States National Accounts* Tables 2.6 and 2.7; prior to 1955 from *Monthly Labor Review* (1956).

A very original analysis by Goodwin gives distance travelled an income elasticity of 1.5, expenditure on travel 1.75, but time spent travelling 0.8.[35] Higher income families travel further, but faster and more expensively. Based on the British National Travel Surveys of 1965 and 1966 he established the following relationships.

Travel (including walking)   miles/person/week d
"   "   "   hours/person/week t
"   "   "   pence/person/week m
Post tax personal disposable
     income   £/person/week M

Then

$$t = 0.8M$$
$$d = 4.8M^{1.5}$$
$$m = 3.6M^{1.75}$$

It follows that

average speed varies with $M^{0.5}$
expenditure/mile varies with $M^{0.25}$
expenditure/hour varies with $M^{0.75}$

In the cities in which, until comparatively recently, our predecessors were living — and this remains true in most cities in the developing countries today — if you wanted to go from one place to another in the city, you walked. Only very few of the richest and the most influential went by carriage or on horseback. The invention of the omnibus (horse-drawn) is attributed to the famous seventeenth century physicist Pascal, but not many of the inhabitants of Paris at that time could afford to use it. In these cities dependent mainly upon walking, or even in the earlier and more expensive days of mechanical transport, there were the strongest incentives, as we have seen to bring together, in areas of high density, residences, workplaces, and public buildings.

Then came a stage, before the use of the car become widespread, of increasing availability and use of public transport, buses, trams, suburban railways, and subways. The Metropolitan Railway in London commenced service in 1863, with steam-driven underground trains. "The window sill was inches deep in soot" observed Sherlock Holmes and Dr Watson, when they succeeded in tracking down the house overlooking the Metropolitan Railway in South Kensington where the corpse had been placed on the roof of a train, to remain there till jolted by the points at Aldgate East. As the economy advanced,

35. P. B. Goodwin, University Traffic Unit, London University and Greater London Council, private communication.

more people could afford public transport, and to live further from their work (the cost of transport of course being a significant but certainly not the only factor in their choice of a place of residence). In smaller towns more people lived within walking or cycling distance of their workplaces. So far this period the demand for public transport is a fair indication of the demand for urban passenger transport in general (other than walking or cycling). With more recent data we also have to take private car transport into account.

First we must allow for the effect of city size on demand for transport. Then, in any one metropolitan area, we may expect the per head demand for public transport first to rise with increasing real incomes and size of city, then to pass its maximum and to fall with its displacement by private cars.

An interesting set of data for Germany in 1931, when there were few private cars and the economy was very depressed, for per head use of urban public transport in twenty cities of size down to sixty-three thousand population showed numbers of journeys per head rising with approximately the 0.75 power of population, the average length of journey with the 0.2 power.[36] There are indications however that for the larger cities, with more use of rail transport, the exponent falls below 0.75.

British experience in the 1930s was summarized (Table 110) in round figures.[37]

Table 110. Population & Public Transport.

Population of city	Under 50,000	250,000	500,000	1,000,000 & over
Public transport journeys/person/year	125	250	400	500

Up to 500,000 population these figures indicate an exponent of 0.4–0.5, lower for larger cities. On the other hand Netherlands cities in 1950, when private cars were still few, over a range from 10,000 to 836,000 population, showed an exponent of 1, that is, journeys per head proportional to population.[38] It may be that in other countries the exponent declines in larger cities because of increased opportunities for employment, shopping, and so on, in their suburbs, which were not present in the Netherlands cities in 1950.

Between 1954 and 1974 use of urban transit systems in U.S.A. fell

36. Buckner, International Statistical Institute, Proceedings of 1933 Conference.
37. Garden Cities and Town Planning Association, quoting F. Pick, London Transport. Evidence before Barlow Commission on Regional Policy, 1938.
38. Netherlands Economic Institute, *Die Entwikkeling van het locaal pesonenvervoer in Amersfoort* (1955).

48% and of railway commuter and taxi services by twenty-eight per cent.[39]

A survey of British cities in 1962 showed no clear relation between size of city and number of vehicular work journeys per head.[40] But the proportion (omitting those who walked or cycled to work, a high proportion in the smaller towns) who used public transport for their work journeys rose with size of town (Table 111).

Table 111. Population and Public Transport.

Population	Over 500,000	150,000-500,000	80,000-150,000
Number of towns	4	6	5
Proportion of work journey by public transport (median)	90	73	60

Very high figures have been attained in Japan (Table 112).[41] Excluding the small amount of traffic carried by private cars (it is not so much that the citizens cannot afford cars, but that they cannot obtain parking space) public transport traffic was as follows:

Table 112. Public Transport in Japan.

	Tokyo Area		Osaka Area	
	1955	1963	1955	1963
Population (million)	12.9	17.0	8.2	10.5
Journeys/person/year	399	562	358	480
Proportion by rail %	59	57	56	53

A survey in the United States covering twenty-five cities with populations down to four hundred thousand showed that the percentage of travellers entering the central business area by car averaged a little over sixty per cent, the proportion not significantly related to size of city, except for the three largest cities surveyed (Philadelphia thirty-seven, Chicago thirty-two, and New York seventeen per cent. The Los Angeles figure was sixty-six per cent.[42]

Australian capital city figures show (Table 113) only slight relationship to size of city, and rapid increase in car travel since 1970. Work

39. *United States National Accounts* Table 2.7.
40. *National Institute Economic Review* (May 1963).
41. Kagayama, *Traffic Quarterly* (Oct. 1965).
42. *The Exploding City,* published by *Fortune* magazine.

Table 113. Percentage of Journeys (Averages of Capital Cities) Australia.

	Work Journeys		School Journeys	
	1970	1974	1970	1974
Car	59.1	66.2	16.0	22.1
Public Transport	27.6	22.2	26.8	25.7
Walking and cycling	13.3	11.6	57.2	52.2

journeys to Central Business Districts, however, were over sixty per cent by public transport.[43]

Demand for urban travel by vehicular means is expected and is found to be a function of (i) income, (ii) family possession of no car, one car, two or more cars, (iii) how many of the household are going out to work, and (iv) suburban or central residence. These factors, unfortunately for the analyst, are closely interrelated. It is the higher-income families who on the average possess more cars, have more working members and schoolchildren, and reside in the suburbs.

Data for London (Table 114) classified not by the size of the family, but by the number of wage-earners, and by income, show that, for a given number of wage-earners, the second car leads to about as much additional traffic as the first, and that there is a pronounced income effect, not of course on work journeys, but on shopping and social journeys.[44] This may be in part due to the higher income families living further away from shopping centres and schools.

A similar Traffic Survey analysis, showing also the relative numbers at different income and car-ownership levels, is available for Melbourne in 1964 (Table 115). The figures relate to areas of median accessibility to public transport. The results are indeed strikingly similar to those for London.

Public transport obviously was the main means of transport for the no-car households, but it also constituted twenty to twenty-five per cent of the journeys for one-car and some ten per cent for the multiple-car households.

The Detroit data (Table 116) (whose compilers admit to some understatement, as recorded above) make it possible to analyze separately the effects of suburbanization and car ownership.[45] The number of journeys increases both with distance from centre and with car ownership, but apparently tending towards an upper limit.

43. Australian Bureau of Statistics, The Journey to Work and School (1976), Reference 17.5.
44. *London Traffic Survey,* Second Report (1966).
45. *Detroit Metropolitan Area Traffic Study* (1953).

Table 114. London, 1962: All journeys (excluding those on foot or by bicycle)/household/day (in areas enjoying normal rail and bus accessibility).

Family income	Households with 1 resident employed			Households with 2 or more residents employed		
	No car	1 car	2 or more cars	No car	1 car	2 or more cars
Below £1,000	2.06	4.05		3.54	5.74	
£1,000—£2,000	3.07	5.29	7.61	4.51	6.70	8.46
Over £2,000		6.63	10.95		7.68	11.46

Table 115. Vehicular Journeys Melbourne.

JOURNEYS/HOUSEHOLD/DAY

Household income $/year	Percentage of all households			One Earner households			Two Earner households		
	No car	1 car	2 or more cars	No car	1 car	2 or more cars	No car	1 car	2 or more cars
Under 2,500	22.2	12.4	0.5	2.19	4.15		4.69	4.97	
3,500—5,000	12.2	28.7	5.7	2.95	5.21	8.18	4.73	6.38	8.65
Over 5,000	2.1	8.3	7.8		7.79	11.76		8.07	11.63

Table 116. Vehicular Journeys/Household/Working Day, Detroit 1953.

Distance of residence from centre (kms)	NO-CAR HOUSEHOLDS		ONE-CAR HOUSEHOLDS		MULTI-CAR HOUSEHOLDS	
	All	Including public transport	All	Including public transport	All	Including public transport
Under 1.6	1.28	1.03				
1.6 to 4.8	1.88	1.37	5.07	1.12	8.56	.89
4.8 to 9.7	2.39	1.59	5.75	.99	8.66	.79
9.7 to 14.4	2.39	1.29	6.79	.75	11.14	.69
14.4 to 19.3	2.55	1.35	7.50	.64	10.45	.72
19.3 and over	2.52	1.07	7.83	.80	10.91	.78
ALL AREAS	2.22	1.39	6.83	.83	10.44	.78

Dependence upon public transport, for any given level of car ownership, is considerably less than in Melbourne.

The journeys other than by public transport for the no-car households represent lifts given by friends and relatives, and the occasional loan or hire of a car.

However a detailed study of the British city of Reading led to the conclusion that it was "unnecessary to include household location in the modelling of vehicular trip generation".[46]

Journeys between home and workplace and return constitute some forty-four per cent of all journeys.[47] It is these journeys, nearly all concentrated into rush hours, which are the main source of traffic congestion. The percentage distribution of journeys averaged over fifty American cities, is given in Table 117.[48]

e 117. Distribution of Journeys. Journeys from —

	Home	Work	Social & Recreational	Shopping	Other	Total
neys to:						
ome	—	19.5	9.2	5.6	6.5	40.8
ork	20.2	4.9	0.2	0.3	2.3	27.9
al & ational	8.7	0.5	1.7	0.4	0.7	12.0
ping	5.2	0.7	0.3	0.8	0.5	7.5
r	6.9	2.3	0.6	0.4	1.6	11.8
AL	41.0	27.9	12.0	7.5	11.6	100

A more detailed analysis of destinations of "Other" journeys for Chicago (where they constitute more than the 11.8 per cent average of all journeys) shows that 58 per cent of them were described as being on "Personal Business", 12 per cent to restaurants, 11 per cent to schools, and the remainder to carry other passengers or "joy-riding".[49]

From the sources previously quoted for Chicago and Detroit (remembering that there is estimated to be some deficiency in the Detroit figures) we can see the effects of different land uses in

46. Department of the Environment, *Transport and Road Research* (1976), p. 3.
47. Oi and Shuldiner, *An Analysis of Urban Travel Demands* North Western University Transportation Centre.
48. Curran and Stegmeier, *Public Roads* (Dec. 1958).
49. *Chicago Area Transportation Survey*, Vol. 1, pp. 37 and 65.

Table 118. Person-Trips Generated Per Day (Thousands).

| | CHICAGO | | DETROIT — Per square km net land use | | | | | | | |
| | Per '000 m² of floor area | Per sq.km of net land use | Central business district | Rest of inner zone | ZONES DISTANT FROM CENTRE, IN KM. | | | | | Whole area |
					1.6-4.8	4.8-9.7	9.7-14.5	14.5-19.3	Over 19.3	
Residential	34	12.0	181	46	16	14	10	7	3	7.2
Manufacture	23	12.2	38	52	23	12	9	9	2	9.1
Transport	20	2.1								
Commercial: retail 75 service 58 wholesale 16		44.8	444	51	48	54	69	80	45	66.4
Public buildings	38	13.1	234	90	22	7	11	8	4	8.1
Open space	—	1.0	—	7	2	1	2	1	—	0.7
Weighted average	36	9.5	376	55	18	14	12	8	4	8.9

generating traffic (Table 118). Measurement can be per square kilometre of net land use, or per square metre of floor space.

It is commercial land which is the main generator of traffic, even in the outer suburbs. Traffic generation per square kilometre is of the same order of magnitude for land use for residences, manufacture, or public buildings. Except for commercial land, the figures fall off rapidly as we proceed away from the city centre.

From a traffic engineer's point of view the economic optimum density, considered in relation to all traffic costs, is only some 5,400 vehicle destinations/square kilometre/day.[50] There was clearly room for much further decentralization in Chicago and Detroit at the time to which these tables refer.

The patterns of journey distribution by length are shown in Diagram 27 for three types of journeys in Chicago, and work journeys in San Diego.[51] In the smaller and more recently developed city (as we saw in the previous chapter for shopping journeys) relatively fewer people live near their work, but also relatively fewer travel over seven miles. In Athens the average work journey was 3.75 kilometres (36 per cent of journeys were below 1.5 kilometre).[52]

A study of a number of United States and Canadian cities indicates that average work-trip length is generally proportional to the size of the metropolitan area population to the power of 0.3.[53] Social and recreation trip lengths vary with the 0.7 power of work trip lengths. However an older and more compact city such as New Orleans may show an average work trip length far below that expected from its population. This report also suggests that the distribution of work-trip lengths might be expressed by a gamma function.

A trip length distribution diagram for the whole city may conceal however important differences between its zones. Data for London in 1971 (Diagram 28) show that, while those residing near the centre nearly all have short work journeys — that was why they came here, in most instances, to trade dwelling space against travel time, as shown in Chapter 14 — those who live further out show a longer but less regular distribution pattern.[54] Journeys to the city centre (indicated by the secondary peaks) are more numerous than to neighbouring destinations; this was only to be expected. At a distance of twenty-

50. A. Black, "Optimizing Density of Development with Respect to Transportation Cost" *Highway Research Record* 207 (1967).
51. *Chicago Area Transportation Survey* and Hall, *Highway Research Bulletin* 203.
52. *Ekistics* (Aug. 1965), p. 108.
53. Alan M. Voorhees and Associates, *Factors and Trends in Trip Lengths* (United States Highway Research Board, 1968), p. 9.
54. Greater London Council, private communication.

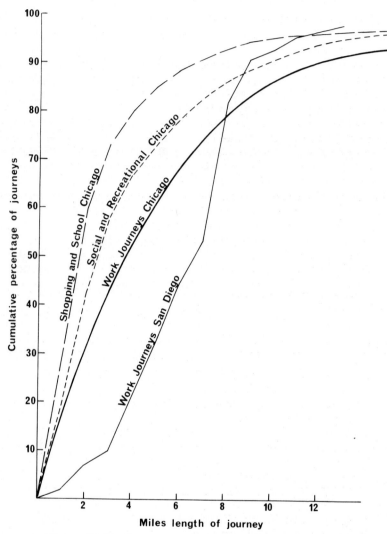

Diagram 27. Distribution of trip lengths in Chicago & San Diego.

eight to thirty kilometres from the centre, short journeys to local employment become relatively more important, but the peak, representing journeys to the centre, is nearly as marked as in the previous diagram.

A full theory of trip length distributions is still beyond our reach.

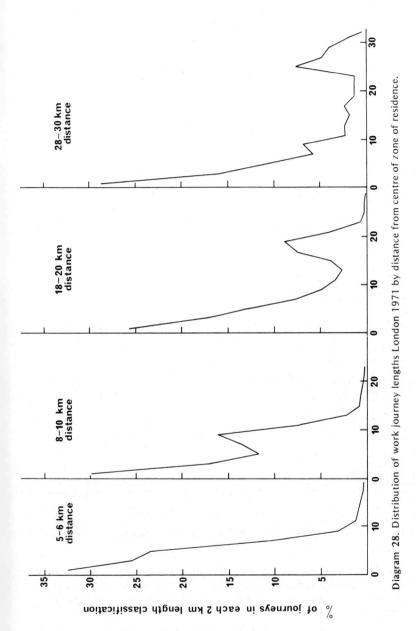

Diagram 28. Distribution of work journey lengths London 1971 by distance from centre of zone of residence.

The distribution of work journeys by duration is less dispersed, because those who make the longer journeys usually have faster means of conveyance. Distribution diagrams are somewhat irregular owing to memory faults (abnormally few people "remember" a journey within the twenty-five to twenty-nine minute range; they usually round it off to thirty minutes). Journeys of course are shorter in the smaller cities, and the distribution more sharply peaked about the median. Those living further from the city centre make longer journeys — up to a point, beyond which they begin to find local employment.

A comprehensive Australian sample recorded (Table 119) journeys by occupational groups and sex (NS indicates no significant figure).[55]

Table 119. Journey Durations Australia.

	Percentage workers at home	Percentage with single journey over 60 mins.	Median duration of single journey (excluding home workers) (minutes)
ALL MALES	13.5	7.0	21.0
Professional and technical	7.7	10.0	23.7
Administrative and executive	10.2	5.4	21.4
Clerical	NS	14.9	28.5
ALL FEMALES	11.1	6.2	19.1
Clerical	7.7	10.4	22.8

The average male journey is not greatly in excess of the female and for both sexes clerical workers have the longest journeys, because so many of them work in the central business district. The classification by city size is shown in Table 120.

Account must be taken of Sydney's difficult topography, broken up by numerous arms of the sea, which has the effect of lengthening the median journey, and also, by the same token, as we saw in Chapter 14, increasing the residential density at which people are willing to settle.

Journeys to school of five to seventeen year olds had a median duration of 13.5 minutes: thirty per cent were by public transport, twenty per cent by car, and fifty per cent on foot or bicycle.

55. Australian Bureau of Statistics, *Journey to Work and Journey to School* (Aug. 1974), Reference 17.5, Tables 2, 8, 9 and 21.

Table 120. Journey Durations by City Size.

| | (Excluding home workers) | | | |
Population of metropolitan statistical area (millions)	Percentage with single journey over 60 mins.	Median duration of single journey minutes	Percentage of journeys by public transport
Sydney	2.9	15.3	30.5	29.7
Melbourne	2.6	10.0	24.5	24.4
Brisbane	0.9	7.0	23.3	20.8
Hobart	0.16	NS	18.3	19.5
Non-metropolitan		3.0	11.5	5.5

In the section of this chapter on demand elasticity, reference is made to Goodwin's systemization, of the longer journeys being on the average by faster transport, that is, income elasticity of time of transport being less than that of distance. Much of Goodwin's apparent "time elasticity" of 0.8 for vehicular journeys appears to represent transfers between the no-car–one-car multiple car categories. More recent British data indicate that, at a given level of car ownership, time spent on travel shows little response to income above a certain level, may indeed fall (Table 121).[56] Increased car ownership reduces the amount of time spent walking while raising vehicular travel time correspondingly so as to end up with an upper limit averaging some seventy-five minutes, at high income levels. Public transport (mostly long distance railway travel) represents quite a high proportion of time spent on travel by high-income families.

With such results before us, we inevitably have to face the problem of the "value of time", or to speak more precisely, how much money a traveller is willing to trade against one hour's travel time saved, under various circumstances. A review of information and some fresh researches have recently been published.[57] The present writer has undertaken a study reviewing as much as possible of the available information with an underlying idea that an hour's travel time saved is an objective piece of economic welfare or utility;[58] and that the amount of money which any person is prepared to sacrifice to secure it is a measure of the marginal utility of income to him. One of the most elementary propositions of economic theory is that the marginal utility of each unit of income declines as real income rises; meaning in our case that the number of hours against

56. *National Travel Survey 1972–73.*
57. I. G. Heggie, ed., *Modal Choice and the Value of Travel Time* (Oxford: 1976).
58. C. Clark, *Oxford Economic Papers* (July 1973).

Table 121. Travel Time in Minutes/Person/Day (National Travel Survey 1972—3).

Household income £/person/yr	NO CAR HOUSEHOLDS			ONE CAR HOUSEHOLDS			MULTIPLE CAR HOUSEHOLDS		
	Walking	Public transport	Total	Walking	Public transport	Total	Walking	Public transport	Total
Under 250	17.3	9.5	26.8	14.5	4.0	30.1	8.5	4.6	54.8
250—500	20.9	14.4	35.3	17.2	9.0	46.2			
500—750	23.3	16.4	39.7	17.8	12.7	54.6	12.9	12.4	54.1
750—1,000	24.8	27.3	52.1	16.5	14.3	58.9	12.3	8.8	60.9
1,000—1,500	28.1	42.8	60.9	17.1	15.1	67.0	10.8	11.1	65.8
1,500—2,000				17.8	14.9	81.2	12.5	13.3	73.0
Over 2,000	25.4	28.9	54.3	13.2	13.4	73.7	9.3	16.4	66.8

which the earner is willing to exchange one unit of income declines, or the proportion of his income which he is willing to exchange against one hour's travel time increases.

As we shall see below, we are oversimplifying matters when we speak of one "hour". Its effects differ according to whether the travel time saved consists of walking, waiting, or sitting in a vehicle; and whether it comes in units of five minutes, fifteen minutes, thirty minutes or whatever. But fore preliminary analysis we will still make evaluations per hour.

A similar relationship indicating declining marginal utility of income is found when we observe increases of real incomes historically, or in international comparisons, with higher real incomes associated with shorter working hours and longer holidays.[59]

The important question for us, and for others, is the rate at which marginal utility declines with real income. Frisch, in a pioneering study, defined income x as yielding marginal utility y and

$$\frac{dy/y}{dx/x}$$

as "flexibility coefficient".[60]

This coefficient itself declines with real income. Work on international comparisons of consumption analyzed on the linear expenditure system, and other consumption studies, show flexibility coefficients (sign reversed) falling from 3.5 or more in poorer countries, possibly to as low as 1.5.[61]

Valuations in money of travel time were first made by comparing the time sacrifices which travellers were willing to make to avoid toll roads and bridges. One pioneer estimate[62] put the value at \$1.20/hour for cars and \$1.80/hour for commercial vehicles, and another as high as \$2.28 in urban rush hours, \$1.10 for longer journeys.[63] Other methods were developed for analyzing records of choice of mode of travel.

An interesting new idea was to relate values of housing sites to the daily travel time which they were estimated to demand from their occupants.[64] Wabe, in a careful study, eliminated disturbing

59. C. Lluch, A. A. Powell, and R. A. Williams, *Patterns in Household Demand and Saving* (New York: Published for the World Bank by Oxford University Press, 1977).
60. Frisch, *Econometrica* (1964).
61. C. Lluch, A. A. Powell, and R. A. Williams, *Patterns in Household Demand and Saving* (New York: Published for the World Bank by Oxford University Press, 1977).
62. T. J. Fratar, *Traffic Quarterly* (Oct. 1949).
63. Lawton, *Traffic Quarterly* (Jan. 1950).
64. Mohring, *Journal of Political Economy* (June 1961), p. 248, quoting Pendleton.

effects due to density, social composition of the area (small), access to open country (considerable), local employment (not significant), and related 1968 site values to fares, indicating an effective interest rate of 10.7 per cent, and a valuation of travel time at £0.27/hour (about half average hourly earnings at that time).[65]

Muth relates prices of houses in Chicago to distances which have to be travelled on public transport.[66] Fares being uniform, travel costs are therefore time costs only. These were found to be per hour about 0.3 of average hourly earnings both in 1950 and in 1960.

For houses distant from public transport, and therefore dependent on car transport, he calculated marginal travel costs (assumed forty-two journeys/household/month) which, capitalized at six per cent, amounted to $118 in 1950 and $222 in 1960 for each additional mile of distance away from business and employment centres. These figures are of the right order of magnitude to explain the one per cent fall in house prices observed for each additional mile of distance outward.

Comparisons of rail or bus journeys on time saved, against extra money spent on air travel over long distances in Australia indicate (at prices of the 1960s) a time valuation of the order of only $1/hour.[67] But this is a biassed result; travellers by rail and bus are now largely pensioners, students, and others below average income.

It is generally agreed that travellers on work journeys value time (or their employers value it for them) at about their wage or salary rate.[68] What concerns us now is the time valuation in ordinary urban commuter travel.

Using results previously published,[69] and others, a function has been fitted which was found to show quite remarkably close agreement with comparative marginal utilities of income shown by two other studies published simultaneously.[70]

If x is average *post-tax* hourly earnings in $US of 1970 purchasing power (now the usual unit for international comparisons) and y is

65. J. S. Wabe, "Study of House Prices as a Means of Establishing Value of Journey Time, Rate of Time Preferences and Valuation of Some Aspects of Environment in London Metropolitan Region" Applied Economics 3, no. 4 (1971), p. 247.
66. R. F. Muth, *Cities and Housing: a Spatial Pattern of Urban Residential Land Use* (Chicago: Chicago University Press, 1969), p. 309.
67. *Oxford Economic Papers* (July 1973).
68. A. Dervany, "Revealed Value of Time in Air-Travel" *Review of Economics and Statistics* 56, 1 (Feb. 1974), p. 81, and others.
69. *Oxford Economic Papers* (July 1973).
70. L. D. Taylor, D. Weiserbs, "Estimation of Dynamic Demand Function" and Philips. *Review of Economics and Statistics* 54 (Nov. 1972), p. 231.

the marginal utility, measured in travel hours exchangeable for it, of one unit of income in 1970 dollars, then

$$log_e y = 9.39x^{-.232} - 7.654$$

Illustrative applications are shown in Table 122.

Table 122. Valuation of Travel Time.

x (average post tax hourly income in 1970$)	1	2	5	7.5	10
y (hours exchangeable for 1970$)	5.675	1.411	.304	.171	.117
(value of one hour's travel time in 1970$)	.177	.709	3.29	5.88	8.58
Ratio of time valuation to earnings	.18	.35	.66	.78	.86

This is a transformation of the equation as originally published. In general, time savings have been undervalued. Common sense tells us that they become relatively more important as real incomes rise, though we might not have guessed to what extent. But there is some confirmation for these high figures. An ingenious analysis of petrol prices and average speeds, making various assumptions on the cost of casualties, puts a valuation on time of £0.76–0.89/hour in 1973 (when average hourly earnings were about £1.[71] Chicago toll-ways charging two cents/mile allow average speeds (with some police collusion) to be raised from sixty to seventy miles/hour, giving a time valuation as high as $8.7/hour.[72] These two latter results contain some elements of travel during working hours, which biasses them upwards, but still largely represent journeys to work.

There are some interesting indirect methods of valuing travel time. Ernest Bevin, as Minister of Labour, made a very interesting statement (unfortunately the evidence from which he was speaking cannot be traced) as follows. "When you can get a person from home to factory in half to three-quarters of an hour as against one to two hours, you increase production by 9 to 10 per cent."[73]

On this reckoning, an hour's travel time costs as much as 0.45 hours of product, in fatigue and mental stress. A careful study made on the Phillips Lamp workers at Eindhoven in the Netherlands

71. Gosh, Lees, and Seal, *The Manchester School* (June 1975), p. 141.
72. Professor Sjaastad, University of Chicago, private communication.
73. *Hansard*, 137 (27 Nov. 1940), p. 294.

by Schut showed that each additional hour's travel per day imposed a cost in fatigue and sickness measured at two per cent of earnings, and in increased labour turnover (a cost falling on the employer) of one per cent.[74] He concluded in general that the "indirect costs" of travel amounted to as much as sixty per cent of the direct costs.

On the comparative valuation of time spent in vehicles, walking, and waiting, there is still little agreement. Taking valuation of time spent in vehicles as 1, the medians of a number of British studies show 2.5 for walking time and 2.8 for waiting time. But in Norway, in a colder climate, these relationships are reversed.[75] A marginal reduction in travel time is valued four times as highly for in-vehicle as for walking or waiting time. Norwegians "enjoy walking".

Also, as mentioned above, the valuation of travel time savings depends on the size of the units in which they come. Small savings, of the order of five minutes, are "not perceived". Increasing savings seem to bring increasing returns, making possible an increasing variety of uses of leisure. Heggie, in a study in Vancouver, established valuations (Table 123).[76]

Table 123. Valuation of Travel Time.

Minutes saved	5	10	15	20
Cents valuation: all journeys	.3	5.4	12.2	22.1

He found an unexpected income relationship, with time valuation declining with income. But his sample was obtained from the university. In this case the higher income earners were already probably possessed of abundant leisure.

"The influence of time is non-linear — journey time would have to be reduced below 40 minutes before there were any impact on the proportion travelling to the centre [of London] — journey times would have to fall below 30 minutes before there were any appreciable increase in this proportion."[77]

Now we come to the final crux of the problem. If we know the distribution of residential population between the different zones of a metropolitan area, and likewise know the distribution between zones of employments (or of shops, or of other journey destinations), are we in a position to make estimates of the information, so much needed

74. Quoted by Kathie Liepmann, *Journey to Work.*
75. S. Hansen, *The Value of Commuter Time in Oslo* (London: Highway Economics Unit, Department of the Environment, 1970).
76. I. G. Heggie, ed., *Modal Choice and the Value of Travel Time*, p. 40.
77. J. S. Wabe, "Commuter Travel into Central London" *Journal of Transport Economics and Policy* 3, no. 1 (1969), p. 65.

by traffic engineers and city planners, of the numbers of journeys from each zone to each other zone? The answer is, as might have been expected, only partially.

Some have attempted to do this by means of "gravity models". By analogy with the law of gravity in physics, it is assumed that the volume of traffic between two areas is proportional to the product of their populations, divided by the square of the distance between them. An important early study in this field was made in Munich in 1952.[78] In this case an exponent of -1.7 was preferred to the inverse square law, another study proposed an exponent of -2.6.[79] The original studies were based simply on the populations of the two zones; more refined studies have set out to estimate. for example. work journeys from the product of the residential population in the zone of origin and the amount of employment in the zone of destination, and so on.

A "trip distribution index" (that is, for any given area of residence, the proportion of journeys to each zone of destination divided by the proportion which employment in that area bears to all employment in the metropolitan area) is found (in Pittsburgh) to be very closely determined by distance, but not on the inverse square law.[80] The exponents for distance (Table 124) vary between occupations, on the obvious but neglected principle that it is the lowest paid who can least afford to travel.

Table 124. Trip Distribution Index Exponents Pittsburgh.

Occupation	Exponent
Labourers, domestic and service workers	− 1.85
Craftsmen and operatives	− 1.47
Clerical and sales workers	− 1.12
Management and professional workers	− 1.08
All occupations	− 1.33

Lowry also fitted parabolic equations for the effects of distance on lengths of various types of shopping journeys.

The exponent for distance was also tested on data from the 1962 London Traffic Survey for the London Borough of Willesden.[81]

78. Feuchtinger and Schlums, *A Study Concerning the Arterial Road Systems in the Munich Area.*
79. Ikle, *Traffic Quarterly* (April 1954).
80. I. S. Lowry, *Papers and Proceedings of the Regional Science Association* (1963).
81. R. D. Munro, University of New South Wales, private communication.

Willesden is a fairly central (about seven kilometres from the metropolitan centre) low-income district. The exponent was fitted by working in natural logarithms.

Defining —

y = percentage of work journeys to given destination.

x_1 = percentage which employment at the destination bears to all employment in the metropolitan area.

x_2 = distance from Willesden to that destination measured in units of 0.32 km (considered to be the approximate equivalent of minutes of travel time).

then

$$ln\ y\ =\ 6.69 + 1.25\ ln x_1 - 2.39\ ln\ x_2$$
$$(0.26) \qquad\quad (0.25)$$

The exponent of -2.39 is undoubtedly high, but might have been lower for a higher-income borough.

Munro drew the interesting conclusion that a reduction in travel time to one of the central destinations of say four per cent (employment and all other variables remaining unchanged) should have the effect of increasing the number of journeys to that destination by nine per cent.

It has been pointed out that the gravity model gives a worse fit in the older cities of the eastern United States than in the western cities, because in the former there is more social stratification by area.

But is it distance which is the controlling factor? Should we not rather be looking at the number of "intervening opportunities" which may or may not be proportional to distance. In Chapter 13 we saw that this principle applied in interregional migration.[82] Its application to urban traffic was first proposed by Morton Schneider in Chicago.[83] The present writer has applied this method to data from London and Copenhagen, Oslo and Birmingham.[84]

The intervening opportunities formula is so simple that it can be expressed in a sentence. Of the total number of journeys originating in any zone the logarithm of the proportion to or beyond any given distance is a linear function of the number of possible destinations at or below that distance.

82. Stouffer, *American Sociological Review* (Dec. 1940).
83. M. Schneider, *Chicago Area Transportation Study, Final Report* II (July 1960), pp. 81–92.
84. Copenhagen from *Traffic Quarterly* (Jan. 1965); Oslo from *Traffic Quarterly* (April 1968); Birmingham from *Traffic Quarterly* (July 1969).

Schneider's mathematical formulation was as follows:

$$v_{ij} \cdot = \text{trips between zones } i \text{ and } j$$
$$v_i = \text{all trips originating in zone } i$$
$$v = \text{trip destinations closer to } i \text{ than is } j.$$

Then
$$v_{ij} = v_i [(1-L)^v - (1-L)^{v+v}j]$$

L should however be adjusted for the number of trip opportunities in the destination area, and the nature of the journey.

It is interesting to find that this principle also has an analogy in physics. In a gas the logarithm of the numbers of molecular paths cumulated to or beyond a given length, is inversely proportional to that length.

Many data on journeys to work have been collected, principally by Census authorities throughout the world, but usually (this applies to the United States Census) the destinations are recorded in far too aggregate a form for such analysis, and most of the information comes from traffic surveys, with some Census data e.g. London boroughs in 1951.[85]

The specification of "possible destinations" conceals undoubted difficulties. We can relate numbers of worktrips to totals of possible employments at different destinations. But this is a crude approximation. What the traveller is looking at are possible employments in his own occupation. A separate analysis for each occupation is of course out of the question and some grouping of occupations is necessary. This might yield diverse results, as with Lowry's work in Pittsburgh (Table 124).

For Birmingham and neighbourhood, though the destination data were too aggregated, separate data could be obtained for manual and non-manual workers, who were found to have very different travel patterns.[86] The results however were unsatisfactory. The central city was found to show much more attraction, particularly for non-manual workers, than could have been predicted from the intervening opportunities formula — probably because its occupational composition was very different from that of adjacent areas.

In general the linear relation on semi-log diagrams (Diagram 29) holds with two important qualifications. In the first place, there is nearly always a break in the linearity (or we may say that we prefer to analyze in terms of two straight lines) near the upper end, that is, the number of people who find employment near their homes is greater than is to be expected from the general intervening opportunities relationship. As we move towards the edge of the metropolitan area this difference becomes more marked, as is to be expected.

85. C. Clark and G. H. Peters, *Traffic Quarterly* (Jan. 1965).
86. *Ibid.*

Thus in the Epsom-Ewell area, some twenty kilometres from Central London (and the site of a famous racecourse) over fifty per cent of the men and seventy per cent of the women find employment locally.

Diagram 29 shows the distribution for Kensington, a London borough only some four kilometres distant from the metropolitan centre, nevertheless still showing high proportions of both male and female workers finding local employment. The lower part of the curve however is almost linear. Less central boroughs show higher proportions of local employment but similar patterns for the lower part of the curve — for the furthest twenty-five per cent of employment opportunities we find some two per cent of males still travelling.

The male–female difference is found everywhere. With their lower pay women can less afford travel, besides often being less able to afford time to travel, in view of their other obligations. So women relate their choice of employment to employment opportunities on a different function to men.

Besides a change of slope at the upper end (extra tendency to find employment near home) most of the diagrams also show an increase of slope at the lower end (the most distant opportunities appear less attractive than expected from the general intervening opportunities relationship). It might at first be thought that this was a function of increasing distance, rather than of running out of opportunities, but a detailed analysis shows that this is not the case.[87]

The London diagrams all show a marked change of slope in the upper corner, indicating the general conclusion that up to twenty kilometres distance from the metropolitan centre over thirty per cent of the men and forty per cent of the women going to work find employment close to their homes, often within walking distance. The remainder however distribute their workplaces approximately in accordance with the intervening opportunities principle.

In London the change of slope at the lower end is much less marked than in Oslo, perhaps because of the greater diversity of opportunities at the greater distances.

Data for fourteen districts in Melbourne in 1964, on the other hand, with 828,000 work trips, of which 314,000 were to the Central Business District, show few indications of people finding employment near their houses, but a marked tendency for the slopes to steepen (not shown in diagram) for the last ten to twenty per cent of the work journeys, once half to two-thirds of

87. C. Clark and G. H. Peters, "The 'Alternative Opportunities' Method of Estimating Traffic" *Chartered Surveyor* 96, no. 12 (June 1964).

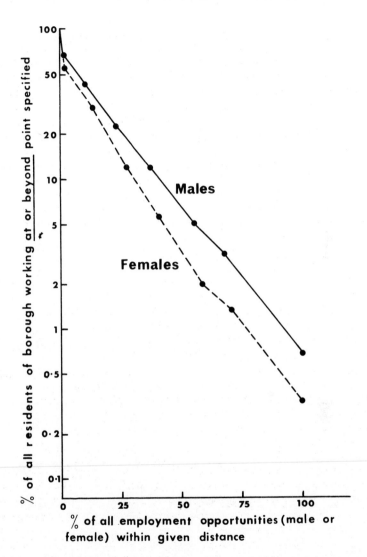

Diagram 29. Alternative employment opportunities, Kensington.

the opportunities have been passed. In this case the distances are greater. Melbourne is a very asymmetrical city, with the built-up zone extending forty-five kilometres from the centre to the south east along the shores of Port Phillip Bay, but only twenty kilometres westwards on the residentially unattractive flat industrial land.

Diagram 30 shows the work journeys of the residents of five representative districts with slopes varying in steepness with distance from the centre, and with the nature of the district; residents of poorer districts can less afford to travel, and thus show steeper slopes on the diagram.

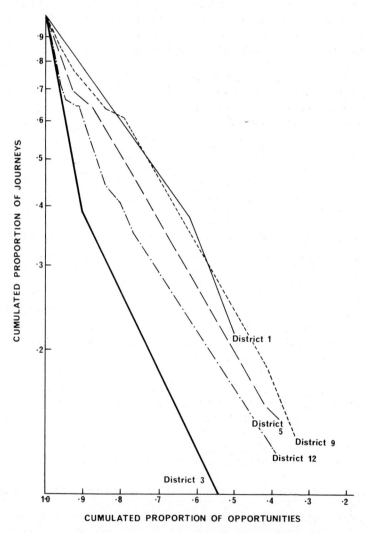

Diagram 30. Melbourne Journeys to Work, 1964.

Table 125.

District reference number	Name	Distance from centre in km.	Nature of district
1	Melbourne	—	Central Business District
9	Malvern	11	Prosperous old established residential district
5	Preston	8	Old declining residential and industrial district
12	Waverley—Dandenong	32	Rapidly developing new residential and industrial district
3	Sunshine—Altona	11	Western industrial district

17

Urban Land Values

On the subject of urban land values there has been an abundance of delusions, with the expected harmful consequences.

The first delusion — very widely held, even by educated men, who ought to know better — is that high urban land values are the consequence of speculation. It is one of the most elementary propositions of economics that speculation does not alter the ultimately attained price of the object traded, but that it does alter the process by which this ultimate price is reached. If land values are increasing, and if there were no speculation, the increases would come in sudden large jumps. Speculation exercises a smoothing effect on the movement of prices and is, on the whole, economically beneficial. Much attention is drawn to occasional high gains by speculators — nobody draws attention to the fact that speculators frequently make losses.

The second delusion is that high urban land values serve no useful economic purpose, and that they ought, somehow, to be suppressed. Urban land prices, high or low, serve an absolutely vital economic purpose in apportioning the claims for land, between those who have greater or less need for central, or other sites. A regulation of land prices which had the effect of allowing a user with less urgent needs to occupy a central site would cause serious economic loss.

The third delusion is that urban land values are always rising. This is a simple error of fact. There is plenty of evidence of some urban land values falling, sometimes even in current money terms, certainly in real terms (i.e. after allowing for changes in the general purchasing power of money). As long ago as 1911 a leading authority was writing "The owners of property yielding the highest rents in the city usually anticipate nothing but continued increase in rents, and seldom realize that the business centre of a city can shift, until declining rents bring the fact forcibly to their attention".[1]

The fourth delusion is that the aim of governments should be

1. R. M. Hurd, *Principles of City Land Values* (New York: Arno Press, 1970).

and will be a reduction of urban land values. When more than half the electors own their own houses, as in the case now in a number of countries, their profound desire is that land values should go up, not down. Politicians, whatever they say, will act accordingly. The politician's ideal of course would be a fall in the price of land for those who have not yet bought their houses, and business sites, with a rise in the price of land for those who have; but somehow this is difficult to arrange.

The fifth delusion is that "urban renewal" is necessary, and should be publicly subsidized, when population and business in any urban zone decline, and land values fall. As shown in Chapter 14 "urban renewal", so widely practised in the United States, has done great harm; though considerations of economic externalities justify some limited assistance to property owners in such areas.

The sixth delusion concerns town planning. Town planning is necessary because there are abundant "economic externalities" (see Chapter 8) in urban land use, for which the optimum solution cannot be attained by market forces. But many people fail to realize that any town planning decision may be the source of great profit to some or great loss to others. Those who made the final decisions on town planning should be men of exceptional integrity, and indifferent to political and financial pressures. Is this always the case?

The seventh delusion concerns the costs of developing roads, water, sewerage, and the like, municipal taxes or rates, and interest during holding period, which, it is generally supposed, are "added" to the price of the land. Not so. They represent deductions from the price originally payable for the undeveloped land, or, in the case of a permanent rate or tax, a deduction from the price which the ultimate buyer is willing to pay. This again is one of the simpler propositions in economics — the incidence of tax depends on the comparative steepness of the supply and demand elasticities. Tobacco, for example, has a high supply elasticity and therefore a tax on tobacco falls on the consumer. Land, on the other hand, has no supply elasticity (only in quite exceptional circumstances can you "make" more land) and therefore rates and taxes on land must fall on the seller. The question is however sometimes raised whether this proposition can be altered by town planning. Insofar as the town plan is rigid, this proposition remains true. If however the town planning authorities release more land when the price goes up, this may cause some of the incidence of municipal taxation and other charges to fall on the buyer.

The eighth delusion goes back to the nineteenth century and Henry George, but still has its followers. The value of all services performed by public authorities, according to this fallacious doctrine, in spite of so much evidence to the contrary, must be capitalized in the price of land, and therefore an adequate tax on land would suffice to pay for all public services and would render all other taxation unnecessary. We shall see below the proportion which the rents of land bear to national product, a proportion far lower than the cost of public services. We must be aware however that there is a half-truth in the Georgeite case. So long as we do not set our sights too high, land is a very suitable object of taxation, for the simple reason that, unlike labour, enterprise, and other sources of wealth, land cannot be discouraged by taxation. Whatever happens, the supply of land does not change.

The final delusion arises out of the attempt to carry the above doctrine too far, and to secure for public revenue the entire net rent of the land, by extremely high taxation, or by outright nationalization or municipalization, still advocated by many. Taxation must not be raised to a point where it leaves the owners of land no real incentive to rearrange, develop, or sell it. Public ownership of land would be an administrative nightmare, with millions of transactions to be performed, rendered all the more difficult by the public authority owning the land, and someone else owning the buildings on it.

Before proceeding further to examine the available information on prices of urban land we should clear up two points mentioned in dealing with the "delusions" above. First there is the possibility of "making" land when its expected selling value is high. In the exceptional case of the Netherlands (which is only restoring however what was dry land a few centuries ago) considerable quantities of land have been obtained for agriculture, though at an uneconomic cost. Apart from this there is what might appear to be an unusual opportunity in Bombay, where shallow water in Back Bay lies close to high-value commercial sites. Reclamation costs (at 1968 prices) were as high as $US800/square metre, a price which few if any commercial enterprises would be willing to pay.[2] Filling in swamp-land (which is not the same as reclamation from the sea) near Dacca in Bangladesh cost only US$2–3/square metre.[3] Both the Indian and Bangladesh costs have been converted on the exchange rate; for their true purchasing power they ought to be multiplied by a factor of three or more. In Hong Kong, where the highest commercial land prices (again in the 1960s) went up to $US600/

2. Reserve Bank of India, private communication.
3. Eddison, *Pakistan Development Review* (1963), pp. 557–59, and Adamjee Mills, private communication.

square metre, there has been some reclamation, for public purposes, including the airport, but it does not seem to have been feasible as a private investment.[4] Projects for "making" land in the United States of America by platforming railway tracks, on the other hand, were estimated to cost (at prices of the 1960s) only \$100–150/ square metre.[5]

Many people still find it hard to believe that land taxes or municipal rates reduce the price of land. The following is a simple demonstration of this principle.

- Let the rate of tax, assessed on the selling value of the land, be t
- Let the normal rate of return on commercial investments be i
- Let the full expected net economic rent from the land before tax be E
- Let the selling price of the land untaxed be F and current selling price of the land be V

Then
$$F = E/i$$
$$V = (E-tv)/i$$
$$\therefore V = E/(t+i)$$
and $$V/F = i/(t+i)$$

So the price of the land is reduced by the ratio which i bears to $(t+i)$, and can be brought down to any specified level by high taxation.

Those still unconvinced by this simple piece of algebra can be shown this actually happening (Table 126).[6] In some (not all) Australian states municipal revenue (including most water, sewerage, and cleansing charges) is assessed entirely on the value of the land,

Table 126. Rates & Land Values.

Rates as percentage of assessable land value		Land values (excluding exempt properties) \$ per head of population
Brisbane	7.1	2,298
Other Queensland cities and towns	9.0	1,615
Torres	23.2	98
Charters Towers	69.1	179
Mt Morgan	114.6	66

4. Flaxman, *The Director* (Oct. 1964).
5. *Resources* (Resources for the Future: 1969).
6. *Queensland Local Government Statistics,* 1977–78.

excluding buildings. In the case of old towns based on previous mining or (Torres in the table below) pearling activities, some population remains behind, largely dependent on pensions and social services. In such cases, municipal rates have to be high to pay for necessary services; this reduces the price of land; rates than have to go higher still, and a downward spiral sets in, with remarkable consequences.

In the world-wide inflation of the mid-1970s land and property values everywhere became extremely unstable, rising violently, and then in many cases falling back again. The data which follow are mostly from the more stable periods of the 1960s and early 1970s. Though prices now are higher all round, these should serve to indicate relative values.

Information on urban land values is usually obtained from official valuations, made for taxation purposes. In many cases they are below the true selling value of the land, and it cannot always be assumed that the extent of undervaluation is uniform. Private studies are rare. The work is laborious, and has to be done by experts sacrificing their commercially valuable time. A limited number of results have been published in the form of "isovalic" diagrams, maps with contour lines linking points of equal price, on the analogy of meteorological diagrams. These are found to be remarkably uneven. Even a few additional metres distance from a shopping centre makes a very great difference to the value of a site. In other words, shoppers put a high negative value on the inconvenience of having to walk even a short distance from the main shopping centre. This is even more true of proximity to the Stock Exchange and other financial centres.

Property values in the City of London have been said to fall by as much as one-sixth for each additional five minutes' walking distance from Lloyd's or the Stock Exchange.[7] *Apropos* the difficulty of finding tenants for a new office building in Moorgate "A hundred yards is too far to expect a stockbroker to sprint from Throgmorton Street", said the *Sunday Times*.

In pre-motorized days these price gradients appear to have been even steeper. In New York in 1911 the prime Wall Street site was worth $400/square foot ($4280/square metre), but in most directions this value was halved by 100 metres distance, and travelling only a little over 250 metres eastward reduced land value to $75/square foot, westward to $25. Values fell less rapidly northwards along Broadway.[8]

7. *Financial Times* (London), 7 May 1962.
8. R. M. Hurd, *Principles of City Land Values.*

Subject to these irregularities however we may seek general patterns of land values in relation to distance from the city centre.

Once again, the proverb about the owl of Minerva flying in the evening (quoted in Chapter 14) is applicable. Useful generalizations have been established late in the day, soon to be overthrown by fresh events.

The first generalization was that land prices fell with increasing distance from the city centre, not exponentially, as do residential densities, but on a negative double-log or power function.[9]

It appears however that Winkler's generalization is applicable only to small cities and to past data. Under such circumstances, a remarkable theoretical justification for the double-log relationship was provided by E. S. Mills.[10] On the key assumption that all employment is in the central business district, and making certain reasonable further assumptions about travel costs, congestion, wages, and so on, he deduces land rents per working day for various distances from the city centre (Table 127). These can be converted to capital values on the assumptions of 250 working days/year and ten per cent rate of return ($1000/square mile/ working day rent converting to $0.955/square metre capital value). Plotted on double-log scale, this gives a relation close to a straight line, with a slope of -2.1.

Table 127.

Miles Distance from city centre	Capital value $/metre^2
1	63.0
2	13.8
3	6.34
4	3.26
5	2.15
6	1.56
7	1.19
8	.95
9	.76

On closer examination of the double-log diagram for larger cities, and with more employment away from the central business district we shall find, firstly, a certain convexity, meaning that, in the

9. Winkler, International Statistical Institute (Municipal Statistics Section), 1957 Conference Proceedings.
10. E. S. Mills, *Studies in the Structure of the Urban Economy* (Baltimore: published for Resources for the Future by John Hopkins Press, 1972), p. 117.

immediate vicinity of the city centre land values fall less rapidly than indicated by the power function.

Subject to the above qualification near the city centre, the next development is for the double-log function to become a semi-log or exponential function, akin to that found for residential densities.

But this again is changing, as are residential densities, with a tendency for both residential densities and land values now to become almost uniform over wide areas, subject to a limited area of high value land in the central business district.

The final stage, already observed in Chicago, is when land values in many of the outer suburbs actually rise above those of the inner suburbs.[11] Such an inversion however is not peculiar to Chicago. In the ancient city of Cairo, land prices, in Egyptian £/square metre, stand at fifty in the commercial centre, fall to six in the inner residential areas, and rise again to thirty in the outermost residential areas.[12]

We may first look at some examples of the double-log relationship. Studies of small cities are few, and results from the Japanese city of Okayama (two hundred and sixty thousand population in 1953) are interesting in showing a fairly good power relation (land values proportional to the -1.5 power of distance from the city centre) except for the first half kilometre from the centre, where land values are lower than indicated by this relation.[13] In this city however, the fall in residential densities with distance from the centre is *not* exponential, and there is no clear relationship between land values and residential densities.

The city of Topeka (population 119,000 in 1960) showed an approximate double-log fitting, with a slope of -1.35.[14]

It is probable that much higher exponents prevailed in the past, or prevail in cities in the developing countries now, where most journeys have to be on foot, judging from some historic figures (Table 128 for Paris).[15]

Table 128. Land Values in Paris.

Distances from Notre Dame in km		5.5	6.5	8.5	10.5	12.5	16.5
Median land values francs/m^2	1871	6		1	.75	.6	.3
	1921	50	20	6	4.5	2	.4

11. Yeates, *Economic Geography* (Jan. 1965).
12. A. Meguid, private communication.
13. *American Journal of Sociology* (March 1955).
14. Knos, *Distribution of Land Values in Topeka* (University of Kansas, 1962).
15. Bastié, *La Croissance de la Banlieu parisienne.*

These give approximate double-log fittings with exponents as high as -2.7 in 1871 and -4.3 in 1921.

In the case of Paris however the concentration of land values may have been accentuated by encirclement by fortifications, much of whose sites were still unbuilt in 1921. Land seven to ten kilometres from the centre rose five-fold in *real* value between 1929 and 1962.

The figures from Sydney (quoted in Chapter 14, Table 87) show an approximate linearity on a double-log diagram (if we assume average distance within Sydney Municipality to be about 1.5 kilometres, and in other districts less than five kilometres from the centre at about four kilometres), subject to a flattening of the relationship for distances over thirty kilometres from the centre. But the curve has an abnormally low slope, only about -1 (that is, land prices are in simple inverse proportion to distance from the city centre).

An exponent of -1.5 was found for Washington in 1963, with the double-log (power function) giving a better fit than alternatives;[16] but in explaining land prices the distance term was also multiplied by a term for local income to the power of 0.62.

Income bore no relation to distance from the central business district, so Muth found in Chicago, once the effect of the age of the housing had been eliminated.[17] This of course is a substantial variable, and Brodsky's coefficient for income may have also captured some distance-related effect.

There must of course be some convexity; if the double-log relationship were followed to its logical conclusion, land values at the city centre would be infinite. But there is more to it than that. If we attempt to fit a double-log relationship in the immediate neighbourhood of the city centre we always find a low slope.

Such convexity is clearly apparent in an unusually detailed study (Table 129) of land values in central San Francisco.[18]

The downward trend of real values through time is clearly apparent.

Convexity is also apparent in central Glasgow (Table 130), a compact city, from a map showing assessed site rentals, on which can be drawn approximately fitting circles.[19]

In Athens (Diagram 31) convexity is apparent not only below one kilometre from the centre, but also appears again after five kilometres.

16. H. Brodsky, "Residential Land and Improvement Values in a Central City" *Land Economics* 46, no. 3 (Aug. 1970), p. 229.
17. Muth, *Cities and Housing: a Spatial Pattern of Urban Residential Land Use* (Chicago: Chicago University Press, 1969), pp. 8–9.
18. Wendt, Real Estate Research Program, Research Report 18, University of California.
19. D. R. Diamond, *Lund Studies in Urban Geography,* Series B, No. 24.

Table 129. Central San Francisco Land Values.

			Distance from Centre (Market and 5th Street) Km		
	Centre	0-0.5	0.5-0.8	0.8-1.1	1.1-1.6
Number of observations	1	8	15	13	8
$'000/front foot at 1950 prices[1] —					
1927	20.1	9.7	6.4	5.7	3.9
1950	12.0	6.5	4.1	3.7	1.7
1960	9.6	5.5	4.7	4.9	2.0

1. 1927 values × 1.58; 1960 values × 0.8.

Table 130. Site Rents in Glasgow.

Radius of circle km	.18	.40	.56	.80
Assessed site rent £/m²/year	17.1	8.5	4.3	2.1

If we fit a line to the central part of the curve we obtain a slope of -1.6.[20]

The tendency to convexity is of course the opposite to the tendency described above, to change from the double-log to the exponential distribution, which would appear as a *concavity* in the double-log diagram. However, in an interesting manner, both tendencies appear in the diagram for Tokyo, the world's largest city with the highest land values, which is slightly S-shaped, that is, convex near the centre and becoming concave in the outer suburbs, when plotted on a double-log (Diagram 32).

The data for 1960 and 1965 are classified not by distance but by travel time from the city centre, and are averaged readings from diagrams giving separate data along each of the four main railway routes.[21] The 1970 data are read approximately from privately published diagrams. The latter are in kilometres, and for comparison one kilometre is equated to two minutes.

An exponential decline, formulated in a different manner, is shown for St Louis, where land prices are estimated to fall ten per cent for each mile distance from the city centre.[22] (The price of land in the

20. J. Papaionnou, Doxiadis Institute, private communication.
21. "Economic Survey of Japan 1966–67" published by the *Japan Times* (Tokyo).
22. K. Wieand, "Housing Price Determination in Urban Ghettos" *Urban Studies* 12, no. 2 (1975), pp. 201–202.

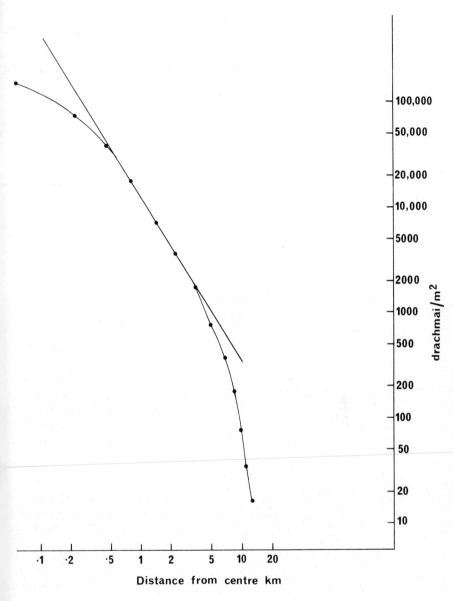

drachmai/m²

Distance from centre km

Diagram 31. Land values in Athens 1964.

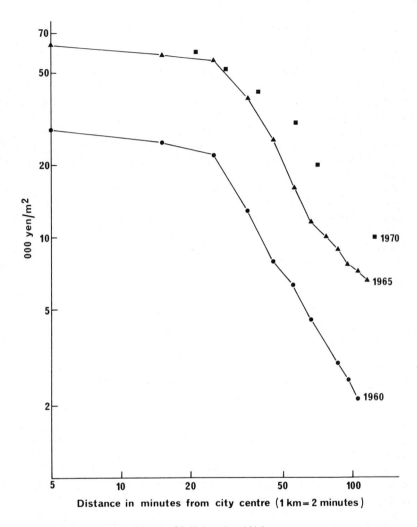

Diagram 32. Tokyo Land Values.

Table 131. Land Values Tokyo 1970.

Isovals '000 yen/m²	60	50	40	30	20	10
Approximate average radius of isoval km.	10.5	14	19.5	28	35	61

black quarter is raised above this equilibrium level by a factor which may be as high as 1.25.)

Muth generalizes that on the average in United States cities, prices of houses fall two per cent per mile distance from the city centre (one per cent in some parts of Chicago).[23] This may be of a similar order of magnitude to the St Louis result when we bear in mind that land constitutes generally some fifteen per cent of the price of a house, if — but only if — the quality of housing does not also vary with distance. If the quality of housing improves in the outer suburbs, then the price of a house of given quality falls more than two per cent per mile.

Land values in Los Angeles (Table 132), as perhaps was to be expected, advanced in 1960 to the next stage, away from the exponential distribution to nearly an L-shape, with a small high-value central area, a secondary outer zone of higher values (the preference of manufacture for this zone was discussed in Chapter 15), with all other land values low, and nearly uniform.[24]

Table 132. Los Angeles Land Values 1960.

Distance from City Hall (miles)	0-1	1-2	2-5	5-7	7-10	10-12	12-14	14-18
Land value $/m²	17.5	14.0	10.8	20.5	9.8	7.6	9.0	7.6

The values are averages from three radii, drawn northwestward, northeastward, and southeastward from City Hall. All land uses (residential, commercial, and so on) are aggregated.

We come to the final stage, as mentioned above, in Chicago, where the land values in most of the outer suburbs are now actually above those of the older inner suburbs.[25] The process of development in Chicago can be observed from the early nineteenth century onward.[26] Land values rose throughout the nineteenth century, with the value-distance relationship rising in roughly parallel lines, with a slope of about -1.7 to a maximum in 1890–1910, followed by persistent falls (in real terms) in all inner areas, except the business centre.

These falling real land values in the old inner suburbs of Chicago frequently (but by no means always) represent black (or Puerto Rican) areas — though the causation is usually the reverse — blacks settle in an area because it is cheap, not that land values fall because the blacks have settled there. In fact in the early stages of the

23. Muth, *Op. cit.,* pp. 8–9, and 309.
24. Brigham, Rand Corporation Memorandum RM 4043RC.
25. Yeates, *Economic Geography* (Jan. 1965).
26. University of Chicago, Department of Sociology, private communication.

formation of a "ghetto" land values usually rise. A striking example was found when Puerto Rican settlement was building up in New York in the 1950s centred on West 90th Street (the present writer resided near that neighbourhood for some months in 1958).[27] Migrants, living five or six to a room, were paying rents up to $70/square metre/year when neighbouring properties were being let for $15–30.

We turn next to the important question (on which we have little information) of the extent to which proximity to a metropolitan area affects land values in adjacent rural and semi-rural areas. In what appears to have been a unique study P. A. Stone showed that such residential land values were closely determined by the interaction of two variables: distance from the metropolitan centre, and the number of dwellings per acre permitted by the local planning authorities (zoning authorities in the United States) – such authorities' decisions sometimes depending on local custom, sometimes apparently arbitrary, but in any case highly variable between different plots of land.[28] Thus, at a distance of twenty miles (thirty-two kilometres) from Central London, Stone found some land with permission to build over thirty, some to build under five dwellings to the acre (0.4 hectare). On 1960–64 data (land prices have greatly risen since then, but it does not appear that relative positions have changed) Stone found (for a given number of dwellings permitted per acre) negative exponential relationships.

Price of land '000 £/acre 1960–64 y
Permitted (zoned) dwellings/acre x
Distance from city centre in km. z

Then adjacent to London
$$y = (7.67 + 1.33x)e^{-.0221Z}$$
and adjacent to Birmingham
$$y = (6.0 + 0.8x)e^{-.0295Z}$$

As was to be expected, at a given distance from the city centre, land values adjacent to Birmingham were lower than those adjacent to London (compare terms in brackets), and falling off more rapidly with distance (compare exponents).

At that time residential land prices in remoter areas were about £2000/acre.[29] It is interesting to calculate, from the above formulae, the distances from the metropolitan centres at which land values could be expected to have fallen to this level (a theoretical result,

27. *Fortune* (Dec. 1957), p. 148.
28. P. A. Stone, *Estates Gazette* (11 Jan. 1964) and *Urban Development in Britain*, p. 133.
29. J. McAuslan "Residential Land Values 1962–65" *Chartered Surveyor* 98, no. 11 (May 1966).

not to be expected in fact, owing to the influence of other near-by metropolitan areas). Substituting *y=2* and *x=5* in the above questions, we find London's influence extending over eighty-nine kilometres, Birmingham's over fifty-five (ratio relative populations of the metropolitan areas was 3.35:1). A Canadian study showed that proximity to Toronto still had some effect on rural land prices at a distance of seventy-two kilometres.[30]

If we attempt to analyze Stone's London region data (ignoring planning restrictions) on a double-log diagram we obtain a sharply convex result (that is, rate of fall of values increasing rapidly with increasing distance).

Where we have previously observed convexity (Tokyo, Athens, and other cities) this may also represent a composite of a negative exponential factor for distance, and a further factor for the declining numbers of dwellings per unit area sought by home-builders, or permitted by planning authorities.

In England in 1967–69 – both absolute and relative values have changed considerably since then, but plot sizes probably have not yet adapted themselves, as they might have been expected to do after a period of comparatively stable prices – outside the London and Birmingham neighbourhoods, residential land prices ranged from £30,000/hectare in the south-eastern counties to £8,000 in East Anglia.[31] The average number of sites/hectare showed a corresponding range from twenty-one to nine. Plotting these and intermediate values on a double-log diagram, it appears that average size of plot responded to price of land per unit area with a price elasticity of 0.66 – an interesting figure.

Perhaps the most significant determinant in the price which buyers are willing to pay for residential land, it is suggested, is its accessibility to employment, with accessibility to shopping, schools, recreation, and so on as secondary considerations.[32] (The converse proposition, that prices paid for factory sites depend largely on accessibility of labour supplies is less probable; while not insignificant, labour supply is only one consideration among several in determining the value of factory sites).

"Accessibility" is measured by a method which is the counterpart of the measurement of "economic potential" (see Chapter 9) as a determinant of the regional location of manufacture, except that in this case the distance between two points is expressed in

30. Sargent, *The Rural Land Market,* Ontario Agricultural College.
31. J. McAuslan "Residential Land Prices 1965–69" *Chartered Surveyor* 102, no. 3 (Sept. 1969).
32. Nicholas Clark and T. Patton, Tewksbury Symposium 1970 (Department of Civil Engineering, Melbourne University).

terms of expected travel time in minutes (obtained from detailed analysis of traffic surveys). The "accessibility" of any point is thus obtained by summing all employments (later refinements should no doubt distinguish types of employment) within possible access, each divided by the number of minutes of travel time required to reach it. The initial research related such accessibilities to residential densities. On the further link to land prices researches are still in progress. An accessibility diagram for Melbourne showed a range of thirty-eight thousand down to twelve thousand (sum of employments/minutes travel time). It was suggested that the latter figure represented the lower limit at which land became attractive for residential development in a large city; in smaller towns a limited amount of development is taking place at lower accessibilities. A double-log fitting for Melbourne showed residential densities varying with the 2.5 power of accessibility in 1961, the 2.7 power in 1966 (Census years). In both cases an accessibility of twenty-eight thousand was related to a residential density of seventy-seven persons/ hectare (130 square metres/person, well above average density), while the supposed lower limit of twelve thousand units accessibility was related to densities of ten persons/hectare in 1961 and eight persons/ hectare in 1966 — near-rural densities.

The exponent for travel time of -1 was found to give a better fit than several alternatives tried.

An alternative measure suggested by Schneider[33] was e^{-k} (distance). It was found that this also gave a good fit for any value of k between 0.003 and 0.016.

Accessibilities in Tokyo (in 1970) were calculated approximately (Table 133), using only employment data from the city wards (*ku*), neglecting employments in the neighbouring semi-rural areas, and equating one kilometre to two minutes travel time. The results, of course, came out enormously higher than for Melbourne. They were *not* however proportional to land prices. Accessibility however showed quite a close proportionality to distance to the power of -0.6.

Table 133. Tokyo Accessibilities and Land Prices.

Distance from centre km	0-5	5-10	10-15
Approximate accessibility '000	700	400	300
1965 land prices '000 yen/m²	62.8	57.4	54.8

33. In G. C. Hemmens, ed., *Urban Development Models* (United States Highway Research Board Special Report 97, 1967).

An international comparison is attempted (Table 134) of urban land prices, at various specified distances from the city centre. The values were obtained by approximate interpolations of the sources quoted above, except for India, Korea, Monaco, and Lagos, which were obtained from various private sources.

The unit of measurement was the American dollar of 1970 purchasing power, which is the basis of our most important source of information on international price comparisons.[34] Simple exchange rates can be very misleading, especially for the low-income countries, where the internal purchasing power of money has been found sometimes to be three times or more than that indicated by its exchange rate. The same authors have published "Exchange rate deviation indexes" (conversion factor from exchange rate to real purchasing power).[35] The original data must first be converted, by the country's own price index, to their 1970 equivalents; then converted to American dollars on the exchange rate; then adjusted by the exchange rate deviation index.

The figure for Monaco is included to show what can happen in a tax haven, while the immunity lasts. Apart from this exceptional case the very high values in Tokyo, even at thirty kilometres distance, are noticeable. The value for Lagos is remarkably high. Sydney, London, and Los Angeles show similar orders of magnitude.

International differences were dramatically illustrated by a Japanese writer who calculated the number of years' pay the average wage earner would have to disburse to buy a plot of land of 150 square metres (only enough to build a small house) within forty minutes' travel time from the city centre in three capital cities.[36]

Bonn	0.5 years
Paris	2.8 years
Tokyo	6.4 years

One of the principal economic functions of urban land prices is to sort out those most urgently in need of (and able to pay for) central sites, against those content with a site further out. Most factories are in this latter category, as we saw from the low slopes of their employment distribution curves, as compared with other land uses (Chapter 15).

Their need for central sites is less urgent than is that of certain kinds of commercial and financial activities — indeed, about the only

34. I. B. Kravis and others *International Comparisons of Real Product and Purchasing Power* (Baltimore: Johns Hopkins University Press, 1978).
35. *Economic Journal* (June 1978), pp. 216, 232–37.
36. *Nihon Keizai Shimbun* (Tokyo) 7 May 1974 (English Edition).

Table 134. International Urban Land Price Comparisons.

		Factors for converting original data in national currency to $US of 1970 purchasing power				Land prices at specified distances from city centre in purchasing power of 1970 $US/square metre							
		National price change original date to 1970	Exchange rate 1970 $US/unit national currency	Exchange rate deviation index 1970	Combined factor	Distance in km 2.5	5	7.5	10	15	20	25	30
Australia (Sydney)	1973	.815	1.12	1.13	1.03	42		23	16	12	8	6	6
France (Paris)	1962	1.35	.181	1.26	.308				12	12			
Germany[g]	1973	.75	.25	1.22	.229		11						
Greece (Athens)	1964	1.17	.033	1.64	.064	200	48	29	4				
India (Calcutta)[a]	1970		.1325	3.34	.443			65					
Japan (Okayama)[b]	1939	.455	.00278	1.49	1.88	5	1						
Tokyo	1970		.00278	1.49	.00414				250	195	160		
Korea (Seoul)[c]	1978	.341	.00323	2.24	.00247		160						
Monaco[d]	1962	1.35		1.26	1.70	1,350							
Nigeria (Lagos)[e]	1964	1.42	2.80	2.46	9.78				100				
Switzerland (Zurich)	1936	2.55	.232	1.09	.645	16	2						
United Kingdom (London)[f]	1963	1.35	2.80	1.39	5.25			37	28	22	16	14	13
United States (Los Angeles)	1960	1.41	2.80	1.41	1.41	20	16	21	28	13	11	11	

a. Described as "Middle Class Residential Land". "Highclass land" priced at $130–200, and maximum commercial land $1,100. Values in Delhi about $1,100 for commercial; Poona $30; in Calcutta it is reported that cash transactions (enabling the vendor to avoid capital gains tax) are at prices some one-third lower.
b. Valuation made in 1952 at 1939 prices
c. "Residential" area; central business district $1,400
d. Original measurement in American dollars
e. Central business district $1,350
f. All residential lands irrespective of numbers of residences permitted by planning authorities
g. Residential land (Statistisches Jahrbuch)

advantage to factories of a central site is better access to labour supplies, and this advantage is rapidly diminishing with the increasing dispersal of residential population. It is not surprising therefore to find factory land prices in London at an almost uniform level (Table 135) up to a distance of thirty kilometres from the centre.[37] Beyond this point difficulties of access to labour, and other facilities, cause a rapid fall in price.

Table 135. London Factory Sites 1962—65. $ of 1970 Purchasing Power/m^2.

Distance from Charing Cross km	0-3	3-13	13-24	24-32	32-40	40-50
Site value $/m^2	163	145	140	127	78	43

The land values were calculated from sale prices of factories less an allowance of £21/square metre floorspace for the estimated replacement value (depreciated) of the structure; and converted to 1970 dollars by the same factor as in the above table.

Factory rents in London were compatible with the above land prices — except that old factories in East London let at rents indicating almost zero land values.[38] Factory site values in the English Midlands were estimated at about half London values, and in the North West as low as one fifth.[39]

Factors in the above table (or calculated similarly) are used in comparing some other factory site values in the same units of dollars of 1970 purchasing power/square metre. Paris shows a value in 1962 of sixty-two for industrial land "near the suburbs".[40] The inner Sydney suburb of Redfern in 1963 showed a figure of twenty-one (2.5 times as high as adjacent residential land).[41] In the principal Sydney industrial suburbs in 1971 the figure stood at twenty-five, and thirty kilometres distant at fifteen.[42] In Melbourne in 1971 some high values up to seventy were recorded for the inner suburbs; but in the suburbs, where the main industrial development has been taking place (about twenty kilometres from the centre) land prices were 11—16.[43] The German average, at ten, was below the residential

37. G. H. Peters, *Estates Gazette* (14 Jan. 1967).
38. J. H. Dunning, *Economic Planning and Town Expansion: A Study of Basingstoke* (Southampton: Workers' Educational Association, 1963), p. 111, and E. Burney, *The Director* (April 1964).
39. E. A. Vallis Estates Bursar, Oriel College, Oxford, private communication; but reducing his estimates for replacement costs.
40. Bastié, *La Croissance de le Banlieu parisienne.*
41. G. M. Neutze, Australian National University, private communication.
42. Messrs. Gray and Johnson, private communication.
43. *The Bulletin* (Sydney), 6 March 1971.

average.[44] Factory site prices in the developing countries (calculated in the same units) appear to be higher than might have been expected. A factory site in Mexico City ten kilometres from the centre in 1958 cost thirty-six in 1970 dollars,[45] and in the Parel District of Bombay (taking replacement cost at 100 rupees/square metre) the site value was fifty-seven.[46] In Bangladesh sites near Dacca cost twenty-nine, and at twenty-five kilometres distant, or in Chittagong or Khulna, the price was nine.[47] In countries where most of the labour force has to walk to work factory sites need to be more concentrated. Also the smaller towns in Bangladesh, it was pointed out, "cannot provide the infrastructure and services essential to competitive industrial operation".

Analysis of the price of commercial sites is much more difficult, because the price gradients are extremely steep, but also because we are dealing (so far as the city authorities permit them) with multi-storey buildings. Net rents (after allowing for interest, depreciation and maintenance on the structure, municipal rates, and so on) may be expected to bear a more or less constant ratio to land prices in the case of factory sties, but certainly not in the case of multi-storey buildings.

Data for office rents in Sydney at distances up to fifteen kilometres from the centre fit fairly well to a double-log curve, with rents proportional to the -0.3 power of distance from the centre.[48] Allowing fifteen per cent on estimated construction costs (at that time of a little over \$200/square metre) the relation becomes convex at fifteen kilometres, the rent only just about covering the cost of the structure, leaving a very low site rent; but up to a distance of three to four kilometres site rents *per unit of floor space* vary approximately with the -0.5 power of distance. Per unit of site area the slope is expected to be steeper, though there are practical limits to the extent to which the floor space/site area ratio can be increased. After allowing \$30/square metre/year (at 1971 prices) for interest, depreciation, maintenance, rates, and so on, on the structure, and then capitalizing net rents at ten year's purchase, city centre land prices, in Sydney and also in smaller Australian cities, per square metre of *site,* are of the order of magnitude of five times capitalized net rents per square metre of *floor space.*

"Central" office sites in 1971, converted to American dollars as in the above table (current values in Australian dollars multiplied by

44. *Statistisches Jahrbuch.*
45. Searle Drug Company, private communication.
46. *The Times of India* 21 January 1961.
47. Eddison, *Pakistan Development Review* (Winter 1963), pp. 557–60.
48. Jones, Lang, and Wootton (Real Estate) Circular, 1 March 1971.

1.10) ranged from $4,150 in Sydney and $1,650 in Melbourne to $900 in Brisbane. These prices had risen about five-fold since 1961, though the general consumer price level had risen only thirty-two per cent.

By 1977 commercial land prices in the centre of Tokyo had reached the figure of 2.5 million yen/square metre, that is, $5000 of 1970 purchasing power.[49] Prices up to one-third of this were paid for the most select residential land.

In 1976 floor space rents for "prime" office accommodation in the "City" (financial centre) of London were as high as £217/square metre/year, having fallen from £277 in 1974.[50] "Secondary" office accommodation however was at £91 and £112 respectively. Moving two or three kilometres to the other business centres of Mayfair and Victoria reduced "prime" rents to £130 and "secondary" to £80.

If we assume that office rents, in the smaller and remoter towns represented no more than the interest and other annual costs on the structure,[51] than the differential or net rent in favour of London "City and West End" (approximately the areas described above) at 1970 prices was £66/square metre/year, or $US220 of 1970 purchasing power (the largest provincial cities showing only a small fraction of such net rents). Before however we capitalize this net rent, or the 1976 figures, at ten, or any other number of years' purchase, we must bear in mind the high and increasing charges for municipal rates, which have the effects of bringing down land prices. In 1976 the share of gross rent taken by rates was of the order of forty per cent in Mayfair and Victoria, as against a little over twenty per cent in 1970. In the City the figure rose from eleven per cent in 1970 to seventy per cent in 1976, the latter figure representing something like eighty-five per cent of the net rent. In provincial cities rates in 1976, as in 1970, were of the order of thirty per cent of gross office rents. The highest "prime" rent in the City of London may be capitalized to some $1,350/square metre of 1970 purchasing power.

The price paid for residential land must include a large element of "servicing" (provision of roads, water, sewerage, grading, terracing, electricity supply, and so on) so that a significant minimum price is payable for building land even when "raw" land has no more than agricultural value. At prices of the 1960s development costs in the United States have been stated at $1.4/square metre (public utilities

49. *Financial Times* (London), 30 May 1977.
50. Debenham, Tewson, and Chinnock, Chartered Surveyors, Circular, April 1976.
51. *The Guardian* (London), 23 April 1971.

only)[52] or $1.6/square metre in 1964 on large blocks[53] (it would be expected to be higher on smaller blocks) of 1,560 square metres. An Australian estimate of 1971, excluding taxation, but including a substantial profit for the developer, on blocks of 1,000 square metres, is $4.3/square metre.[54] Detailed statistics recorded by the German authorities show a surprising variation with size of town, presumably owing to the lower standards required in the smaller towns.[55] Converting at the current exchange rate of four Deutschemarks to the dollar, development costs (difference between "raw" land and land ready for building) rose steadily from $0.75/square metre in village below two thousand population to 2.1 for ten to twenty thousand population, 5.3 for one to two hundred thousand population, 8.4 for cities over 0.5 million population. Most building however appears to have been in the smaller towns, and the general average was only 2.25 (9 Deutschemarks). Between 1962 and 1976 it rose from 5.3 to 21.4, while building costs rose only by a factor of 2.12, indicating rapidly increasing standards.

Finally we consider historical trends of land values which certainly, as pointed out above, have not always been rising. Particularly the improvements in transport and in the level of real income in the late nineteenth century, leading to reductions in urban densities, led also to a relative fall in site rents.

A most ingenious method has been devised (Table 136) for measuring the total non-agricultural (except for public buildings)

Table 136. Site Values 1845—1931.

Revaluation year	Rateable value of dwellings England & Wales $m	Of which estimated site rent £m	Site rents of dwellings £/population	Site rent of dwellings per head as percentage of net national incom per head
1845	36.6	6.0	0.36	1.8
1861	53.2	18.9	0.94	3.4
1876	90.5	28.8	1.18	3.6
1893	131.9	59.2	1.99	5.1
1910	196.2	67.8	1.89	4.2
1931	394.5	122.2	3.06	3.2

52. Harrell, Harris, and Tolley, *Review of Economics and Statistics* (May 1968), p. 246.
53. Schmid, *Converting Land from Rural to Urban Uses.*
54. A. E. Gray, *The Bulletin* (Sydney, 25 November 1971.
55. *Statistisches Jahrbuch,* 1968, p. 443.

site rents in England and Wales in the nineteenth century.[56] (Scotland and Ireland were not covered; this omission is allowed for by taking per head incomes as the basis for the last column of the table.)

For the period 1845 to 1910 Singer reviewed the rating assessments, distinguishing reassessment years from others. In the years in which there was not a reassessment, the increase in rateable value showed the new structures constructed, less demolitions; the net value of construction of new structures in the reassessment years was also estimated from the average of the two adjacent years. The value of the increases in the reassessment years, less new construction, represented the assessors' estimates of the rise in value of all structures constructed before that year and still standing, due to rising land values, plus rising replacement costs, less depreciation. Singer adjusted this figure for physical depreciation, and for rises in replacement costs due to rises in building costs.[57] The residue is estimated to have represented increases in urban site rents. Singer estimated an opening value for these rents at £3 million per annum in 1845, and cumulated the subsequent increases. The present writer has extended the series to 1931 and raised the opening figure to £6 million, and also made a further small adjustment for the increase in the site value of the land when it is used for construction for the first time, which escaped Singer's calculations.

The results are very interesting. They show site rents rising from two per cent of income in the 1840s to a maximum of five per cent in the 1890s, then falling again to three per cent by 1931. This corresponds to capital values of more than a year's national income in the 1890s, and about sixty per cent of a year's income in 1931.

The present writer brought these figures up-to-date to 1964 for residential land only (Table 137) by comparing recorded average selling prices of houses with replacement costs.[58]

Much lower estimates are made by Revell (it is not clear whether he is referring to residential or to all land).[59]

Between 1964 and 1970 average residential land prices rose by a further seventy-five per cent to £2.08/square metre, rising to a maximum of £6.12/square metre in 1973, falling back to £4.20 in 1975.[60]

On non-residential land little systematic information is available. An unpublished study of the remarkably complete (though badly

56. H. W. Singer, *Econometrica* (1941).
57. Derived from G. T. Jones, *Increasing Return.*
58. *Land Values* (Sweet and Maxwell, for Acton Society Trust, 1965).
59. Revell, *Review of Income and Wealth* (Dec. 1966).
60. *Economic Trends* (Feb. 1971) and *Housing and Construction Statistics.*

Table 137. Residential Site Values 1938—64.

	1938	1953	1957	1960	1964
Value of residential sites £ billion	3.0	10.2	10.5	17.6	29.8
As percentage of national income: Residences at replacement value including sites	129	165	155	142	146
Residential sites	62	74	59	85	121

filed) records kept by Manchester City Council since the 1890s of sales of land and buildings near the city centre, after making estimates of the depreciated value of the structures, gave money and real land values.[61] The old-style factory and warehousing premises, in which Manchester then abounded (no longer), surprisingly, reached their maximum real site value in the 1930s, followed by a heavy fall. The main explanation is simple enough; there was no vehicle access space, except perhaps for a yard with just enough room for a horse-dray.

Some conflicting data for the United States indicate, since 1929 in relation to national income, falls in the aggregate value of residential and commercial land, (greater dispersal of residences and businesses) and a heavy fall in agricultural land.

These aggregates are confirmed by some individual illustrations. The maximum site value[62] in 1911 in New York's financial district of $400/square foot was not regained in *money* terms[63] (quite apart from real value) until 1964. The business centre of Chicago had the same money value ($220/square foot) in 1967 as in 1929,[64] while the corner of 63rd and Halstead, in 1929 at $100/square foot "probably the world's highest value outside central business districts" had fallen to $30 in 1967, and the average of 16 leading non-central retail centres from $43 to $15. It was only in Chicago's outer suburbs that land values were rising.

Residential sites represented a much lower proportion of national income in Canada, falling from about 10 per cent in the 1920s and 1930s to 7.7 per cent in 1950.[65]

61. E. C. de Varallya Agricultural Economics Institute, Oxford.
62. R. M. Hurd, *Principles of City Land Values.*
63. *Fortune* (Sept. 1964), p. 119.
64. Hoyt, *Traffic Quarterly* (July 1968).
65. Firestone, *Residential Real Estate in Canada.*

German data on average real land prices of all land sold for building in four leading cities, deflated either by building costs or by average incomes (the results have been much the same) from a real land price index of 100 in 1910–12, show a fall to 46 in 1929, 25 in 1936 and 52 in 1964.[66] The 1970 index stood at 107 deflated by building costs, 63 deflated by average income. Between 1970 and 1976 land for building rose fifty per cent ("raw" land only twenty-seven per cent — a measure of the increased services required). Deflated by retail prices, or by building costs, the rise was only a little over five per cent, whereas in terms of income there was a fall of fifteen per cent in real land value.

Dwelling rent (including imputed rent on owner-occupied dwellings) as a percentage of a four-person wage-earning family's gross income is shown in Table 138.

Table 138. Rent as Percentage of Income.

1870–1900	1907	1927	1937	1967	1975
20-25	19.8	12.2	15.2	10.7	10.4

Japanese urban land values (Table 139), already noted for their height, have shown further extraordinary increases.[68]

Table 139. Japanese Land Price Index on 1955 Base.

	Index	Deflated by Consumer Price Index	Deflated by average wage
1936	308	102	
1955	100	100	100
1960	280	260	207
1965	768	526	352
1970	1,395	732	323
1973	2,286	969	325
1975	2,691	819	272

In terms of wages, it is interesting to note, that the peak was reached in 1965, and the index is now falling. Since 1975 the fall in real land values has continued, in terms of consumer prices, a fall of eleven per cent between 1975 and 1978.[69]

66. *Statistisches Jahrbuch.*
67. G. Hallett, private communication.
68. H. Niida, *Review of Income and Wealth* (June 1978); and Mortgage Bank for 1936–55.
69. *Nihon Keizai Shimbum,* (Tokyo), 24 April 1979 (English Edition).

Index

Abrasimov, 76
accessibility. *See* urban land values, accessibility and
Adelaide, 169, 191, 208
advanced economies, 30, 76-77, 88, 120, 124-25, 127, 132, 159, 160, 162, 185-88
Africa. *See also* names of individual African states
  transport costs, 3, 4, 5, 6, 7, 8
  urban residential densities, 175
agricultural advance, 2
agricultural income, 124
agricultural land, 28-30, 86, 194
  cost in relation to markets, 17, 21
  demand for, 28, 37
  prices of, 29
  rent, 20, 23, 28-30
  scarcity of, 94
agricultural output, 29-30, 100, 123-24
  consumption of, 2
  trading of, 2-3
agricultural production
  effect of transport costs on differentiation of, 18-23, 128
  specialization of, 128, 131
agricultural productivity, 27, 29-30, 123-25, 128
  low, 131
  measurement in Asian economies of, 1-2
agricultural regions, 122
agriculture, 108, 119. *See also* labour force, agricultural; primary production
  location of, 1
agriculture-substitutes, 124, 125
ancient world, 5, 7-8, 10-11, 67
  urban residential densities in, 171-72, 173

Angel, 232
animal transport, 2, 4, 5, 6-7, 10
Argentina, 61
Athens, 271-73, 277, 280
Atkinson, 175
Atlanta (Georgia), 183-84
Auerbach, 59
Australia, 32, 34, 36, 102
  agriculture in, 4
  and transport costs, 5, 7, 8, 22, 27, 32, 34, 36
  manufacturing industries, 90, 99-101
  migration to urban areas, 166, 169
  municipal costs, 74
  railways in, 152-53
  regional employment, 108, 113
  regional income differences, 120, 121
  regional incomes, 75, 149-50
  urban land use, 208
  urban land values, 267-68, 284
  urban residential densities, 184, 185, 186, 191
  urban settlements in, 60, 61
  urban transport and traffic, 230, 235, 241-42, 250
Austria, 58, 120, 121
Aztecs, 14

Bairoch, 77
Bangladesh, 4, 5, 266, 282
Barfod, B., 138, 143
Beckett, 17
Belgium, 60, 61, 158
Belloc, Hilaire, 78
Berry, B.J.C., 43, 54, 56-58, 84, 102
Bevin, Ernest, 255
bicycle transport, 5, 6, 41, 43
birth and death registrations, 162

Blackman, J.M., 155-56
Bleicher, 176
boats, 4, 7-8, 11, 16
Boswell, James, 26
Bowles, S., 167
Bracey, H.E., 52-53, 56, 83
Brasilia, 67, 77
Brazier, H.E., 70
Brazil, 34, 61, 109, 124-25, 159
  migration to urban areas, 163, 166
  regional income differences, 118, 120, 121, 122
  urban growth, 160
Brisbane, 169, 186, 191, 214, 251, 267, 283
Brodsky, H., 271
Brush, J.E., 52-53, 56, 83
Buck, J.L., 2
Bulgaria, 60
Bussiere, Rene, 181-83
bus transport, 185, 223-25, 227, 228, 230-31, 236, 237, 239, 254

Cameroun, 17
Canada, 158
  city size, 68, 72
  manufacturing industries, 99, 101
  regional employment, 108
  regional income differences, 75, 119, 120, 121, 122
  rural settlement pattern, 48, 50, 53
  urban land values, 286
  urban settlement pattern, 60, 61
  urban transport and traffic, 247, 256
Canberra, 67, 77, 111-12, 191
Cantillon, Richard, 14
capital, 129, 153
  and agricultural land, 29-30
  costs, 74-75
  inflow, 137, 140, 150
  movements, 127
capital cities, 68, 77, 78, 95, 111-12, 117, 128, 152-53, 166
  migration to, 167-70
  size of, 61-62
Carrere, Paul, 112-14
carts and wagons, 5, 7, 10, 20, 24, 41
cassava, 17
Chicago, 21, 92, 98, 183-84, 189
  land use, 201, 204, 214, 216
  land values, 270, 271, 275, 286

transport and traffic, 230, 234, 237, 241, 245-47, 248, 255
Chile, 120
China, 24, 48, 51
  transport costs, 2, 4, 5, 6, 8, 16
  urban settlement pattern, 60, 61
  urban residential densities, 171-72, 173
Chisholm, M., 17
Christaller, W., 41-45, 53, 60, 84
cities, 14, 24, 54-56, 58, 64-65, 133. *See also* capital cities; satellite cities; and headings under urban
  disadvantages of, 77-78
  functions of, 114
  growth of. *See* urban growth
city centre
  densities, 175-88, 189, 191, 192, 193-94, 195
  distance from, 176-88, 191. *See also* urban land values and distance from city centre
  employment, 229-30, 279-81. *See also* urban land use and employment
city size, 14, 198. *See also* capital cities, size of
  age of city and, 180-81
  and demand for transport, 240-41
  and income inequality, 78-79
  and journey destinations, 250-51
  and regional income differences, 118, 133-34
  economic functions in relation to, 75-76
  employment and, 112-14, 118
  optimum populations, 66-68, 69, 76-77, 81-84, 154, 169
  social, economic and political disadvantages, 78, 80-81
Clark, Colin, 60, 75-76, 94, 124, 132, 176, 285
Clark, Professor Kitson, 162
Clawson, M., 84
coal, 36, 95
Cobb-Douglas production function, 29
coefficients, 176-77, 179, 180, 181-84, 185-88, 215, 253, 271. *See also* Gini coefficients; regional inequalities coefficients
coffee, 18
Colombia, 120, 130, 159
Common Market, 103, 169

agricultural productivity, 127
growth of non-farm employment, 158
industries covering local demand, 131-32
migration to urban areas, 162-65, 168
regional employment, 108, 112-15
regional income differences, 117, 120, 121
rural settlement pattern, 46-48, 52
urban settlement pattern, 60-61
urban transport and traffic, 235
Frisch, 253
Fuchs, 92
fuels, 21, 27
rise in cost of, 226-29, 236, 238

George, Henry, 265-66
German Statistical Office, 119
Germany, 22-23, 32, 41-42, 60, 61, 84
agricultural productivity, 127
and manufacturing industries, 104
industries covering local demand, 131-32
migration to urban areas, 162-63, 168
regional employment, 107-8
regional income differences, 119, 120, 121
urban land values, 279, 280, 281-82, 284, 287
urban residential densities, 176
urban transport and traffic, 235, 238, 240, 257
Ghana, 4, 5, 15-16, 17, 137-38, 172
Gilboy, E.W., 25, 26
Gini coefficients, 78-79
Goodwin, P.B., 239, 251
Gordon, 145-46
Gottman, 79, 80
Gourou, 14
government expenditure, 153
grain
and transport bias, 15-17, 22-23
as measurement of transport costs, 1-12, 15, 21, 27
economic distance grown from market, 21-22, 27
transport costs, 36
Graunt, 161

gravity models, 257-58
grazing, 4, 22
Great Britain, 5, 7, 16, 23, 24-25, 26, 29, 30, 31, 32, 61. *See also* Scotland; Wales
and city size, 68-69, 70, 71, 73, 75, 80
and manufacturing industries, 92-94, 95, 105-6
growth of non-farm employment, 158
interregional migration, 163, 166, 169-70
interregional trade, 141-42
labour force in manufacturing industries, 111
policies to attract industry to regions, 154-55
regional employment, 107-8, 110, 113, 114
regional income differences, 116, 120, 121
regional multipliers, 143-46, 149
rural settlement pattern, 45, 48-54
urban land use, 202, 204-7, 219
urban mortality, 161-62
urban residential density, 174, 179-80, 189-91, 194
urban settlement pattern, 60
urban transport, 225, 235, 240, 241, 256, 259
Greece, 30, 61, 120, 171, 247, 271

Hagen, Everett, 130-31
Halley, 161
hamlets, 52, 54-56, 58
Harris, Chauncey, 98
Hartland, Penelope, 138-39
Hawaii, 137, 147, 149
Heggie, I.G., 256
Hirsch, 70, 72
Hirschmann, A.O., 154
Hobart, 251
Hollingsworth, 175
Hong Kong, 7, 95, 175, 266-67
Hoover, E.M., 118, 154, 198, 219
Hotelling, H., 40
housing prices, 254. *See also* public housing
Howard, Ebenezer, 68-69
Hungary, 168
Hyman, 232